高等学校英语专业系列教材
Textbook Series for Tertiary English Majors

求知 *STEM*

高等学校英语专业系列教材 求知 STEM

Textbook Series for Tertiary English Majors

总 主 编　石　坚

副总主编　杜瑞清　陈建平　黄国文　李　力

编 委 会　（按姓氏笔画排列）

丁廷森　石　坚　刘守兰　刘晓红

吴　念　宋亚菲　张美芳　张维友

李　力　李海丽　杜瑞清　杨瑞英

陈建平　周　仪　周玉忠　姜秋霞

段　峰　高广文　高庆选　黄国文

廖七一

策　　划　张鸽盛　饶邦华　周小群

Introduction to Contemporary Linguistics

当代语言学导论

郑 超 编著

重庆大学出版社

内容提要

本教材以生动的表述、风趣的举例、明快的文笔将当代语言学各个领域的理论奥妙娓娓道来，旨在让学生熟悉这门学科的研究对象、方法和成就，以及其哲学渊源、文化底蕴和科学走向。全书共分 15 章，每章后面编有两类练习题，第一类侧重复习基本理念，第二类具有一定挑战性，启发独立思考，培养科研能力。练习之后介绍一位有突出贡献的语言学家，并推荐一批有影响的书籍。全书后面附有术语解释与汉译，方便学习与复习。

本教材适用于大学英语专业本科或研究生阶段的语言学导论课程，可供一个学期的教学。

图书在版编目(CIP)数据

当代语言学导论/郑超编著.—重庆:重庆大学出版社,2006.3(2022.7 重印)

(求知高等学校英语专业系列教材)

ISBN 978-7-5624-3605-8

Ⅰ.当… Ⅱ.郑… Ⅲ.语言学—高等学校—教材 Ⅳ.H0

中国版本图书馆 CIP 数据核字(2006)第 008531 号

求知高等学校英语专业系列教材

当代语言学导论

郑 超 编著

责任编辑:周小群 韩 杰 版式设计:牟 妮
责任校对:邹 忌 责任印制:张 策

*

重庆大学出版社出版发行
出版人:饶帮华
社址:重庆市沙坪坝区大学城西路 21 号
邮编:401331
电话:(023)88617190 88617185(中小学)
传真:(023)88617186 88617166
网址:http://www.cqup.com.cn
邮箱:fxk@ cqup.com.cn(营销中心)
全国新华书店经销
POD:重庆新生代彩印技术有限公司

*

开本:720mm×960mm 1/16 印张:15.5 字数:286 千
2006 年 3 月第 1 版 2022 年 7 月第 12 次印刷
ISBN 978-7-5624-3605-8 定价:39.00 元

总　序

　　进入 21 世纪,我国高等教育呈现快速扩展的趋势。为适应社会、经济的快速发展,人才的培养问题已经比我国任何一个历史时期都显得更为重要。当今,人才的能力和素质的衡量越来越多地采用国际标准,人才的外语水平自然地也越来越受到培养单位和用人单位的重视,由此引发了对大学外语教学模式、教材和检测机制的新一轮讨论,掀起了新一轮的大学英语教学改革。作为外语师资队伍和外语专业人才培养的高等学校英语专业,相比之下,在教学改革思路、新教材开发和新教学模式探讨等诸方面均显得滞后。尽管高等学校外语专业教学指导委员会英语组针对当前高校发展的新形式和外语专业人才培养的新规格、新模式和新要求,修订出了新的《高等学校英语专业英语教学大纲》,并结合 21 世纪外语人才培养和需求的新形势,制定了由教育部高等教育司转发的《关于外语专业面向 21 世纪本科教育改革的若干意见》,就英语专业的建设提出了指导性的意见,但在实际工作中这两个文件的精神尚未落实。

　　为此,重庆大学出版社和外语教学界的专家们就国内高等学校英语专业建设所面临的新形势作了专题讨论。专家们认为,把"大纲"的设计和"若干意见"的思想和理念变为现实的一个最直接的体现方式,就是编写一套全新理念的英语专业系列教材;随着我国教育体制的改革,特别是基础教育课程标准的实施,适合高等学校英语专业教学需要的教材也应作相应的调整,以应对中小学英语教学改革的新要求;高等学校学生入学时英语水平的逐年提高和就业市场对外语人才需求呈多元化趋势的实际,对高等学校英语专业的人才培养、教学模式、课程设置、教材建设等方面也提出了严峻挑战,应对这些挑战,同样可以通过一套新的教材体系来实现。

　　迄今为止,国内尚无一套完整的、系统的英语专业系列教材;目前已有的教材出自不同的出版社,编写的思路和体例不尽相同;现有的教材因出版时间较早,内容、知识结构、教学方法和手段已经不能适应新的发展要求;传统的教材设计多数基于学科的内在逻辑和系统性,较少考虑学习者的全面发展和社会对人才需求的多元化。

　　自 2001 年开始,在重庆大学出版社的大力支持下,我们成立了由华中、华南、西南和西北地区的知名专家、学者和教学一线教师组成的《求知高等学校英语专业系列教材》编写组,确定了系列教材编写的指导思想和总体目标,即以《高等学校英语专业英语教学大纲》为依据,将社会的需求与培养外语人才的全面发展紧密结合,注重英语作为一个专业的学科系统性和科学性,注重英语教学和习得的方法与规律,突出特色和系列教材的内在逻辑关系,反映当前教学改革的新理念并具有前瞻性;锤炼精品,建立与英语专业课程配套的新教材体系,推动英语专业的教学改革,培养高素质人才和创新人才。

系列教材力求在以下方面有所突破和创新：

第一，教材的整体性。系列教材在课程类型上分为专业技能必修课程、专业知识必修课程、专业技能选修课程、专业知识选修课程和相关专业知识课程等多个板块。在考虑每一种教材针对相应课程的特性和特色的同时，又考虑到系列教材间相互的支撑性。

第二，学生基本技能和实际应用能力的培养。在课程的设计上充分考虑英语作为一个专业来培养学生的基础和基本技能，也充分考虑到英语专业学生应该具备的专业语言、文学和文化素养。同时，教材的设计兼顾到社会需求中对英语专业学生所强调的实际应用能力的培养，除考虑课程和英语专业的培养目的，课程或课程体系应该呈现的学科基本知识和规范外，充分考虑到教材另一方面的功用，即学生通过教材接触真实的语言环境，了解社会，了解文化背景，丰富学生的实践经验。在教材编写中突出强调"enable"，让学习者在实践中学习语言、文学、文化和其他相关知识，更多地强调学习的过程，强调学生的参与，以此提高学生的实际应用技能。

第三，学生的全面发展。对高等学校英语专业学生而言，英语不仅是一门工具，更重要的是一个培养学生人文素质和跨文化意识的学科专业。系列教材强调合作性学习、探索性学习，培养学生的学习自主性，加强学习策略的指导。通过基础阶段课程的学习，使学生在语言知识、语言技能、文化意识、情感态度和学习策略等方面得到整体发展；在高年级阶段则更多地注重学生的人文精神、专业理论素养、中外文学及文化修养的培养。

第四，教材的开放性。一套好的教材不应该对课堂教学、老师的施教和学生的学习拓展有所制约，应给使用教材的教师和学生留有一定的空间，要让学生感到外语学习是一件愉快的事，通过学习让人思考，给人以自信，引导人走向成功。系列教材的总体设计既考虑严密的学科系统性，也考虑独具特色的开放性。不同地区、不同类型的学校，可以根据自己的生源和培养目标灵活地取舍、选用、组合教材，尤其是结合国内高等学校中正在探讨的学分制，给教与学一个多维度的课程体系。

我们希望通过这套系列教材，来推动高等学校英语专业教学改革，探讨新的教学理念、模式，为英语专业人才的培养探索新的路子，为英语专业的学生拓展求知的空间。

《求知高等学校英语专业系列教材》编委会
2004 年 8 月

前　言

　　语言学是英语语言文学专业学生必修的一门学问,全国英语专业 8 级考试从 2004 年起已经增加了语言学方面的内容。作者所在的广东外语外贸大学(以下简称广外大)拥有国家文科基地——外国语言学与应用语言学研究中心,科研、教学力量雄厚,作者本人长期担任语言学导论课程的教学,秉承前辈专家们的学术传统,逐渐摸索出自己的教学风格。2002 年重庆大学出版社组织编撰大学英语专业系列教材,广外大推荐将本人的教学思路发展成语言学导论课程的教材。教材稿成形后,作为内部讲义,已经试用 4 年,受到学生肯定,在使用中又经过了逐年仔细修订。

　　教材的体例和特色:

　　本教材突出反映了当代语言学的理论概貌和前沿进展,注意以生动的表述,风趣的举例,明快的文笔将当代语言学各个领域的理论奥妙娓娓道来,旨在让学生熟悉这门学科的研究对象、方法和成就,及其哲学渊源、文化底蕴和科学走向。

　　全书用英语编写,穿插有少量汉语例句。共分为 3 大部分,15 章。

　　教学内容主要包括:

　　第 1 部分:含第 1 章"人类的语言"和第 2 章"语言科学"。内容主要为介绍当代语言学的来龙去脉,回顾两千年来东西方对语言本质的探索与思考,突出介绍柏拉图、亚里士多德、荀子、索绪尔、乔姆斯基、韩礼德的语言观,语言学研究方法,三个研究层次(观察、描写、解释),语言学各分支间的关系等。

　　第 2 部分:含第 3 章"语音与语音体系",第 4 章"词的构造与标记",第 5 章"短语结构",第 6 章"从形式到意义",第 7 章"从意义到功能",第 8 章"交际中的功能结构"和第 9 章"意义与使用",介绍语言学各主要分支,包括语音学、音系学、形态学、句法学、语义学、功能语法、语用学等,注意各分支间的衔接,并且将一般语言学导论教材中不专门提到的功能语法的核心内容,以一章篇幅插在语义学与语用学之间介绍,显得恰如其分,试用时受到学生欢迎。

第3部分:含第10章"语言的本能",第11章"语言的约定",第12章"语言的习得",第13章"第二语言",第14章"共性与差异"和第15章"环球语言",各有侧重地综合介绍心理语言学、神经语言学、社会语言学、语言习得、语言类型学、应用语言学、批判应用语言学等跨学科领域的重点内容。

每章自成一体,不是对诸多理论条条框框式的罗列,而是引导学生从不同视点,如科学与文化,形式与功能,意义与使用等,纵览语言学这一"大观园",感受到科学探索的脉搏和理性思维的节律,内容繁而不杂,追求"小景之中,形神自足","择焉虽精而语焉犹详"(冯友兰语)的境界,在深入浅出、化解难点上具有自己的风格。

每章后面编有两类练习题,第一类侧重复习刚学过的概念、定义、定律,以翻译、填空、答问、写摘要为主,第二类为一组挑战性的思考题和论述题,启发独立思考,融会贯通所学知识,培养科研能力。

此外,每章的练习之后另辟出一栏,介绍一位在该领域有突出贡献的语言学家或语言哲学家,他们分别是索绪尔、叶斯帕森、赵元任、布龙菲尔德、乔姆斯基、菲尔默、蒙太古、韩礼德、维特根斯坦、平克、拉波夫、伦内伯格、克拉申、格林伯格、威多逊。章末还附有相关领域的书籍介绍,重点推荐两三本适合初学者阅读的国内外佳作,以及数本虽有一定难度,但颇具钻研价值的专著。所推荐的国外文献大都是国内书店有售,高校图书馆也应有藏书的。全书后面附有术语解释与汉译,方便学习与复习。

综上所述,本教材在运用先进信息技术、提高兴趣、便利学习方面具有鲜明特色,主要用于大学英语专业本科或研究生阶段的语言学导论课程,可供一个学期的教学。

作者衷心感谢桂诗春教授的培养和指导,是桂先生把我领入语言学总论的广袤领域,手把手教我如何备课,如何做电脑演示课件,如何在教学中把握好各种理论的精要,如何化解讲授中的难点;作者也十分感激宁春岩教授、何自然教授、李行德教授、王初明教授在他们各自曾执教的普通语言学、语言哲学、第一语言习得、第二语言习得等研究生课程中对自己的教导和指点,书中许多内容源于他们的深邃思想;同时,作者还要感谢广外大及其英文学院两级领导,尤其是担任丛书副总主编的陈建平副校长几年来对本书编撰的积极支持和热情勉励;最后对重庆大学出版社外语分社对自己的长期信任和温馨鼓励,说一声道谢。

广外大语言学博士生徐佳欢在本书编写过程中作了大量高效、细致的工作,包括编写部分练习题、编词汇表、收集资料、反复校阅书稿等,她扎实的语言学基础和英语实力给本书的学术质量增色不少。美国亚利桑那大学语言学博士,现在广外大任教的冯蔚老师给了作者不少颇有见地的指点，并帮助修改语音学与音系学部分，付出了很多时间和精力。广外大长期担任语言学研究和教学工作的王文心博士也在平时的交流中给了作者很多启发。美籍教师 Mrs Louise Gustafson 仔细校阅了全稿。还有广外大的一些老师，曾在广外大求学或来广外大作学术访问的各地学者，作者指导的研究生和广外大语言学专业的本科生们都对本书的试用提供了大量有价值的反馈，他们中主要有何晓炜教授、鲁守春博士、余盛明博士、龙翔副教授和贾婷婷、黄春兰、谢昌香、黄辉、李燕玲、朱海群、李雪莲、徐俊、韩艳梅、翁素贤、周沫、陈伟、王华、刘吉林、张波、陈向丽、罗雪梅、陈劲波等同学。尤其要提到的是作者曾指导的刘娟同学，本书第9.4节中一些生动的内容借鉴了她的优秀学士论文中的构思。广外大语言信息系的蒋铁海副教授指导一批学生为本书开发了学习网站，许多研究生、本科生参加了网站内容的创作和编辑，其中贡献较多的有李平原、翁向明、曾广斌、徐可人、李建辉、王姝、蒙洁群、陈松青、李巧郎、金天、赵文静、王英、房垚、方晓国、李倩、左传果、陈洁等同学。这本书正是所有这些同行和朋友们通力合作的结晶。

　　本课题得到了广外大外国语言学及应用语言学研究中心（教育部人文社科重点研究基地）资助，谨此致谢。

　　在本书的编撰过程中作者先后阅读了不下百种国内外学术著作，这些参考文献均在与书配套的学习网站中列出，其中一部分适合学生阅读的还在各章后面作了推荐，在此谨对文献作者们表示敬意。

　　作者期待通过这本教材结识更多的语言学爱好者，并通过我们的学习网站开拓更广的合作，让我们在砥砺、切磋之中分享求知的甘辛，共建友谊的虹桥，让我们去告诉更多的人，语言学是值得每个信息时代的地球人去探访、去珍爱的宝库。

Contents

The people of Earth, tired of pleasing a demanding God, decided to build a tall tower as an easy way to Heaven. Begun on the plains of Babel, the tower soon rose to great heights.

God, viewing the audacity of His people, confounded their language, creating chaos and confusion. Unable to understand each other, the people scattered throughout the Earth, prevented from building another tower to Heaven.

a story from *the Old Testament*

Chapter 1

Human Language

Human beings are capable of changing the world. Human beings are proud of their incomparable power and intelligence among all the creatures on earth. Then, what attribute does a human being possess that exemplifies this outstanding ability to cause change? It cannot be his muscle. Some other species are more muscular. It cannot be his sensory organs. Some other species excel at perceiving ultrasonic waves or infrared rays, which is beyond human inherent capability. Upon examination, human superiority lies in his unique endowment—the ability to talk, or rather, to communicate by means of language.

With language, people convey thoughts and feelings to each other, and transmit their accumulated knowledge and beliefs to their children. Without language, other species are unable to formulate and exchange logical ideas, let alone figure out the mysteries of the world they inhabit, and change the world for any intended purpose.

The power of language has been duly noted since the remote antiquity. Ancient Jews, for example, credited their belief in language in the Talmud: "God created the world by a word, instantaneously, without toil or pains". Mystical as it is, this piece of scripture points to "the primacy of language in the way human beings conceive of the world" (Widdowson, 1996). In almost all ancient cultures we can find a mythology concerning the role of language: it facilitates gods to exercise their will; it satisfies the mortal desire to praise the Almighty; it also empowers earthlings to challenge the heaven (e. g. the myth of the Tower of Babel). Indeed, language is a vehicle of power, for control, for creation, and for change.

The Cambridge Encyclopedia of Language uses the following description to highlight how central language is to human lives:

We look around us, and are awed by the variety of several thousand languages and dialects, expressing a multiplicity of world views, literatures, and ways of life. We look back at the thoughts of our predecessors, and find we can see only as far as language lets us see. We look forward in time, and find we can plan only through language. We look outward in space, and send symbols of communication along with our spacecraft, to explain who we are, in case there is anyone there who wants to know.

Language is our constant companion. Whether we are speaking or thinking, whether we are awake or in a dream, it always stays in our mind. It is so natural, so familiar to us that most of us seldom sit down to think about its essence, which is, actually, among the hardest puzzles for us to unravel. We are just beginning to explore how the human mind operates to organize the experiences and ideas of man into a verbal form anytime he speaks or thinks.

The study of human language is called linguistics. It is a widely practiced academic discipline, with boundless possibilities for application. Any college students whose major is related to language should not ignore it. As a domain of science, linguistics plays an essential role in the information age. Just as the industrial age liberated human hands and sensory organs with fuel-driven machinery based on the development of mathematics, physics and chemistry, the information age will liberate the human brain and vocal organs with the development of artificial intelligence by virtue of the inspiration from linguistics. The purpose of this course is to familiarize beginners with the different branches, topics and focuses of linguistics, as well as reviewing the viewpoints of some important schools and influential researchers in the domain. This will help students lay the foundation of their academic career and pave the way for their specific research in the future.

Let's begin with an analysis of some major aspects of the discipline, along with how today's linguists think of their research object — language.

1.1 Language and languages

Linguistics deals with human language as a whole or as particular languages. If we talk about language as a whole, it is the system of human communication which consists of the structured arrangement of sounds (or their written representation) into larger units, e. g. morphemes, words, sentences, utterances. If we speak of languages, e. g. the French language, the Korean language, they are particular systems of human communication used by people living in different parts of the world. What we are talking about now are just general descriptions of language and languages, but not their scientific definition. The exploration of "what is language" is one of the major tasks of modern linguistics, which has not approached a satisfactory answer yet.

Sometimes a language is spoken by most of the people in a particular country, e. g. Japanese in Japan, sometimes a language is spoken by people of different countries, e. g. English, and sometimes a language is spoken by only a part of the population of a country, e. g. French in Canada.

In some cases, there is a continuum from one language to another. A dialect of a Language on one side of the border may be very similar to a dialect of another

Language on the other side if these two Languages are related. This is the case between Sweden and Norway and between Germany and the Netherlands.

Any particular language is in essence a set of varieties. There are local varieties — dialects and accents (the former differ from each other in pronunciation, vocabulary, and even grammar; the latter only in pronunciation), social varieties — sociolects (= social dialects, used by people of different classes, ages, or sexes), historical varieties — temporal dialects (e. g. the 17th century English), stylistic or occupational varieties — registers (e. g. formal English, scientific English), and even individual varieties — idiolects. Usually a language has an officially declared or generally considered standard dialect (e. g. Putonghua in China, General American in the United States).

Recent centuries have seen a change of attitude in language studies, from prescriptive to descriptive. Prescriptivism is the view that one variety of language has an inherently higher value than others. Those who observe the rules of this favored variety are said to speak or write "correctly". In the past, the unchanging form of Latin was held in high prestige in European education, and was regarded as a universal framework for other languages to adapt to. For instance, a prescriptive "rule" in English used to be that one should say *It is I* rather than *It is me*, because the verb *be* is followed by the nominative case in Latin, not the accusative. This "rule" is directly against the fact that people usually say *It is me* in modern English unless in some very formal situations. Moreover, *be* is followed by the accusative in some other languages, e. g. Arabic. These examples show that Latin rules are not universal — it is the prescriptivists who once attempted to impose the rules upon English.

Most of today's language researchers and teachers no longer support the opinion that behavior in a particular language should be prescribed. Instead, they turn to another tenet — descriptivism, which holds that usages of different varieties should be observed and recorded instead of being judged with some imposed norms. Unlike Latin, furthermore, a living language is never frozen, so its linguistic description should catch up with its development.

One approach in descriptivism is to investigate the knowledge of language in people's brains. It has been found that such knowledge, complex though it is, is equally shared by all human beings. Language (not in written form) has its own way of development in a child's mind. The process of this development is remarkably unique.

1.2 Language and human beings

Suppose a creature from another planet finds our earth and visits it. He will encounter language wherever there are human beings. Human language as a terrestrial phenomenon may not arouse his attention at first, for any sounds from human mouths would be intermingled with other noises. If this alien creature is intelligent enough and fairly observant, he may gradually notice that the human oral sounds are different from all other sounds in that they are apparently produced when there is a need for communication, so he guesses they must be meaningful. We don't know how much time he will spend before he can successfully distinguish human language from meaningless noises, but we know it will not be an easy job.

However, even though our imagined visitor can recognize that human sounds are used for communication, he still cannot understand them. For him, what he has heard is just a string of voices. The string seems to be a continuum with different patterns of rhythm and tone variation, and occasional breaks. If he is an excellent space detective, he may conjecture that there must be a structural hierarchy behind the phenomena, and the rhythm and tone patterns and breaks may serve as clues to uncover it. So, he sets out to divide the string of voices into proper segments of different levels. For example, he hears a human being produce this string of sounds to another:

I like your necklace. It is really beautiful. Where did you buy it?

He can identify two tiny breaks in the string because human speakers usually make a brief stop between two sentences. Thus he may infer that the whole string consists of three groups of meaning. He takes the first group (*I like your necklace*) for further analysis. With the help of the rhythm and tone patterns, he will possibly find that this group is composed of four smaller units "I", "like", "your", and "necklace".

Gosh! Our cosmic guest has done some linguistic work! Linguists on the earth indeed analyze the internal structure of language in the same way, but the actual hierarchy discovered by them is more complex: between the sentence and the word there is another category — phrase. For instance, the words "your" and "necklace" comprise one phrase, which further merges with the word "like" into a larger (and higher) phrase. This analysis can guarantee the understanding (like what→like your necklace). If that outer space linguistic novice fails to figure out this phrasal structure but mistakes "like your" for a phrase, then he won't be able to make out the meaning of the whole group of sounds. Even if he has correctly analyzed the sentential hierarchy, he still needs to spend a huge amount of time and energy figuring out the arbitrary combination of sound and meaning for each constituent of the structure: What do "I", "like", "your", and "necklace" stand for? Which of them is the name of something? Which denotes an action?... All he must decipher is knowledge of language, mainly involving the systematic internal structure of a sentence and the relationship between sounds and meaning. What an arduous job it is before he can understand a single sentence!

A newborn human baby faces the same situation. Everything in the human world is strange to him. He must screen language from all kinds of noises. He needs to break the string of sounds from his parents' mouth into syntactic constituents. He ought to associate a sound combination with a definite meaning. If he is a cub of another species on the earth, to master so complex a knowledge system is totally impossible. But since he is a human baby, he is bound to succeed. He doesn't need to cudgel his brains to unravel the structural riddles of the language as the imagined space creature does. He exerts no conscious effort in decoding the language he is exposed to. In fact, he perceives the existence of language around him spontaneously since his cradle days and gradually picks up this language as his mother tongue as he grows. Human children generally produce single-word sentences (e. g. they may say "Car" when they want a toy car) between 12 and 18 months of age. Then, they start to form elementary phrases and two-word sentences (e. g. "Want car"). By the age of two and a half, most children are able to make adult-like sentences such as "Can I have that toy car, daddy?" A child will not start this process too much earlier, no matter how enthusiastically his parents teach and encourage him; similarly, his speech ability will not develop at a fairly slower rate, no matter how little care he gets from adults (e. g. suppose he has been deserted by his parents). For human beings, acquiring a language as one's mother tongue is an effortless, time-predictable process, contrasting sharply with the painstaking, deliberate process of our imagined outer space decoder. For human beings, it seems as if the knowledge of language does not need to be deliberately taught but grows naturally from the mind during a certain period in childhood, just as teeth grow from gums.

1.3 Knowledge of language: endowed or conventional?

The universal success of all human individuals in acquiring a language as their mother tongue has aroused long-standing interest among scholars of different cultures in the world history. The following are two oldest questions put forward by Greek philosophers more than two thousand years ago, which remain unanswered.

1. What is knowledge of language?

2. Where does it come from?

Plato (427?—347 B. C.), one of the most influential Greek scholars, thought that man's knowledge came from universal truths. In order to demonstrate his idea, he asked:

How can every human being develop a rich system of linguistic knowledge on the basis of limited and fragmentary empirical evidence?

This famous question, called "Plato's problem", still obsesses the minds of today's linguists. To interpret it plainly, let's think of the process for a person to acquire music. At first he has to listen. If he has only been exposed to some simple songs, he will have no hope of becoming a composer of very complicated symphonies. The acquisition of language is totally different. All the sentences a baby hears are very simple, limited and incomplete as evidence of the involved structural system of human language. How can he become so proficient in manipulating the system and producing/understanding varieties of very complicated sentences as he grows?

Plato's problem remains a tough nut for today's science to crack. The famous American linguist Noam Chomsky pointed out in 1973, "... the fundamental empirical problem of linguistics is to explain how a person can acquire knowledge of language."

Plato gave a dualist explanation to his own question. He believed that there was a universally correct and acceptable logic of language for man to follow in expressing his ideas. Such an ideal logic existed before one's birth. The varieties of dialects Plato's compatriots actually spoke were, in his view, simply decayed or degenerate versions of a once-perfect system of communication, which could be approached by recalling. Accordingly, knowledge of language was not learned but recalled. That was why every adult could develop a rich system of linguistic knowledge in spite of the poverty of empirical evidence in his childhood.

Aristotle (384 — 322 B. C.), another great Greek scholar who was Plato's most brilliant student, held a totally different view from his teacher. He insisted that knowledge of language was arrived at by convention and agreement of the speakers of a given language. For example, *aēr*, the Greek word for *air*, was not based on some innate relationship between airiness and certain sounds, but was simply a combination of sounds arbitrarily agreed upon among Greeks to express the notion of air.

Decades later there rose a similar voice on the other side of the globe. Xun Zi (313? — 238 B. C.), a famous philosopher in ancient China, argued that a name was accepted through public agreement, and the appropriateness of naming a thing lay in convention[1].

Then, whose voice is right? How do we determine the source of language knowledge? Does it come from the mysterious universal truths or from convention? These two epistemological trends have confronted each other for more than two thousand years. Today we still see linguists standing in either Plato's or Aristotle's camp, but the names of the camps have changed. Those in the former now call themselves nativists or mentalists, who have, however, made an essential revision of Plato's tradition: from dualism to monism. They still hold that human beings do have an inborn knowledge of language which must be universally correct and acceptable, but the location of such innate knowledge is no longer mysterious — not beyond us but within us — just in our genes. Since all animals have some qualities genetically inherited from generation to generation, e. g. spiders inheriting skills of spinning webs, bees inheriting skills of collecting nectar and producing honey, why can't human beings inherit a certain universal logic of language to facilitate their particular language acquisition? These revisionists of Plato's innateness hypothesis, with Chomsky as their leading authority, make the following declaration:

There is a biological, physiological entity inside our brain which decides what we speak.

Chomsky has given a name to this entity — UG, or, universal grammar. His epistemology of the knowledge of language goes as follows:

1) Every human being has the language competence, because he has the inborn UG which other species lack.

2) UG is the initial state of the human language faculty which alone cannot enable a human baby to speak. A baby needs to be exposed to the linguistic environment of a certain language and accumulate experience.

3) Due to the effect of later experience, the baby's mind develops from the initial state into the steady state, which corresponds to the competence of speaking a specific human language.

According to UG theory, every speaker is endowed with a set of principles which apply to all languages and also a set of parameters that can vary from one language to another within certain limits. For example, all human languages have the subject (S), verb (V), and object (O), which may be decided by one of the universal principles, but these three constituents are in different orders in the sentences of different languages. In English and Chinese, the dominant order is SVO; in Japanese, SOV; in Arabic, we can find VSO;... These variations are regarded as different values of the parameter of word order. Therefore, acquiring a language means applying the principles of UG to a particular language, and learning which value is appropriate for each parameter.

UG theory, to a certain extent, reflects the persistent belief that there must be an absolute norm of perfect language. People need such a norm to tell good sentences from bad sentences in any particular languages. Plato thought this perfect norm existed before and beyond one's life. The way to approach it was to recall one's prenatal knowledge. Prescriptivists once attempted to establish such a norm through academic authority, forcing people to conform through education. Chomsky undoubtedly opposes the idea that man's linguistic behavior should be prescribed by some man-made norms, but he believes that it should be prescribed by UG, man's genetically endowed standard. It is genetic so it can grow mature in its own way in every human mind, without a need for recalling.

Opposing to Chomsky's camp are behaviorists or empiricists, whose opinions are identical with Aristotle's. They maintain that one's brain is blank when he is born, and that it has nothing specific to contribute to his linguistic knowledge. Some of them even doubt the necessity to assume the existence of any perfect knowledge as a linguistic standard. They hold that if convention plays the crucial role in the establishment of linguistic rules, then disparities in convention may produce different varieties. All the varieties should be regarded as equal, and each of them has enough reason to be accepted in a given situation. Only on some formal occasions should a "standard" variety be needed. After all, the power of language exists in its countless varieties, not relying on any universal standard.

A new school called connectionism is also worth mentioning. It argues that the mental-neural mechanisms responsible for both lexical and grammatical processing are not unique to language, and those who feel man cannot acquire a particular language without any innate endowment underestimate the power of the neural mechanisms, which are capable of doing a lot of things much more involved than acquiring a language. Connectionists have designed some large-scale computer tests to demonstrate that knowledge of language is an accomplishment after birth rather than an innate endowment.

1.4 A marvelous scope to explore

Now you have a glimpse of the big garden named modern linguistics. All the flowers of the garden have their roots in the fertile soil called language. Language is as common as water and air for every person. Did you expect that the study of it would be so sophisticated and exciting before you took this course?

A textbook leading to such a dynamic field should not be as stiffly organized as those introducing some fully matured disciplines like classical physics and chemistry, where it is possible for students to encounter on every page an unassailable axiom, law, or formula, waiting for them to digest and memorize. Linguistics itself is not stiffly organized at all. Its scope, for example, has never been finalized. Language study used to be treated as an adjunct to other disciplines, such as philosophy, religion, or literary criticism, without an independent scope of inquiry in its own right. Less than two hundred years ago, researchers who, for the first time in history called themselves linguists, focused their interest on the comparison between languages and the exploration of the historical change and variation of some ancient languages. Their main concern was diachronic. Early in the 20th century, a great linguist named Ferdinand de Saussure diverted the focus to synchronic analysis, i. e. to the research of the facts of language agreed upon or shared by the members of a language community at a given point in time. From 1957, Chomsky, the founder of generative grammar, has revolutionarily advanced the frontiers of linguistics several times, attracting hundreds of scholars to join his ranks, as well as provoking other hundreds to challenge his theories. The scope of linguistics is still expanding. Everywhere within the scope you can find new problems, and seldom will the solution to a problem be unexceptionable. Everywhere you hear the calls for a breakthrough. You are always free to join a discussion, air your own opinions, argue with an expert, challenge an authority, and then, if you think it necessary, return to a bookshelf to recharge yourself, sharpen your reason, and further your inquiry.

Remember the far-reaching influence of Plato's problem? In the field of linguistics we see a profound tradition of philosophy, where posing a significant problem is more valued than its solution. Some problems touch upon the origin and essence of the human world and human mind, and their solutions need the successive efforts of numerous generations. As Halliday, an excellent modern linguist, once pointed out in a lecture, language is the most complicated among all the objects of research in the world. When you delve into this field, your curiosity will always be in full play.

Linguistics offers such a marvelous scope for you to explore. Now you have approached its doorway. Don't hesitate! Get in and have a look!

NOTES

1] The Chinese original from Xun Zi's (荀子) thesis *Zhengming* (正名 "Justifying the name") is "名无固宜,约之以命,约定俗成谓之宜".

EXERCISES

I. Translate the following quotations into Chinese.

Language touches every part of our lives; it gives words to our thoughts, voice to our ideas, and expression to our feelings. It is a rich and varied human ability—one that we can use without even a thought, that children seem to acquire automatically, and that linguists have found to be complex yet describable.

(from G. Tserdanelis & W. Wong: *Language files*)

Linguistics is the study of the nature, structure, and variation of language, including phonetics, phonology, morphology, syntax, semantics, and pragmatics.

II. Fill in the blanks with the names of linguists.

1) _____ held that there was a universally correct and acceptable logic of language for man to follow in expressing his ideas.

2) _____ argued that knowledge of language was arrived at by convention and agreement of the speakers of a given language.

3) In ancient China, a famous philosopher named _____ reasoned that a

name was accepted through public agreement, and the appropriateness of naming a thing lay in convention.

4) According to _____, knowledge of language is the result of the interaction of UG and later experience.

5) _____ advocated the diversion of the focus of linguistic study from diachronic to synchronic.

III. Give a summary of less than 150 words to Section 1.2 *Language and human beings*.(You need not to mention the imagined outer space visitor, the description of whose terrestrial trip serves just as a hook to the main ideas.)

IV. Questions for discussion.

1) What distinguishes human beings from other animals? Some philosophers think it is the ability to make tools. Some others think it is the ability to acquire a language. Which side do you take? Give your own reasons.

2) Do you think it possible for an intelligent species on another planet to have a language similar to ours? What prerequisites should these creatures meet if such a language does exist?

3) Do you think language is just a means of communication for human beings? Are there other roles for language to play?

4) Compare the role of physics and chemistry in the Industrial Revolution with the role you think linguistics can play in the Information Age.

5) List several countries you know which have more than one official language.

V. Challenging work.

1) Observe a one-year-old child by visiting his/her family every other week. Record his/her progress in acquiring Chinese. Deliver a report to your class before the end of the term.

2) Write an essay on the following topic:

Does language need a norm?

■■■

F. de Saussure (1857 — 1913)

Ferdinand de Saussure was a great Swiss linguist at the turn of the 20th century. Though he was enormously influential as a teacher, lecturing at the École des Hautes Études in Paris from 1881 to 1891 and as professor of Indo-European linguistics and Sanskrit (1901 — 1913) and of general linguistics (1907 — 1913) at the University of Geneva, he did not have his ideas published during his lifetime because of his persistent search for perfection. Three years after his death, a compilation of notes on his lectures by two of his students, Bally and Sechehaye, was published with the title the *Course in General Linguistics*, which soon became the most influential linguistic works at that time.

Saussure established the structural study of language, emphasizing the arbitrary relationship of the linguistic sign to that which it signifies. He also contended that language must be considered a social phenomenon, a structured system that can be viewed synchronically and diachronically but he insisted that the methodology of each approach is distinct and mutually exclusive. He also introduced two terms that have become common currency in linguistics — "parole", the speech of the individual person, and "langue", the systematic, structured language existing at a given time within a given society. Saussure advocated more importance to be attached to "langue" rather than "parole", and suggested that the synchronic rather than the diachronic approach be adopted by the linguists at his time. His creative ideas on the theoretical and methodological orientation of language research have been so widely accepted that he is generally regarded as the father of modern linguistics.

Linguistic Stars

■■■

Reading recommendation

Beginner-friendly：

S. C. Poole. An Introduction to Linguistics. Macmillan Publishers Ltd, 1999；外语教学与研究出版社,2000（刘润清　导读）

H. G. Widdowson. Linguistics. Oxford University Press 1996；上海外语教育出版社,2001

胡壮麟,姜望琪. 语言学教程(修订版). 北京大学出版社,2001

戴炜栋,何兆雄. 新编简明英语语言学教程. 上海外语教育出版社,2002

More challenging：

V. Fromkin, et al. An Introduction to Language. the 7th edition. Holt, Rinehart and Winston Inc. 2002；北京大学出版社,2004

D Crystal. The Cambridge Encyclopedia of Language. Cambridge University Press, 1995,2003；外语教学与研究出版社, 2002(王克非等　导读)

A lady was regarded as of slightly poor mentality. A doctor asked her to put some pictures into categories. She put flowers, trees, and a dog into the same category. "Because they are all around the house," she explained.

Please analyze the mental state of this lady.

Chapter 2

Linguistics as a Science

The moment you begin your second lesson of the present course, you rank yourself among the explorers in the field of language studies. The first step toward a successful explorer is to read a lot, to think a lot, and to debate a lot.

You should read a lot because you need to know what other explorers have studied in the field. During your reading, you should always pay attention to term definitions, research questions, school names, theoretical models, arguments, and examples.

You should think a lot because you cannot get any insight into any problem without your independent analysis and reflection. Otherwise, you will drift at loose ends between different doctrines of different schools. You can have a notebook to reorganize what you have learned from different perspectives as well as to collect your own ideas and sort them out with neat logic.

You should debate a lot because it is the best way to approach a thorough comprehension of what you have dealt with. You cannot be a mere listener if you set foot in linguistics; everywhere you will encounter questions, hypotheses, and disputes, and you have to choose your own stance. Therefore, debating is the best way to make progress.

Furthermore, even if you have developed the good habits of reading, thinking and debating, you will still not be a qualified researcher. What you will need to master is scientific methodology. What we are to discuss here are some of its basic processes.

2.1 Speculation

Ancient people knew less than us — citizens of the age of information — about the world, but they were no less self-confident in judging things. Plato, the great ancient Greek scholar who we have talked about, discussed everything he noticed of the universe. Once he addressed himself to the origin of language. His answer was that at some ancient time there was a "legislator" who gave the correct, natural name to everything. In his book *Cratylus*, he wrote, "the legislator made language with the dialectician standing on his right hand." We need not infer that Plato conceived words, like coins, to be issued from the mint of the state. But he obviously meant that language was the product of intelligence, and that languages belonged to states but not to individuals.

In 1770, an essay competition was held by the Prussian Academy in Berlin on the topic of whether mankind alone could have evolved language. The winner was J. G. Herder (1744—1803). His essay *The Origin of Language* outshone his rivals' partly owing to his fresh, poetic diction. He knew the emotional force of the natural sounds poetry and music may carry, and that such sounds, as he pointed out in his article, could even be made, felt and exchanged among animals (except the voiceless fish). Babies could also make natural sounds, for example, cry, but such sounds could never develop into a language. What a baby acquires from adults is language, not natural sounds. Thus, there were two different oral capabilities man possessed. One was natural sounds (rhyme, pitch, intonation, etc.) which carried emotion; the other was language which carried thought. He emphasized that language was not the direct gift of God because he found it was far from perfect in the beginning. Instead, he postulated that God gave man the impulse to speak. With this impulse, man developed language from simple to complex, in parallel with the development of his power to think.

Both Plato and Herder were excellent thinkers. Their ideas were influential for centuries. But what they did, unfortunately, has nothing to do with today's science. Neither Plato's "legislator" nor Herder's "God" can be proved or disproved: they are either imaginative or supernatural. Therefore, what they conceived could not be truths but speculations.

Scholars eventually realized that such theories were unable to be tested. When the Linguistic Society of Paris was founded in 1866, its rules forbade discussion of the origin of language, in this way to divert its members' academic practice from the traditional philosophical speculation to authentic scientific research.

Both philosophers and scientists ask questions. They ask questions because they believe there is a thing called truth and they hope to find it. Ancient philosophers asked numerous questions about the world, a majority of which were later probed by science. The rest remain beyond the scope of scientific research for different reasons. Some are only significant in theology, for example, "What was the language spoken in the Garden of Eden?" Some are bound to be fruitless such as "what is the first sentence of the first language in human history?" because of the inaccessibility to any crucial evidence relating to the matter. Some famous philosophical reflections are highly logical but not scientific, either due to scarcity of evidence or supernatural presuppositions involved. Then what is meant by scientific research? Science attaches importance to evidence, which ensures that a scientific study will be repeatable and its conclusion will be useful in explaining and changing the world. When science brought great change to Europe during the Industrial Revolution, people became more and more impatient with any fruitless philosophical enquiry and turned to pursue "hard" science. It is with the same enthusiasm that a majority of today's linguists declare proudly that they are scientists.

This conversion to science is not meant to discourage speculation, which is as indispensable in modern linguistics as in Plato's and Herder's days. In fact, a perfect answer to a puzzle in nature has often been the brainchild of a great scientist, such as the case of relativity in physics and perhaps, of Goldbach's conjecture in mathematics. An ingenious speculative brainchild in scientists' eyes, however, is no more than a hypothesis, which needs to be tested with evidence. Evidence comes from scientific observation, with reliable instrumentation and computation. In science, no one can be so romantic and arbitrary as to presuppose an untestable factor in his theory.

Although any supernatural hand seems to be denied in science, one aesthetic proposition is an exception. It is the Galilean thesis "nature is perfect", by which scientists' speculation has often been inspired. As is emphasized by Chomsky (2001), the task of the scientist is to demonstrate this thesis, "whether studying the laws of motion, or the structure of snowflakes, or the form and growth of a flower, or the most complex system known to us, the human brain." In other words, if the universe were not harmonious as we expect it, then no phenomenon would be predictable, and all scientific rules would be groundless. Therefore, universal harmony is embraced as the foundation of modern linguistics as a science.

2.2 Starting from observation

A scientific researcher should be observant. In science, everything starts from observation.

For example, the first scientific attempts to discover the history of the world's languages were made at the end of the 18th century. Many language scholars at that time had noted similarities between various European languages, and they had known that some languages had developed from one provincial variety or another of Latin. There had been few exciting discoveries until an English amateur linguist, Sir William Johns, published his works in 1786. Johns had served in the colonial government of India, where he had carefully studied Sanskrit, the ancient learned language of India. He found systematical similarities between a remarkable number of vocabulary items in Sanskrit and their equivalents in European and Middle Eastern languages phonologically. He was shocked by the phenomena he investigated. Then he produced the bold hypothesis that all these languages might have "sprung from some common source, which, perhaps, no longer exists. " His hypothesis aroused many scholars' interest in pursuing this common source as well as opened up a new area in language studies — historical linguistics. Researchers began to collect data from different languages of the world, and compare their similarities and differences systematically, so as to see whether there were correspondences between them. Their work in the 19th century led to the recognition of several big language families, and those languages researched by Johns were proved to be members of the most widely dispersed family, called Indo-European family. Their splendid achievements marked the beginning of scientific language research, characterized by its own procedure: from phenomenon to hypothesis, from data analysis to description and explanation. It values insightful speculation based on observation and investigation, but does not encourage the philosophical tradition in language studies, i. e. speculation without seeking for evidence.

2.3 Doing your own research

Can we make some discoveries in linguistics by ourselves? Yes. Linguistics involves the revelation of the features of every language and the comparison of these features at different levels from different perspectives, as well as the universal principles of language as a whole. Its scope is so huge and so closely related to the human mind and human society that secrets behind phenomena are abundant enough for any researchers to make a discovery of their own. Not just the researchers today, but also those in the future will have their own opportunities, because language develops and its speakers keep changing. There will always be something new for us to reveal in such a dynamic process, provided that we are careful in observation, skillful in selecting a valuable perspective and insightful in analyzing the collected evidence.

Many postgraduates of linguistics have made their own discoveries in their degree studies. One of them in Guangzhou, China, for example, noticed a sentence structure unaccepted by the native speakers she interviewed but not rejected by almost all English learners in China, including many university teachers of English. Below is an example of this structure.

(2.1) *The house is easy to catch fire.*

The asterisk (*) before the sentence is used to mark ungrammatical sentences as the convention in linguistics. Can you make out the ungrammaticality of this sentence?

Then how about another sentence below? Is there any structural difference between the two sentences?

(2.2) *The house is easy to blow up.*

This striking contrast between L1 (= first language) and L2 (= second language) syntactic knowledge was analyzed with theories that postgraduate had reviewed:

> *Every person's lexical knowledge of his first language is tacit and natural, with a tendency to influence, often unknowingly, his second language learning. This influence is called transfer.*

When a Chinese learns the English word *easy*, he may naturally match it to the word 容易 in his native language, and unconsciously associate all his lexical knowledge of 容易 with it. In Chinese we can say:

(2.3) 这座房子容易着火。

(2.4) 这座房子容易爆破。

In (2.3), the phrase 着火 after 容易 is a verb plus an object, while in (2.4), the phrase 爆破 after 容易 is a transitive verb only, with the subject 这座房子 as its logical object. Both structures are legal in Chinese. But in English, *easy* is different from the Chinese 容易 in that it only requires the same structure as in (2.4) but refuses the structure in (2.3). Therefore, a native speaker of English will accept (2.5) but reject (2.6).

(2.5) *John is easy to please* (= It is easy to please John)

(2.6) *John is easy to please others.*

Thus that Chinese postgraduate made a real discovery of her own: (2.1) reflects a typical first language transfer among learners of English as a second language in China. Since few learners at advanced levels of English proficiency may get rid of this strong influence from their mother tongue, this phenomenon is a typical example of fossilization, i. e. a process in which incorrect linguistic features become a permanent part of the way a person speaks a second language.

What this student has achieved is not unattainable for all of us. We can also develop insights from observations. In fact, more exploration can be attempted on this student's achieved results. The following is a specific proposal.

In one's mind, there is a "dictionary" called lexicon, where all the words one knows of his mother tongue are stored, with their related information such as their meaning, grammatical function, pronunciation, etc. Whenever a native speaker of English uses the word *easy*, the syntactic information of the word stored in his mental lexicon will be retrieved, telling him that if *easy* is used as a predicative adjective, it must merge with a transitive verb in its infinitive form, with its logical object as the subject of the sentence. Contrastively, whenever a native speaker of Chinese uses the word 容易, his mental lexicon will give him different syntactic information. What is the information? — Now we have a research question.

Let's start to answer the question by analyzing the existing data.

Since native Chinese speakers accept both (2.3) and (2.4), we can infer that the syntactic information of 容易 embraces that of the English word *easy*, as reflected in (2.2) and (2.5). Besides, *easy* does not allow a verb-object phrase after it but 容易 does (as in (2.3)). Furthermore, can the verb-object relationship of 着火 be overlooked as a matter of word-formation and regarded as an intransitive verb? If yes, then can we conclude that an intransitive verb is also allowed in Chinese after 容易?

Further observation may lead us to the comparison of examples similar to the following:

(2.7) 约翰容易讨好。

(2.8) ?约翰容易微笑。

(2.9) *约翰容易走路。

Are 讨好, 微笑, 走路 intransitive verbs? Why do they sound differently in degrees of acceptability? What criterion can be established to describe the syntactic properties of 容易 in the mental lexicon of native speakers of Chinese?

What we have completed is just a small step: analysis of the research question.

It seems a new discovery is ahead but to achieve it requires more effort. We will stop here and leave this actually unfinished research task to our readers.

2.4 Three adequacies

How can we appraise the extent of success in scientific study? There are three levels to consider, namely observation, description, and explanation. What a linguist seeks can be summarized as three adequacies.

1) observational adequacy

Successful research is expected to be adequate in observation. It is characterized in linguistics by correctly specifying what is observed to be phonologically, morphologically, syntactically, semantically, or pragmatically well-formed or ill-formed. The observation should be duplicable and the conclusion should be generally applicable. The research should exhaust all the phenomena observable, but any statistically ignorable exception is still allowed unless it leads to a new conclusion and thus develops or falsifies the present results.

2) descriptive adequacy

Proper description is based on adequate observation, and a piece of scientific work in language study is descriptively adequate if it provides a principled account of the native speaker's intuitions about the structure of the linguistic phenomenon observed. For example, the effort in historical linguistics to reconstruct the features of a common source language of the Indo-European family is made toward such a goal.

3) explanatory adequacy

Explanatory adequacy is the ultimate goal of any scientific exploration. In linguistics, a theory attains explanatory adequacy just in case it provides a descriptively adequate grammar for every natural language, and does so in terms of a maximally constrained set of universal principles which represent psychologically plausible natural principles of mental computation(Radford,1988).

Such a goal requires the earnest work of a great number of generations, because language is so complicated a mental entity, so dynamic a cultural process, and so subtle an emotional representation. To reveal the rules behind it is far more difficult than to reveal the interrelationship and operation of any other physical phenomena in the nature.

Now let's turn back to the beginning of this chapter and reread the clipping above the title. Please have a discussion of the mental state of that lady of "slightly poor mentality". Maybe she was used to confining herself to the vicinity of her house, so she set up a principle for categorizing the doctor's pictures — whether or not the objects were around the house. She was mentally normal in her observational behavior and descriptive behavior, though her principle had too narrow a perspective which restricted her explanation of the objective world. Don't laugh at her! Sometimes our own research may turn out to be more tragic than hers — with wrong observations resulting in a more absurd principle!

2.5 Testing a theory

If you have a principled account of the objective rules underlying a certain phenomenon, you will be a theory founder. A theory in science must not be pure speculation but testable at observational, descriptive, and explanatory levels. The usual way of theory testing is to derive a prediction from it, and carry on a controlled investigation to see whether the prediction works. A familiar example from history is the test of Einstein's theory of relativity, which was conducted by some astronomers who successfully observed a then-unbelievable phenomenon during a total solar eclipse: they saw stars behind the sun. Their witness evidenced the prediction that light will move along a curving route beside a great mass like the sun, in the light of relativity. In linguistics, there are also many theories constructed following the scientific tradition. Chomsky's UG theory is a case in point. This bold model is testable. It presumes that every human baby is born with the initial state of language faculty, which means that the inborn knowledge of language structures exists in everyone's brain, and helps a person acquire a specific language as his mother tongue. Recently some German doctors conducted an experiment with an advanced medical device called functional magnetic resonance image (FMRI) scanner, to see if there was any difference in the brain when their subjects were processing some newly-learned rules of a language they had not known, compared with their processing of some other rules, also just learned, but not similar to any natural language rules at all. They did observe differences: when their subjects were dealing with unfamiliar language rules, their Broca's area, a region in the brain which was known to scientists to be closely related to language (please refer to Chapter 10 for more about it), became very active; when they were handling non-linguistic structures, the region turned inactive. The results of this experiment indicated that there must be something universal in the human brain that can facilitate the acquisition of language, so these German doctors declared that they had found evidence for UG's existence.

2.6 The "tourist map" of linguistics

Starting with the next chapter we will briefly visit different domains of contemporary linguistics. Our "sightseeing tour" consists of two stages. The first stage covers the main branches of linguistics, which are mutually related by the following triangle:

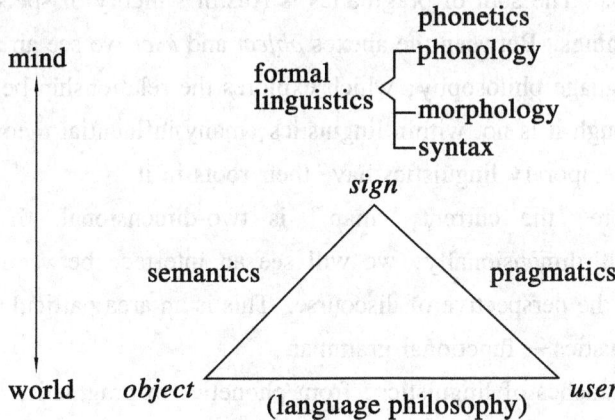

Fig 2.1   The interrelationship of the main areas of linguistics

If linguistics is compared to Disneyland, Fig. 2.1 can serve as a tourist map. The apexes of the triangle are language signs, objects the signs refer to and users of language. The areas above the apex *sign* are phonetics, phonology, morphology and syntax, which are only related to signs. Phonetics deals with the physical foundation of human language — articulation, which is a relatively independent area. In fact, some western universities even have "the department of phonetics and linguistics", indicating that they take phonetics as a parallel domain with linguistics. The other three branches belong to a general domain — formal linguistics, or core linguistics, whose interest is concentrated on the formal structure of linguistic signs. Phonology studies the distribution of sounds in a language and the interactions between those different sounds. Morphology is the study of word-making and word-marking. Syntax studies the organization of words into phrases, and phrases into sentences.

The area concerning the relationship between sign and object is semantics, so it is located on the left side of the triangle. According to de Saussure, the relationship here is mainly of arbitrariness. Semantics focuses its study on meaning, including meaning of words, phrases, and sentences, without considering contextual influence.

On the right side there is the recently-opened-up area — pragmatics, which is concerned with how people use language within a context and why they use language in particular ways. The soul of pragmatics is Austin's theory of speech acts — using language to do things. Between the apexes *object* and *user* we see an area adjacent to linguistics — language philosophy, which explores the relationship between language and reality. Though it is not within linguistics, many influential theories of different branches of contemporary linguistics have their roots in it.

What's more, the current "map" is two-dimensional. If we view the relationships multi-dimensionally, we will see an interface between semantics and pragmatics from the perspective of discourse. This is an area particularly explored by a school in linguistics — functional grammar.

All these branches of linguistics, from phonetics to pragmatics, are introduced between Chapter 3 and Chapter 9, with each branch either occupying one chapter or extending across two or three chapters, sometimes interwoven with an aspect of another branch.

The second stage of our "tour" is the comprehensive introduction to some important aspects of interdisciplinary studies, some having more to do with the mind, some having more to do with the world. Such discussion covers chapters 10-15, mainly within the domains of psycholinguistics, neurolinguistics, sociolinguistics, typology and applied linguistics. Limited space does not permit any thorough introduction to all these subjects. However, as a rainbow of different highlights and applications of these areas, the content of each chapter will be much effective in arousing the learners' interest in delving into a more systematic study of the related discipline in the future. Each chapter features an attractive thesis — language instinct, language convention, language acquisition, second language, universals and diversities, global language, respectively.

Science tells us that nature is a physical continuum, which does not break itself into physics, chemistry, psychology, linguistics... ; these disciplines are not facts but our decisions. They are different perspectives from which we talk about the world. Accordingly, language should be studied as a whole, too. Otto Jespersen, one of the greatest linguists of the 20th century, points out that the essence of language is human activity — activity on the part of one individual to make himself understood by another, and activity on the part of that other to understand what was in the mind of the first. This activity is a continuum, which cannot be split into detached research objects for phonetics, phonology, morphology, syntax, semantics, or pragmatics. These branches of linguistics are just different levels at which we talk about language.

If we draw a clear line between the branches, what we introduce will be dispersed and fragmentary. It will be difficult for learners to collect a concept of linguistics as a whole. We should not therefore ignore the interrelationships and interactions between the branches.

That is the reason why the present course is designed in the present way.

EXERCISES ✍

I. Translate the following quotations into Chinese.

> *Linguistic knowledge as represented in the speaker's mind is called a grammar. Linguistic theory is concerned with revealing the nature of the mental grammar which represents speakers' knowledge of their language.*
>
> *Grammar as viewed here is different from the usual notion of grammar.*
>
> (from V. Fromkin: *Linguistics*)
>
> *Grammar is the ability to use structures accurately, meaningfully, and appropriately.*
>
> (from D. Larsen-Freeman: *A Lecture on SLA*)

II. Fill in the blanks with the names of linguists or organizations.

1) _____ asserted that there was a "legislator" who gave the correct, natural name to everything, and languages belonged to states but not to individuals.

2) _____ pointed out that babies' cry is a sort of natural sounds, which could never develop into a language.

3) A cornerstone of science is _____'s intuition that nature is perfect.

4) _____ first proposed that a language in South Asia be a relative of many European languages.

5) The origin of language as a topic was banned by _____ founded in 1866.

III. Designate the following research questions to different branches of linguistics.

1) What determines whether a string of words in a language is a sentence or simply a string of unrelated words?

2) How do people use language within a context and why do they use it in particular ways?

3) What are words like?

4) What are speech sounds? What is their physical nature?

5) How do sounds behave in languages?

6) Why does one set of words mean one thing and a similar set means something very different?

7) When do two different sentences mean the same thing? How can one sentence mean more than one thing?

IV. Designate the following research questions to the different interdisciplinary domains introduced in this chapter.

1) How similar are the process of listening and reading?

2) When did spelling start diverging from pronunciation, why, and what was people's reaction?

3) How do we decide what is a dialect or an accent and what is a language?

4) What mechanisms operate during speech production to ensure that all the words come out in the right order and with the right intonation?

5) How do speakers signal their identity in the language they use, and why do people who live in specific communities sometimes speak in a similar way?

6) Examine the text of a play for evidence of implicit messages, and consider what the playwright is deliberately conveying about the attitudes and personality of the characters.

7) How should we teach a foreign language?

8) To what extent do children vary in their language acquisition and usage? And why?

V. Give a summary of less than 150 words to Section 2.1 *Speculation.*

VI. Questions for discussion.

1) What is the difference between science and philosophy in methodology?

2) What can be regarded as a scientific theory?

3) Why should language be studied scientifically?

4) What is the role of speculation in linguistic studies?

5) The following are all essential factors in scientific research. Can you list more? Can you point out their interrelationships and interactions?

speculation   observation   description   explanation

phenomenon   data   hypothesis   evidence

induction   deduction   testability   falsifiability

VII. Challenging work.

1) Give an example (in any scientific study, unnecessary to be restricted to linguistics) to show how a learner may drift at loose ends between different doctrines of different schools due to lack of independent thinking.

2) Do you accept the following sentences in Chinese? Why?

    (1) 张三容易动怒

    (2) 张三容易苦笑

    (3) 张三容易跳高

    (4) 张三容易走神

    (5) 张三容易犯傻

3) Write an essay on the following topic：

Is linguistics also a subject of arts?

■■

O. Jespersen (1860—1943)

Otto Jespersen was an internationally influential Danish linguist. He was born in Randers in northern Jutland and attended Copenhagen University, earning degrees in English, French, and Latin. He also studied linguistics at Oxford.

Jespersen was a professor of English at Copenhagen University from 1893 to 1925. Along with Paul Passy, he was a founder of the International Phonetic Association. He was a vocal supporter and active developer of artificial international languages such as Esperanto. He was also involved in the delegation that created the artificial language Ido and later developed the Novial language, which he considered an improvement.

He was most widely recognized for some of his books. His monumental work *A Modern English Grammar on Historical Principles* concentrated on morphology and syntax. His *Growth and Structure of the English Language* is a comprehensive view of English by someone with another native language, and still in print, over 60 years after his death and nearly 100 years after publication.

More than once he was invited to the U. S. as a guest lecturer, and he took occasion to study the country's educational system. As a foremost authority on English grammar, he helped to revolutionize language teaching in Europe.

Linguistic Stars

■ ■

Reading recommendation

Beginner-friendly：

G. Yule. The Study of Language. 2nd edition. Cambridge University Press, 1996；外语教学与研究出版社,2000(戴曼纯,何兆雄　导读)

More challenging：

J. Aitchison. The Seeds of Speech：Language Origin and Evolution. Cambridge University Press, 1996；外语教学与研究出版社, 2002(陈国华　导读)

A. Wray, K. Trott, A. bloomer, S. Reay, and C. Butler. Projects in Linguistics：A Practical Guide to Researching Language. Edward Arnold (Publisher) Limited, 1998；外语教学与研究出版社,2001(严辰松　导读)

N. Chomsky. New Horizons in the Study of Language and Mind. Cambridge University Press, 2000；外语教学与研究出版社,2002(程工　导读)

桂诗春,宁春岩.语言学方法论.外语教学与研究出版社,1997

Beware of *heard*, a dreadful word,
That looks like *beard* and sounds like *bird*.
And *dead*: it's said like *bed*, not *bead*—
For goodness sake don't call it "*deed*"!
Watch out for *meat* and *great* and *threat*
(They rhyme with *suite* and *straight* and *debt*).

by T. S. W.

Chapter 3

Speech Sounds and Their System

Sound is the most widely used medium in human language. The use of sounds involves three phases in the communication process. First, a speaker encodes meaning into sounds and utters strings of them. Then, the sounds are transmitted in the air. Finally, a listener perceives them and decodes them into meaning.

The science of speech sounds is called phonetics. It aims to provide the set of features or properties that can be used to describe and distinguish all the sounds used in human language.

In accordance with the three phases just mentioned, phonetics is divided into three sub-fields. Articulatory phonetics studies speech production by the speech organs; acoustic phonetics studies physical properties of speech sounds; and auditory phonetics studies the perception of speech sounds in the human auditory and cognitive system.

A large part of this chapter focuses on articulatory phonetics, which will gradually be intermingled with a brief introduction of the studies of the structure and systematic patterning of sounds in human language — another subfield of linguistics

—phonology, and the close relationship between these two areas.

3.1 IPA

It is often a terrible job for learners of English as a foreign language to tell the differences in pronouncing the letter combination "ough" in such words as *tough*, *bough*, *cough*, *dough*, *thorough* and *through*. Since the written system of a language does not always give a reliable guide to pronunciation, phonetics has its own tool to transcribe speech sounds of different languages. This is the International Phonetic Alphabet (IPA). The first version of IPA was published in August 1888. Its major author was a French linguist Paul Passy (1859—1940). The design principles of IPA were that there should be a separate letter for each distinctive sound, and that the same symbol should be used for that sound in any language in which it appears.

With these symbols, describing the sounds of a language is no longer a troublesome task. Take the English letter combination "ough" as an example again. Its variations of pronunciation in different words can be exactly distinguished with IPA symbols:

English spelling: *Tough   bough   cough   dough   thorough   through*

IPA transcription: [tʌf]   [bau]   [kɔf]   [dəʊ]   ['θʌrə]   [θruː]

The following is a list of the IPA symbols used to represent speech sounds in modern English.

Vowels

Monophthongs		Diphthongs	
[iː] as in *eat*	[ɪ] as in *bit*	[ei] as in *day*
[ɑː] as in *palm*	[e] as in *bet*	[ai] as in *die*
[ɜː] as in *earn*	[æ] as in *bat*	[ɔi] as in *boy*
[ɔː] as in *paw*	[ʌ] as in *cut*	[au] as in *how*
[uː] as in *too*	[ɔ] as in *cot*	[əʊ] as in *go*
	[ʊ] as in *put*	[iə] as in *fear*
	[ə] as in *about*	[ɛə] as in *air*
		[ʊə] as in *poor*

Consonants

[p]	as in *pin*	[f]	as in *fin*	[h]	as in *how*
[b]	as in *bin*	[v]	as in *van*	[m]	as in *more*
[t]	as in *tin*	[θ]	as in *thing*	[n]	as in *no*
[d]	as in *din*	[ð]	as in *this*	[ŋ]	as in *long*
[k]	as in *kin*	[s]	as in *sing*	[l]	as in *low*
[g]	as in *girl*	[z]	as in *zoo*	[r]	as in *red*
[tʃ]	as in *chin*	[ʃ]	as in *shoe*	[j]	as in *yet*
[dʒ]	as in *gin*	[ʒ]	as in *measure*	[w]	as in *wet*

A small insect familiar to all of us is called *bee*. When we give out the name, how many sounds do we produce? "Just one," you may respond. But a phonetician will think you are wrong. "It's two," he will correct you, "The first is a consonant [b]; the second is a vowel [iː]." Similarly, a longer word like *honey* contains four sounds (two consonants, two vowels) instead of "two" as people may feel. A "sound" people say they produce is actually a combination of sounds called a syllable, which is often related to a chest pulse. Each chest pulse is accompanied by increased air pressure, which attains its peak in the central part of a syllable that has more sound quality than the surrounding sounds. Therefore, a syllable is easy to distinguish.

Bee is a single-syllable word, and *honey* involves two syllables. Syllable by syllable, pulse by pulse, the sounds people produce during speech are continuous. To our ears, each syllable is just one continuous "sound". For example, in the English word *dog* there are three sounds [d], [ɔ], [g], which make a closed syllable. In saying this word, no native speakers of English will produce one sound first, then another, then the last. They just move their speech organs to produce a continuous signal [dɔg].

Phonetic analysis is needed as the first step to reveal the secrets of language and mind. In phonetics, a syllable in continuous speech can be segmented into a sequence of sound units, like [d], [ɔ], [g] for [dɔg]. The properties of these separate sounds, or segments in phonetician's jargon, can be described in several dimensions, specifically, the place of articulation and the manner of articulation.

The place of articulation refers to the point in the vocal tract at which the main closure or narrowing is made so as to modify the flow of air from the chest to the mouth in producing a sound. Organs in the vocal tract, such as the lips, teeth, or hard palate, are called articulators.

The manner of articulation refers to the type of constriction or movement that occurs at any place of articulation. Take [p] for example. The [p] sound is produced in three phases: first, closing the lips to shut off the vocal tract completely; second, forcing air out of the lungs to build up a pressure inside the mouth; third, suddenly opening the lips to release the pressure. The sound produced in this manner is a plosive lasting for a very short time.

3.2 Articulation

It is postulated that the remote ancestors of human beings might have used both visual and vocal signals to communicate. As the ideas they exchanged became more and more complex, they tended to use their voice more often than their hands. Their selection of a sound language came so late that there were hardly any early human organs that evolved specifically for verbal articulation except the vocal cords — thin bands of muscle in the larynx at the upper end of a person's windpipe that can be made to move rapidly by the passing of air and thus produce sound. Other organs involved in the production of speech evolved originally for the basic biological needs of breathing and eating, though phoneticians also call them speech organs. They are the lungs, which provide the energy — a stream of air — for the production of speech sounds, the windpipe (or academically, the trachea), the pharynx, the nose, and the mouth. The cavities of the pharynx, mouth, and nose form a long tubular structure called the vocal tract, where the air stream from the larynx is affected by the action of several mobile vocal organs such as the tongue, soft palate, and lips, which work together to make a wide range of speech sounds. The production of different speech sounds through the use of these organs is known as articulation.

Lung air has to be changed into audible vibrations before it becomes speech sounds. A main source of vibration is provided by the vocal cords (or vocal folds),

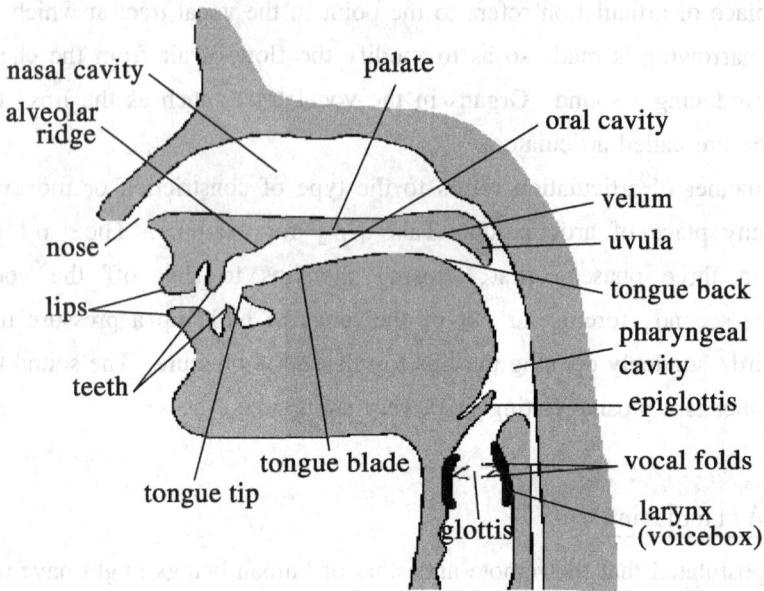

Fig 3.1　Principal organs of articulation

which are two muscular tissues located at the upper part of our trachea—larynx. We can feel the movement of vocal cords in speech production. Press your fingers on your throat around the Adam's apple area and say "ssss" and "zzzz" loudly. At the production of "zzzz", you will feel the vibration of the vocal cords and at the production of "ssss", you will not. Another way to feel this is to cover your ear with your fingers and you will hear the resonance of vibration at saying "zzzz". The vibration of the vocal cords also gives us pitch, which contributes to tone, stress and intonation in language. The faster the vocal cords vibrate, the higher the pitch goes. Our singing behavior involves controlling the vibration of vocal cords to hit high and low notes.

　　Once air passes the larynx, it enters the vocal tract, which functions as a resonance box. We change the shape of this box by moving our lips, jaw, tongue and velum. Different configurations give us different speech sounds.

3.3 Consonants

Speech sounds are traditionally classified as consonants and vowels, though the scientific definition of this dichotomy for all the languages of the world remains a tough job. The most common view is that consonants are sounds made by a closure in the vocal tract, or by a narrowing from which air cannot escape without producing audible friction, and vowels are sounds in which there is no obstruction to the flow of air as it passes from the larynx to the lips. Vowels function as the main sounds of syllables, either alone or combined with consonants.

Let's deal with consonants first.

Two reference points are involved in defining consonantal places of articulation. One is the active articulator which moves; the other is the passive articulator with which the active one makes contact. For instance, the sound [t] is made by placing the tip of the tongue against the gum ridge behind the upper teeth, where the tongue tip is active and the gum ridge, or in phonetician's jargon, the alveolar ridge, is passive.

The following are eleven possible places of articulation for consonants of all human languages, with the first eight workable in English.

1. Bilabial, formed by bringing the lips together, e. g. [p], [m]. Here the function of lips is somewhat complicated: they both can be regarded as the active and passive articulators simultaneously.

2. Labio-dental, formed by the lower lip against the upper teeth, e. g. [f].

3. Dental, formed by placing the tip of the tongue against the upper teeth, e. g. [ð].

4. Alveolar, formed by placing the tip or blade of the tongue against the alveolar ridge, e. g. [t].

5. Palatal, formed by the front of the tongue against the hard palate, namely, the roof of the mouth, e. g. [j].

6. Palato-alveolar, formed midway between the places of articulation for palatals and alveolars: the blade (and sometimes the tip) of the tongue articulates with the alveolar ridge, with a simultaneous raising of the front of the tongue

towards the hard palate, e. g. [ʃ].

7. Velar, formed by the back of the tongue against the soft palate, e. g. [k].

8. Glottal, formed by the vocal cords coming together to cause a closure or friction, e. g. [h].

9. Retroflex, formed when the apex of the tongue is curled back in the direction of the hard palate, as heard in many Indian English accents.

10. Uvular, formed by the back of the tongue against the uvula, as heard in some accents of French.

11. Pharyngeal, formed in the pharynx, the part of the throat above the larynx. Specifically, the front wall of the pharynx articulates with the back wall, as heard in Arabic.

Consonants are also classified according to the manner of articulation, concerning which phoneticians tend to consider several factors.

The first factor is the degree of the constriction of airflow. At least six main classes can be distinguished in English.

1. Plosive, formed by completely closing the air passage and suddenly removing the obstacle, so that the air escapes making an explosive sound, e. g. [p], [d]. It belongs to a broader category called "stop" which includes closures produced by air streams not from the lungs, as encountered in some southern African languages.

2. Nasal, formed with the soft palate lowered, thus allowing air to resonate in the nose, e. g. [m].

3. Affricate, a consonant which starts as a plosive, but instead of ending with plosion, ends with a fricative made in the same place, e. g. [tʃ].

4. Liquid, formed by some obstruction of the air stream in the mouth, which seems not enough to cause any real constriction or friction, e. g. [l], [r]. [l] is called a lateral liquid, because in making it, an obstacle is placed in the middle of the mouth, leaving the air free to escape at one or both sides.

5. Fricative, formed by a narrowing of the air passage at some point so that the air in escaping makes audible frication. e. g. [f], [z]. Some fricatives are also called sibilants, which are made with a groove-like structure in the front

part of the tongue, producing a kind of hissing sound, e. g. [s], [ʃ].

6. Glide, sometimes called semi-vowel because it is typically produced with the tongue moving, or "gliding", to or from the position of a nearby vowel, e. g. [h], [w].

place manner	bilabial		labio- dental	dental	alveolar	palatal	Palato- alveolar	velar		glottal
plosive	p	b			t d			k	g	
nasal		m			n				ŋ	
affricate							tʃ dʒ			
liquid					l r					
fricative			f v	θ ð s z			ʃ ʒ			
glide		w				j				h

Tab. 3.1   The classification of English consonants

The second factor is voicing. Voice is caused by the vibration of the vocal cords. Several pairs of similarly articulated sounds are distinguished in many languages as voiced and voiceless. For example, [p] is a voiceless consonant, and [b] is a voiced one. Other such pairs in English are [t] and [d], [k] and [g], [f] and [v], [s] and [z], [θ] and [ð], [ʃ] and [ʒ], [tʃ] and [dʒ].

The third factor is aspiration. This is the sound of air rushing through the vocal tract, usually found after the release of plosive consonants in some situation. Take the English words *pit* and *spit* for example. If you listen carefully to the pronunciation of "p" in them, you should be able to hear that the "p" of *pit* is followed by a puff of breath which is absent in *spit*. This puff of breath is aspiration. In IPA, aspiration is transcribed by means of a raised "h", e. g. [pʰ], [tʰ], [kʰ]. This phenomenon is more frequently encountered in some other languages. In Chinese Pinyin, for example, the pronunciation of the letters "p" and "b" is quite different from that in English. They are not a pair of voiceless and voiced consonants; instead, both of them are voiceless: "p" in Chinese is voiceless aspirated ([pʰ]) and pronounced in the same way as the English sound "p" in *pit*, while "b" in Chinese is just voiceless ([p]), and pronounced in the same way as the English sound "p" in *spit*.

3.4 Vowels

While the consonant sounds are mostly produced with a constriction in the oral cavity, vowel sounds are articulated with the oral cavity relatively open to the flow of air. Different vowels result from changing the shape of the mouth; all of them are voiced continuous sounds.

The qualities of vowels depend upon the positions of the tongue and lips. For example, to pronounce [iː], the lips are somewhat pulled back and the front part of the tongue is raised high toward the palate. In fact, the position of the tongue in smiling is quite similar to that in producing [iː]. That is why a cameraman often asks his customer to say "cheese" [tʃiːz] in taking a picture. The [iː] sound, therefore, is called a "high, front" vowel. In contrast, the tongue in pronouncing [ɑː] turns flattened and lowered. When a doctor intends to examine the throat of his patient, he may ask the patient to say [ɑː] so that the tongue will be low and easy to see over. The sound [ɑː], therefore, is classified as a "low, back" vowel. It has been claimed that [iː] and [ɑː] are the most basic vowels, which are found in almost all the languages in the world and are the vowels that babies learn first. Vowels with the tongue in a high position like [iː] will keep the mouth fairly closed, so we call them close vowels. Those like [ɑː] that require the tongue to move lower and cause the mouth to open wider are called open vowels.

Similarly, [uː] is a "high, back, close" vowel, because to pronounce it, the tongue is raised toward the back of the mouth while the lips are rounded and pushed forward, almost closing the mouth. Moreover, [e] is labeled as a semi-closed vowel and [ɔː] a semi-open one, with the middle part of the tongue in the raised position when articulating them.

Vowel quality is also largely dependent on the shape of the lips, which may be held in a neutral shape, or spread out so as to leave a long narrow opening between them, or drawn together so that the opening between them is more or less round. In

English, there are four rounded vowels, namely, [uː], [ʊ], [ɔː], [ɔ], which are all back vowels. [ɑː] is the only English back vowel that occurs without lip rounding. Besides, all nonback vowels are also unrounded in English but not so in all languages. French and Swedish, for example, have both front and back rounded vowels.

There is another interesting rule: all the long vowels (transcribed with a diacritic "colon" after the segment, e. g. [iː], [uː]) are tense vowels, and all the short vowels (e. g. [ɪ], [ʊ]) are lax vowels. Though both the sounds [iː] and [ɪ] are classified as "high, front", the long vowel [iː] is articulated with a slightly higher tongue position than the short vowel [ɪ] owing to the higher tension of the tongue muscles in producing it. This is also true for [uː] and [ʊ], and [ɔː] and [ɔ].

In French, Portuguese, Polish and some other European languages, we can see another characteristic of vowels — nasalization, i. e. some of the airflow is allowed to escape through the nose. This can be identified when a French friend greets you with *Bon jour* in the morning: Vowels in French syllables *bon*, *fin*, *dans*, and *brun* are nasalized. Nasalization of a vowel can be transcribed with a diacritic mark ~ over the vowel, as in Bonjour [bɔ̃ʒuːr].

So far we have discussed a number of important criteria for vowel classification, namely the location of the tongue in the mouth, the openness of the mouth, the shape of the lips, the length and tenseness in articulation and the nasalization.

mouth \ tongue	front	central	back	Tongue height
close	iː ɪ		uː ʊ	high
semi-close	e	ɜː		mid
semi-open		ə	ɔː	
open	æ a	ʌ	ɔ ɑː	low

Tab. 3.2   The classification of English vowels

The vowels we have discussed until now are all simple ones called monophthongs, or pure vowels, for which the organs of speech remain in a given position for an appreciable period of time. Another category, called diphthongs can also be encountered in English, Chinese and many other languages. They are transcribed by a sequence of two letters, e. g. [ei], [əʊ], [ai], [aʊ], [ɔi], [iə], [ɛə], [ʊə]. When a diphthong is pronounced, the organs of speech start in the position of one vowel and immediately move in the direction of another vowel. This deliberate glide must be performed with a single impulse of the breath; if there is more than one impulse, the ear will perceive two separate syllables.

Every vowel constitutes a single syllable. The vowel can be a monophthong, a diphthong, or even a triphthong that contains three distinctive qualities, e. g. [aiə] in *tyre*, [aʊə] in *tower*, and [ɔiə] in *loyal*. However, not every syllable contains a vowel. The second syllable of the word *little* ['litl] has no vowel after the plosive [t] but a liquid [l]. Liquids [l], [r] and nasals [m], [n] are sometimes syllabic.

3.5 Phonemes and allophones

From studying the previous two sections you have got a general picture of speech sounds. Maybe you feel it is not an easy job to become familiar with all the features of consonants and vowels, some of which you have never encountered in your mother tongue. Actually, each language has a special inventory of sounds, and no two languages organize their sound inventories the same way. For example, the consonant [b] is not used in Chinese, where the voiceless aspirated [pʰ] is used in contrast with the unaspirated voiceless [p] in distinguishing words (e. g. 怕 vs. 坝). In English, [b] is frequently encountered while [pʰ] and [p] do not appear in the same position (e. g. *pit* pronounced as ['pʰit] vs *spit* pronounced as ['spit]).

Therefore, [pʰ] and [p] are distinctive sounds in Chinese. They are called phonemes. Phonemes have no meaning of themselves, but they are the smallest linguistic unit, whose change will lead to the change of meaning. Look at the following sentence, below which the alphabets between the slant brackets (//) are phonemes.

(3.1) *It is a big pig.*
/b/ /p/

A normal sentence, isn't it? But, if one reverses the distinctive feature — voiced and voiceless — between the initial phonemes of the words *pig* and *big*, he will surely pronounce a wrong sentence:

(3.2) * It is *a pig big.*

[p] [b]

So, a phoneme is defined as the smallest unit of sound in a language which can distinguish two words.

A phoneme of a language may not exist in another language at all, like the case of [b], a phoneme existing in English but unavailable in Chinese. Besides, two sounds may be distinguished as phonemes in one language but turn undistinguishable in another language. (3.3) is an illustration.

(3.3) *She bought a pair of shoes.*

[ʃ]   [ʃw]

The letter combination *sh* in English is pronounced [ʃ] except the case when it is located before /uː/, where it should be pronounced [ʃw] instead. [ʃ] and [ʃw] are different sounds, but their occurrence in English is conditioned by neighboring sounds and thus said to be in complementary distribution. They are called allophones. Allophones are not designated with slant brackets (//). Instead, they are still in ordinary phonetic brackets ([ ]). A pair of sounds with a certain distinctive feature can be two phonemes of a language but allophones in another language. As we have seen, [pʰ] and [p] are phonemes in Chinese but allophones in English.

Allophones like [ʃ] and [ʃw] in English are examples of the positional variant of a phoneme, which is characterized by a complementary distribution. The relationship between [pʰ] in *pit* and [p] in *spit* (both in the initial consonant position of the word) is also a complementary distribution, so they are allophones in English, too. Another category is called free variant of a phoneme, which can be substituted for another without bringing about a change of meaning. For example, in *Stand up*, the lips may remain closed or there may be an aspiration at the end of this utterance; it makes no difference. Thus, the two final sounds [p˺] (˺ stands for unreleased) and [pʰ] are said to be in free variation.

A phonetic property that distinguishes phonemes from one another is called a distinctive feature. Such a feature usually represents a certain controllable aspect of articulation, and is viewed as basically binary, marked as either + or − and enclosed in square brackets ([ ]) as a convention. Each phoneme of a language has a group of distinctive features. Take /m/ as an example. It is [+ consonantal], [+ voiced], [+ nasal], [− lateral], [− affricate], [+ labial], [− round], [+ anterior], [− high], [− back], [− low], [− / + syllabic] ... And [ɪ] is [− consonantal], [+ high], [− back], [− low], [− round], [+ syllabic]... Distinctive features are also different from language to language because each language has its own phonemes to describe. Aspiration, for instance, cannot be used to distinguish phonemes in English, so it is not a distinctive feature in English. It is, however, a distinctive feature in Chinese for distinguishing /pʰ/ and /p/.

What we have discussed in this section are the basic concepts of phonology. What are the differences between phonology and phonetics which we have dealt with earlier in this chapter? Both phonetics and phonology can be generally described as the study of speech sounds. Phonetics is more specifically the study of how speech sounds are produced, what their physical properties are, and how they are interpreted. Phonology, on the other hand, is a description of the sounds of a particular language and the rules governing the distribution of those sounds. Thus we can talk about the phonology of Chinese, English, German, or any other language. Furthermore, phonology is also concerned with the universal properties of natural language sound systems and aims at revealing the general principles of the sound patterns of all languages.

3.6 Stress and pitch

This section discusses the combination and interaction of phonemes from both phonetic and phonological perspectives. Let's start from the syllable.

A syllable can be stressed in actual pronunciation by making it louder, longer, or/and giving it a higher pitch. In languages like English, stress plays a decisive part in word pronunciation. For instance, the word *university* has primary stress on the third syllable, secondary stress on the first syllable, and no stress on the remaining three syllables. It is thus transcribed phonetically as [ˌuːnɪˈvɜːsətɪ]. If a non-native speaker misses the correct location of the levels of stress in pronouncing this word, he may run into trouble in making himself understood.

Stress is not independent of higher-level grammatical structure. Notice that in some noun and verb forms of identically spelled words — for example, the noun *record* and the verb *record* — stress reflects a part-of-speech categorization.

Human speech is colorful not only due to the stress patterns but also thanks to the change of pitch. Pitch is the auditory sensation of the height of a sound. Only in very unusual situations do we speak with fixed, unvarying pitch. When we speak normally, the pitch of our voice constantly changes. Pitch variation is found in all languages, but its function is very different from one language type to another. Broadly speaking, there are two ways in which languages make use of pitch variations in speech. In languages such as English, French, and German, regular sequences of different pitches characterize stretches of speech between pauses and are known collectively as intonation. The differences of intonation may correlate with different types of utterances. In English, when one ends the sentence *Tomorrow at five o'clock then* with a falling pitch, his audience know it is a statement of a fixed time for an appointment; when he ends the same sequence of words *Tomorrow at five o'clock then* with a rising pitch, his audience know it is a question for confirmation of the time of the appointment.

In languages such as Chinese, Vietnamese, Thai, and Zulu, pitch differences help to distinguish one word from another and may be the only differentiating feature between two or more words whose composition is the same in terms of consonants and vowels. Pitch differences used in these ways are called tones and these languages are called tone languages. Their difference from non-tone languages can be illustrated by a Chinese tongue twister *Ma ma ma ma*. It consists of four repeated syllables *ma*. The first syllable should be produced with high-rising tone, the second with high-level tone, the third with high falling tone, and the last with low-falling-rising tone. If the appropriate tone pattern is followed, this short utterance means "A pockmarked lady scolds a horse" (Its corresponding written characters are 麻妈骂

马). The northern dialect of Chinese has four distinctive tones: high-level, high-rising, low-falling-rising, and high-falling; Cantonese, a southern dialect of Chinese, has six: mid-level, low-level, high-falling, low-falling, high-rising, and low-rising; Thai, a Southeast Asian language has five: low-, mid-, and high-falling, high-rising, and low-falling-rising; Zulu, a language in South Africa has the simplest tone system: high vs low.

Stress, pitch, tone and intonation are also called suprasegmentals because they relate to aspects of pronunciation that go beyond the production of individual segments.

If we go still further, we will enter a new domain—morphology.

EXERCISES

I. Translate the following quotation into Chinese.

Phonetics provides the means for describing speech sounds; phonology studies the ways in which speech sounds form systems and patterns in human language. The phonology of a language is then the system and pattern of the speech sounds. We see that the word phonology is thus used in two ways, either as the study of sound patterns in language or as the sound pattern of a language.

(from V. Fromkin & R. Roman: *An Introduction to Language*)

II. Match each of the speech organs on the left with its proper description on the right (Refer to Fig. 3.1 on p 36 if you find the task difficult).

Larynx	The backward continuation of the roof of the mouth, which can be lowered to let air pass through the nose
Pharynx	The bony prominence behind the upper front teeth
Vocal cords	The tube-like passage in the throat which connects the larynx to the upper part of the vocal tract
Soft palate	The roof of the mouth
Hard palate	Two muscular folds in the larynx that vibrate as a source of sound
Alveolar ridge	The passage between lungs and larynx
Trachea	The beginning of the vocal tract, containing the vocal cords

III. Give the IPA symbol for each of the consonants described below.

1) voiced bilabial plosive
2) voiceless alveolar plosive
3) voiceless dental fricative
4) voiced bilabial nasal
5) voiceless labio-dental fricative
6) voiced alveolar (lateral) liquid
7) voiced palato-alveolar affricate
8) voiced palatal glide

9) voiced velar nasal

10) voiceless alveolar fricative

IV. Which one of the four choices below each vowel is not a phonetic feature of that sound?

1) ɜː

    a) semi-closed   b) front   c) mid   d) unrounded

2) æ

    a) semi-open   b) front   c) low   d) unrounded

3) uː

    a) closed   b) back   c) low   d) rounded

4) ə

    a) semi-open   b) central   c) high   d) always unstressed

5) i

    a) close   b) front   c) high   d) rounded

V. Tell which of the following statements are incorrect.

1) The connected passages inside the chest which form the system used to produce speech is called vocal tract.

2) The vocal tract starts at the larynx and includes the pharynx, the mouth, and the nasal cavity.

3) Auditory phonetics studies the physical properties of speech sounds, the way sounds travel from the speaker to the hearer.

4) Segment is the smallest unit that can be identified in continuous speech.

5) A syllable occasionally contains two or three vowels.

6) A word consists of one or more syllables, with a distinctive stress pattern in languages like Chinese, or a distinctive tone pattern in tone languages like English.

7) Allophone is the phonetic variant of a phoneme, which can be substituted for another without bringing about a change of meaning.

8) Phoneme is the smallest unit of sound in a language which can distinguish two words.

VI. Give a summary of less than 150 words to Section 3.3 *Consonants and vowels.*

VII. Challenging work.

1) How do vowels differ from consonants?

2) List some roles played by the suprasegmentals mentioned in this chapter. Cite examples from different languages you know to illustrate these roles.

3) The following is a humorous story written by a famous American Chinese linguist Chao Yuen Ren（赵元任）in Chinese. All the syllables of the words he used are the same, namely, *shi* in Pinyin.

The story in Pinyin：

shíshì shīshì shīshì, shì shī, shì shí shí shī。 shì shíshí shì shì shì shī。 shíshí,
shì shí shī shì shì。 shìshí,shì shīshì shì shì。 shì shì shì shí shī, shì shí shí shí shì,
shí shì shí shī shìshì。 shì shí shì shí shī shī, shì shíshì。 shíshì shī, shì shí shì shì
shíshì。 shíshì shì, shì shí shì shí shí shī shī。 shí shí, shí shí shì shí shī shī shí shí
shí shī shī。 shì shì shì shì。

The story in Chinese characters：

石室诗士施氏,嗜狮,誓食十狮。氏时时适市视狮。十时,适十狮适市。是
时,适施氏适市。氏视是十狮,恃十石矢势,使是十狮逝世。氏拾是十狮尸,适石
室。石室湿,氏使侍拭石室。石室拭,氏始试食十狮尸。食时,始识是十狮尸实十
石狮尸。试释是事。

Suggested work：

1) Read the story in Pinyin to others who have not heard it before, to see whether they can understand your reading.

2) Then read the story in characters, and ask others to comment your pronunciation by referring to its Pinyin version.

3) What features of Chinese as a tone language will you and your partners summarize after handling the story in the above way?

4) Words with the same form but different meanings are called homonyms; words with the same pronunciation but different meanings are called homophones.

How many homonyms and homophones have you identified in this story? Is a tone language richer in homonyms and homophones than non-tone languages? Cite examples to support your opinion.

5) More challengingly and optionally, what phonetic discrepancies may you and your partners see between spoken Chinese and classical written Chinese （文言文）?

6) Discuss how to translate the story into English.

You can exchange your ideas with other readers on our course website.

■■

YR Chao（1892—1982）

Chao Yuen Ren（赵元任）, born in Tianjin with ancestry in Changzhou, Jiangsu Province, China, was one of the leading linguists in the world.

Chao went to the United States with a scholarship in 1910 to study mathematics at Cornell University. He got his PhD from Harvard University in 1918. Then he went to teach physics at Cornell University for one year. In 1920 he went back to China and taught psychology and physics in Tsinghua School. He reentered Harvard University in 1921, first researching phonetics, then teaching as a lecturer on philosophy, and then as a professor of Chinese language. In June, 1925 he returned to Tsinghua and soon became a fruitful researcher on phonology, dialectology, and general linguistics. In 1938 he left China and taught first for a short period at the University of Hawaii, and then at Yale University until 1941. Then he went back to Harvard University, teaching as well as editing dictionaries there for five years, and becoming an American citizen in the meantime. From 1947 he taught at the University of California, Berkeley. He retired in 1962 with the title Professor Emeritus there. Chao was the president of the Linguistic Society of America during 1945, and a special issue of the society's journal, *Language*, was dedicated to him in 1966. Chao went back with his wife and some family members to China for a visit in 1973, soon after the thawing of the relations between China and the USA, and was warmly welcomed by Premier Zhou Enlai and many of his old friends. He visited China again in 1981 and was granted Honorary Professor of Beijing University. Chao passed away on Feburary 24, 1982.

Chao published prolifically on language research, the most influential of which is *A Grammar of Spoken Chinese* (1968). Besides English, Chao could speak German, French, and Japanese. He was the interpreter of the renowned British philosopher Bertrand Russell when he visited China in 1920, and they became lifelong friends since then. Chao was also an excellent composer. His composition *How could I help thinking of her*（教我如何不想她）was a "pop hit" in the 1930s in China. The lyrics were written by Liu Bannong（刘半农）, another linguist who invented the Chinese feminine pronoun 她. His love of music brought him sensitive ears to sounds and tones, which was very helpful for his phological and dialectological study.

In the 1920s, Chao joined the initial work of shaping Gwoyeu Romatzyh（国语罗马字）, but, as a gifted punster, he also wrote the essay *the Lion-Eating Poet in the Stone Den*, which consisted of 92 characters all with the sound *shi* (though in the four different tones of Mandarin), and was incomprehensible when romanized.

■ ■

Reading recommendation

Beginner-friendly：

P. Roach. Phonetics. Oxford University Press 2001；上海外语教育出版社,2003

More challenging：

P. Roach. English Phonetics and Phonology：A Practical Course. 2nd edition. Cambridge University Press, 1991；外语教学与研究出版社,2000（王嘉龄　导读）

Alan Cruttenden. Intonation. 2nd edition. Cambridge University Press, 1997；北京大学出版社,2002

The Guinness Book of Records declared the "longest real word" in the English language to be **floccinaucinihilipilification** (29 letters), defined as *the act of estimating as worthless*. In the 1970s, there were advertisements for **lipsmackinthirstquenchinacetastinmotivatingoodbuzzincooltalkinhighwalkinfastlivinevergivincoolfizzin** Pepsi, coining a 100-letter term. Later, the 71-letter **twoallbeefpattiesspecialsaucelettucecheesepicklesonionsonasesameseedbun** was used in a McDonald's Restaurant advertisement to describe the Big Mac.

Chapter 4

Word-making and Word-marking

When we are asked to define the concept *word*, what come to our mind first may be its written features. An English speaker may think of the letters making up the word; a Chinese speaker may mention the written characters which comprise the word. Actually, however, the written form is none other than a derivative of a spoken word, with the latter used by all but the former shared by literates only. For any human language, its oral system is primary whereas its written form is secondary. Primarily, knowing a word means knowing both its sound and its meaning.

To convey meaning, sounds are combined into words. However, words are not the smallest unit of meaning. They are composed of smaller units of meaning, called morphemes. Some morphemes are added together to make a word. For example, *retell* is a word made up of two morphemes *re* and *tell*. Other morphemes are used to mark the grammatical process by which a word is used, such as tense, plurality, voice, etc. For example, *-ing* is such a morpheme in the present participle *eating*. The study of these meaning-bearing units and the rules governing them is called morphology.

4.1 Morphemes

Morphology deals with word structure. Many words are themselves morphemes, such as *big* and *book*. They cannot be broken into smaller units that in themselves carry meaning. We call them free morphemes.

Many other words are created by joining together two morphemes, e.g. *blackboard*, in which the two morphemes *black* and *board* can be recognized as meaningful words by themselves. So they are also free morphemes.

Another type of morpheme is the bound morpheme, which occurs only when attached to another morpheme, such as *-ly* in *happily* and *un-* in *unhappy*.

Such bound morphemes are called affixes, including the prefixes (e. g. *un-*) and the suffixes (e.g. *-ly*). Words with one or more affixes are called morphologically complex words, the core of which is a root, i. e. the morpheme that remains when all affixes are stripped. A root may either stand alone as a word (e. g. *happy* is the root of *unhappy*) or not (e. g. *ceive* is the root of *conceive*).

The function of an affix can be derivational or inflectional. A derivational morpheme is one that is added to a root to form a new word that differs, usually, in its part-of-speech classification. For example, when the suffix *-ness* is added to the adjective *happy*, the noun *happiness* is formed. Similarly, the adjective *great* becomes the adverb *greatly* when *-ly* is added. These examples suggest that certain aspects of morphology have syntactic implications in that nouns can be derived from verbs, verbs from adjectives, adjectives from nouns, and so on. Besides, the addition of a suffix usually has little effect on the basic meaning of the word. There are a few exceptions, like *-less* in *useless* and *-ify* in *purify* which means "to make pure".

Prefixes as derivational morphemes usually change the basic meaning of a word but do not change its part-of-speech classification. For example, *dis-* in *dislike*, and *in-* in *independence*. Exceptions include *en-* that can change a noun or an adjective to a verb, as in *enjoy* and *endear*.

A bound morpheme that is inserted in the middle of another morpheme is called infix, which is very rare in English. Examples include *-bloomin-* (an euphemism for *bloody*) in *absobloominlutely*, *-fucking-* in *Massafuckingchusetts*, and *-ma-* in *sophistimacated*, and *edumacation*, all used in informal, vulgar speech.

An inflectional morpheme indicates certain grammatical properties associated with nouns and verbs, such as gender, number, case, and tense. Unlike highly inflected languages such as Latin, English has very few inflectional morphemes. In English, the inflectional morphemes are all suffixes. The suffix *-s*, which indicates plurality in nouns as well as the third-person singular in verbs, is an inflectional morpheme; the past tense suffix *-ed*, which is added to verbs, is another.

According to Wilhelm von Humboldt, languages of the world can be classified morphologically into three types: isolating, inflecting, and agglutinating. An isolating language is also called an analytic language or root language, in which all the words are invariable. Chinese, Vietnamese and Samoan are typical cases. An inflecting language is also called a synthetic language or fusional language, in which grammatical relationships are expressed by changing the internal structure of the words — typically by the use of inflectional endings which express several grammatical meanings at once. Latin, Greek, and Arabic are clear cases. An agglutinating language is also called agglutinative language, in which a word typically consists of a neat linear sequence of morphemes, all clearly recognizable. Turkish, Finnish, Japanese, and Swahili are usual cases. Let's look at a group of morphemes in Turkish:

    (4.1) ev — house

         ler — PLURAL

         im — my

         in — GENETIVE

These morphemes, each corresponding to a single meaning, are simply connected linearly to form a word *evlerimin*, which means my houses.

Interestingly, English is not a typical example of any of these three categories.

Ancient English did have rich inflectional rules, since it shared the same origin with German. After England was occupied by French-speaking Norman invaders in 1,066, English became a vernacular and gradually lost most of its inflectional features in its arduous survival over centuries. Today's English is more similar to an isolating language: there are few inflectional endings, and word-order changes are the basis of the grammar. For example, (4.2) and (4.3) are totally different in meaning just because of the change in word order.

(4.2) *The mouse loves the rice.*

(4.3) *The rice loves the mouse.*

Therefore, English is referred to as a poor inflectional language. As a contrast, those rich inflectional languages do not rely so much on word order. For example, both (4.4) and (4.5) in German have the same meaning "The mouse loves the rice", though they are opposite in word order.

(4.4) *Die Maus liebt den Reis*

(4.5) *Den Reis liebt die Maus*

In German a noun's Case is always marked by the inflection of its article. *Die* is a nominative article for the feminine noun *Maus*, whereas *den* is an accusative article for a masculine noun *Reis*. Though *Den Reis* is located at the beginning of (4.5), it remains accusative and cannot be the subject. The subject is *die Maus* though it stays at the end of the sentence. In English, however, definite articles are the same in form, providing no information about the case of each noun. The syntactic role of a noun can only be identified through observing the word order — whether it is before the verb. Similarly, a Chinese nominative noun should be before the verb. For example：老鼠爱大米≠大米爱老鼠

Besides, English has some agglutinating structures as well. In fact, some of the longest words in English are made in this way. For example, *antidisestablishmentarianism* means "the belief which opposes removing the tie between church and state." Actually, it can be made even longer by putting *non-* at the beginning.

4.2 Morphemes in Chinese

Chinese is regarded as a typical analytical language. However, as one of the most widely spoken languages in the world, Chinese also has some inflectional and agglutinating structures.

Does Chinese have bound morphemes? Yes. Some common examples are as follows.

(4.6) 我昨天钓了几条鱼。

(4.7) 你钓了几条鱼?

(4.8) 你昨天钓几条鱼来着?

In (4.6) there is an inflectional morpheme 了, denoting the past tense here because the sentence has an adverbial denoting a specific point in the past——昨天. In (4.7) there is not any adverbial of time, so 了 can be regarded as a morpheme of the perfect aspect. Though the Chinese listeners can tolerate the dropping of 了 as in (4.8), they will expect some other tense marker like 来着 which always appears as an ending of the sentence. Similar structures can be found in (4.9) and (4.10) below, both denoting an aspect instead of a tense.

(4.9) 你钓了几条鱼了? (present perfect)

(4.10) 你现在干什么来着? (present continuous)

Comparing (4.9) with (4.7), we may feel that the sentence-final structures like 了 seem selective, but sometimes they seem indispensable to a certain word sequence:

(4.11) 她饭做好了。(present perfect)

Apparently, the subject-object-verb sequence of (4.11) —她饭做 will not be acceptable unless the aspect morpheme is added after the verb. This phenomenon resembles the morphology in Japanese, in which the verb is normally sentence-final with an agglutinated morpheme.

However, Chinese has no morphological agreement between the subject and the verb, which enables a non-nominative noun to be located immediately before the verb, like the case in (4.11) and (4.12).

(4.12) 她蔬菜不吃茄子。

Similar to English, the Chinese functional bound morphemes also fall into two categories. One is inflectional and with free distribution, such as 着, 了, 过, for verbs and 们 for nouns, all serving as grammatical markers; the other is derivational and distributed with limitations, such as 非 in 非人, 度 in 湿度, and 化 in 丑化, the role of which is to change the meaning as well as the lexical category of the words to which they attach.

As we have seen, Chinese has prefixes like 非, and suffixes like 度, 化, and 着, 了, 过. Does Chinese have infixes? The answer is also *yes*. These infixes can either be inflectional (e. g. 收工——收了工;坐牢——坐过牢) or derivational (e. g. 慷慨——慷他人之慨; 滑稽——滑天下之大稽), both distributed with limitations, however.

Does Chinese have free morphemes? Sure. For example, 一 is a free morpheme because it can appear alone as a cardinal number, or be attached by a bound morpheme 第 to form the ordinal number 第一. Most of the Chinese free morphemes are monosyllabic because Chinese is a tone language. A few Chinese free morphemes are disyllabic, for instance, 葡萄, 匍匐, 玻璃, etc.

4.3 Compounding

Compounding is a process that forms new words not by means of affixes but from two or more independent words. The words that are the parts of the compound can be free morphemes, words derived by affixation, or even words formed by compounding themselves. Below are some examples in English of these three types.

girlfriend	air-conditioner	passerby
blackboard	cutting-machine	aircraft carrier
soap opera	troublemaker	greenhouse effect

From the list above we see that in English, compound words are not represented consistently in writing. Sometimes they are written together, sometimes they are written with a hyphen, and sometimes they are written separately.

Compounds are different from phrases in that they symbolize an integrated concept. Phonologically, they have primary stress on the first word only, while individual words in phrases have independent primary stress. Some examples are listed below. (Primary stress is indicated by ´ on the vowel.)

compounds	phrases
dárkroom	dárk ròom
mákeup	máke úp

If you ask an English speaker what is a word in English, he can give you a clear definition: a word is the smallest unit of language that people can understand if it is said or written on its own. An English teacher can assign a composition task to his students by saying "Write an essay of about five hundred words". If a Chinese teacher described the requirement of his homework in this way, his students might be confused. Unlike the case in English, Chinese words are not separated from each other, and it is really hard for Chinese people to differentiate either between *zi*（字）and *ci*（词）or between a compound and a phrase.

Zi in Chinese is usually interpreted as characters, but a character is a visual icon used in written Chinese. Do you think Chinese enables spoken communication by the oral exchange of little visual icons? Then how about those illiterates? Can't they speak to each other? Of course they can. For them, *zi* is not a written character at all but a monosyllabic morpheme or a part of a disyllabic morpheme in their utterances. A monosyllabic morpheme in Chinese may either be a free one (e. g. 兵；怒) or a bound one (e. g. 了；们).

The speech sound *jin*（今）, for example, is a *zi* or a morpheme in Chinese which means *today*. But the concept *today* can also be expressed by two morphemes as *jintian*（今天）. *Jintian* is undoubtedly a word, and how about *jin*? Is it a word or not? If a student is asked to write an article of 500 words in Chinese, how will he count the number? Therefore, "word" is by no means a clear and intuitive notion in Chinese.

There is a term in Chinese for "word"—*ci*. Most of *ci*'s are disyllabic, but not all disyllabic terms in Chinese can be analyzed as one word. For example, 绿叶 consists of two characters and two morphemes, and it also consists of two words, a noun and a modifying adjective, either of which can be substituted with other words of the same part of speech. We can say 红叶，黄叶，绿草，绿花 etc. But 绿豆 is an exception. Referring to a particular kind of food called *mung bean* in English, 绿豆 is a single word because we cannot substitute another adjective for 绿 or another noun for 豆 without losing the idiomatic meaning. Such a word is actually a compound because it is formed from two independent words and has an integrated meaning, whereas the two-word combinations such as 红叶, 绿草 are not compounds but phrases.

A compound in Chinese can be distinguished from a phrase in an interesting way — to see whether the words in it still keep their own meaning. For example, 冬瓜 is a compound because it cannot be understood separately as 冬天的瓜, but 冬雪 is a phrase because it means 冬天的雪. Similarly, 大方 is a compound because it does not denote both *big* and *square*, but 贫富 is a phrase because it just stands for *poor* and *rich*.

There are different semantic relationships within the morphemes comprising a compound. For example, *sunrise* can be analyzed as noun-verb, *safety belt* as modifier-noun, and *makeup* as verb-complement. For Chinese compounds, the internal relationships are more colorful, as is illustrated by Table 4.1 below.

type	further analysis	Chinese compounds	English meaning
noun-verb		地震	earth-quake
modifier-noun	meaning-limiting	摇篮	cradle
	describing	国营	State-run
modifier-verb		仰望	look up at
verb-complement	action-object	打靶	target practice
	cause-effect	推翻	overthrow
coordinative	echoing	拼搏	struggle bravely
	oppositional	买卖	business
	contrasting	江山	land
	parallel	耳目	spy

Tab. 4.1   Internal relationships of Chinese compounds

A more interesting morphological phenomenon in Chinese is that different semantic analyses may lead to ambiguities for some compounds. For example, when 生气 is interpreted as a verb-complement compound, it means *get angry* (e. g. 她生气了) ; when it is interpreted as a modifier-noun compound, it means *vitality* (e. g. 讨论会充满生气) .

4.4 Idiomatic power

Words are combined into phrases. Some phrases are temporarily made, while others are prefabricated. When you think something is easy, for instance, you may say *It's a piece of cake*. If you do not like something, you may say *That isn't my cup of tea*. A piece of cake, your cup of tea, they are good metaphors! But they are not your own creation. They are fixed sequences of words with a fixed meaning that is not composed of the literal meanings of the individual words. We call them idioms.

Modern linguistic research suggests that language is intrinsically less literal than we have always assumed. It is abundant in idiomatic expressions. Some of them are metaphoric (e. g. *I'm really tied up*.), some are allusive (e. g. *The ruling party met its Waterloo in the new election*.), but a majority are institutionalized. These set phrases are different from the traditionally defined idioms. They are just common utterances which are frequently used by all native speakers in a certain situation. Everyone can list a lot of examples like the following:

> *in the days to come*
> *second to none*
> *as much as possible*
> *I see what you mean.*
> *It's very kind of you to say so.*
> *It's my fault.*

All these prefabricated chunks of a language are stored in the mental lexicon of its native speakers, and retrieved anytime they are needed. Other kinds of chunks include collocation. Native speakers know clearly which words can idiomatically be used together. They know they should say *have a try*, *make a phone call*, *take a risk*, *do one's hair*, *hit the spot*, as well as *a nail in the wall*, *a cabin on the farm*, and so on. With such idiomatic knowledge one needs not to be always creative when they intend to express themselves. Besides, when one finds it hard to express his ideas effectively, he resorts to his brain for proper institutional phrases, which are also a significant aspect of foreign language learning.

Now we have crossed the borderline of morphology and stepped into the domain of phrases, where problems are mostly dealt with in the light of the principles of syntax.

EXERCISES

I. Translate the following quotations into Chinese.

Morphology is the study of word-making and word-marking. On the one hand, morphology examines meaning relationships between words and the ways in which these connections are indicated. On the other, morphology looks at how grammatical relationships between words are marked. Different languages focus on different word relationships, and they make use of different patterns of marking.

(from G. Tserdanelis & W. Wong: *Language files*)

The study of the internal structure of words, and of the rules by which words are formed, is called morphology.

(from V. Fromkin & R. Roman: *An Introduction to Language*)

II. Fill in the blanks with the linguistic terms you have learned.

1) Words are not the most elemental sound-meaning units. The most elemental grammatical units in a language are _____.

2) _____ morphemes like "a-", "pre-", "-ly", "-ness", which have only grammatical meanings, are limited in number, about 100 in English.

3) _____ are different from phrases in that they symbolize an integrated

concept. Phonologically, they have primary stress on the first word only, while individual words in phrases have independent primary stress.

4) Modern linguistic research suggests that language is intrinsically less literal than we have always assumed. It is abundant in _____ expressions.

5) Languages of the world can be classified morphologically into three types: isolating, inflecting, and _____.

III. In the following sentences, judge whether each morpheme is (a) a free morpheme, (b) a derivational bound morpheme, or (c) an inflectional bound morpheme.

1) The older gentleman voted wisely.

2) The Children skipped rope and played games joyfully.

3) 他们赛跑拿了第一。

IV. Give a summary of less than 150 words to Section 4.1.

V. Challenging work.

1) Morphemes are generally defined as minimal units of meaning, but some morphemes in English such as -ceive and -mit cannot be assigned any intrinsic meaning. They are regarded as separate grammatical units because they can be combined with other morphemes into meaningful words such as receive, perceive, conceive; transmit, permit, submit. Can you list more such examples? Have you noticed any similar case in Chinese?

2) Observe the following reduplicated modifiers of adjectives in Chinese

绿油油　羞答答　娇滴滴　活脱脱　怯生生　明晃晃　好端端

响当当——当当响　　平展展——展展平

Suggested research questions:

a) Do these reduplicated words produce any special effects to the audience?

b) Can these words be substituted with any other words?

c) Do they belong to the core vocabulary of Chinese?

d) Were they used long ago? Are they used more frequently today or less?

Write a summary of your research.

L. Bloomfield (1887 — 1949)

Leonard Bloomfield is considered one of the best Linguists of all time. He devoted his entire life to a thorough-going study of language, its structure and its use. His influence dominated the science of linguistics from 1933 — when his most important work, *Language*, was published — to the mid-1950s.

Bloomfield was born on April 1, 1887, in Chicago. He graduated from Harvard College at the age of 19 and did graduate work for 2 years at the University of Wisconsin, where he also taught German. His interest in linguistics was aroused by Eduard Prokosch, a philologist in the German department. Bloomfield received his doctorate from the University of Chicago in 1909.

After teaching German at the University of Cincinnati for a year, Bloomfield became assistant professor of comparative philology and German at the University of Illinois, where he remained until 1921. Then he became professor of German and linguistics at Ohio State University. He was one of the founders of the Linguistic Society of America in 1924. In 1927 he went to the University of Chicago and worked there as professor of Germanic philology till 1940, when he became professor of linguistics at Yale University. He died in New Haven, Conn., on April 18, 1949.

Bloomfield adopted Ferdinand de Saussure's concept of language structure. Influenced by the behaviorist psychologist A. P. Weiss whom he met when he worked at Ohio State University, Bloomfield took a logical positivist approach to science, holding that a mechanistic rather than a mentalistic approach to human phenomena was necessary if the disciplines concerned with man were to be truly scientific.

The period from the publication of *Language* in 1933 to the mid-1950s is commonly called the "Bloomfieldian era" of linguistics. His masterpiece *Language* (1933) is a standard text. It had a profound influence on linguistics, for it was a clear statement of principles that became axiomatic, notably that language study must always be centered in the spoken language, as against documents; that the definitions used in grammar should be based on the forms of the language, not on the meaning of the forms; and that a given language at a given time is a complete system of sounds and forms that exist independently of the past — so that the history of a form does not explain its actual meaning.

Though Bloomfield's particular methodology of descriptive linguistics was not widely accepted, his mechanistic attitudes toward a precise science of linguistics, dealing only with observable phenomena, were most influential. For a long period most American linguists considered themselves in some sense Bloomfield's disciples, whether they actually studied under him or not, and a great deal of American linguistic work has taken the form of working out questions raised and methods suggested by Bloomfield. His influence waned after the 1950s, when adherence to logical positivist doctrines lessened and there was a return to more mentalistic attitudes.

Reading recommendation

Beginner-friendly:

陆国强. 现代英语词汇学. 上海外语教育出版社,1999

Chao Yuen Ren. A Grammar of Spoken Chinese. Berkeley: University of California Press, 1968. (汉语版:赵元任著,吕叔湘译《汉语口语语法》,商务出版社,2002 (1979))

More challenging:

P. H. Matthews: Morphology. 2nd edition. Cambridge University Press, 1991; 北京:外语教学与研究出版社,2000 (汪榕培 导读)

J. L. Packard. The Morphology of Chinese: A Linguistic and Cognitive Approach. Cambridge University Press, 2000; 外语教学与研究出版社,2000 (石定栩 导读)

XP

A Chinese student: *Could you show me what English is?*
An American linguist:
... Yes. English is NP plus VP.

Chapter 5

Phrase Hierarchy

5.1 Trees

This chapter will lead us to step across a new threshold — syntax.

For many students, syntax seems to be an awesome subject because it is, as they lament, "full of trees". Actually, those so-called trees are fairly useful tools in revealing the relationship between different constituents within a sentence.

Such trees are not plants but diagrams, which connect things with lines to show how they are related to each other. A familiar example to us is the family tree — a drawing that gives all the members of a family, and shows how they are related to each other. Fig. 5.1 is such a tree.

Such a tree diagram cannot be used to show the relationship between students sharing a dorm flat. We can give each student a number, so if a new dorm manager is not familiar with their names, he can treat them as No. 1, No. 2, No. 3... in his record. This number relationship is linear, free of levels. The relationships within a family tree are different. A family has different levels, i. e. generations; one level may dominate the levels below it and be dominated by those above it. This tree relationship is non-linear but hierarchical.

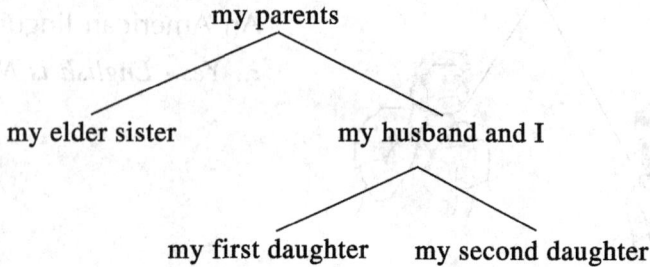

Fig. 5.1　A family tree

Similarly, a labeled tree diagram in syntax shows the way words are arranged to form sentences or phrases. For example, the tree diagram of the sentence *They hate Bill* is as follows:

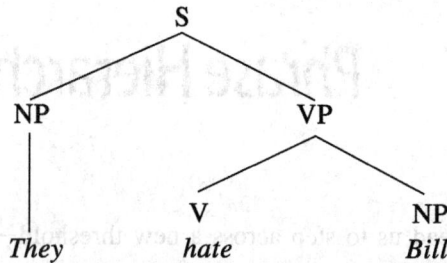

Fig. 5.2　A syntactic tree

Analogically, S (standing for sentence) in Fig 5.2 is the mother of the NP (noun phrase) and VP (verb phrase) immediately below it, and the grandmother of the V (verb) and NP immediately below the VP. These V and NP are the daughters of the VP as well as the granddaughters of S. These different "generations" represent different levels. The sister constituents *hate* and *Bill* belong to the lowest level, while *They* is a constituent of a higher level, with the whole VP *hate Bill* as its sister. Like a family tree, a syntactic tree of a sentence reveals that the relationship between the phrases of a sentence is not linear but hierarchical.

Besides a labeled tree-diagram, this hierarchically arranged structure within a sentence can also be represented in the form of labeled bracketing:

(5.1) [$_s$ *They* [$_{VP}$*hate Bill*]]

In addition, it is necessary to point out an important difference between a family tree and a syntactic tree. The former is used here to facilitate the understanding of the hierarchical characteristics of the latter, but they have an opposite sequence in their development. The growth sequence of a family tree is top-down: mother gives birth to her children; however, the growth sequence of a syntactic tree is bottom-up: one word merges with another to form a phrase, which sounds as if children gave birth to their mother! This bottom-up process in sentence production is called merging.

5.2 Merging

The simplest way of forming a phrase is by merging two words together: for example, by merging the word *hate* with the word *Bill* in (5.1), we form the verb phrase (VP) *hate Bill*.

Furthermore, the two words of the VP play different roles — head and complement. The head of a phrase is the key word which determines the properties of the phrase. In our example, *hate* is a verb, hence the head of the VP. It expands to a VP by merging with a complement *Bill*. More technically, we say that a phrase is the projection of the head. Here by projection we mean expansion. (see Fig 5.3)

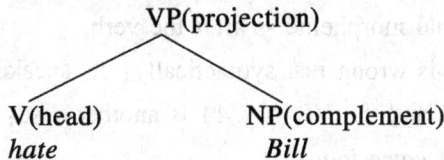

VP(projection)

V(head)   NP(complement)
hate   *Bill*

Fig. 5.3   Projection: from V to VP

Sometimes a phrase consists of the head only, without any overt complement, such as the two NPs *They* and *Bill* in our example. We have to regard such single words as phrases, or rather, the maximal projection of themselves.

Consider the example again. If we change the subject *They* with *He*, will it still be a correct sentence?

Surely not, for we never say

(5.2) *** He hate Bill.*

Instead, we say

(5.3) *He hates Bill.*

The inflectional morpheme -s affixed to the verb *hate* in (5.3) carries some necessary syntactic information — third person singular present-tense. With-s, the verb agrees with its third person singular subject. With this inflectional morpheme, the three words in (5.3) form a sentence. Without it, like the case of (5.2), there will be no sentence but just three separate words. So the I (inflectional morpheme) plays an essential role in merging an NP and a VP into a sentence. Such a role can be compared to that of glue in sticking things together. I is the "glue" to "stick" a VP to an NP so as to make a sentence. A sentence, therefore, can be regarded as the maximal projection of I. Hence, a sentence, or rather, an NP + VP, is labeled as IP, a more accurate label than S. Thus we would like to substitute IP for S in a tree diagram from now on.

5.3 Functional categories

Let's turn back to examine (5.2) *He hate Bill.* It is undoubtedly a wrong sentence, but we can still see its content clearly, can't we? Why? Because these three words all have descriptive content (they are therefore called content words). All the necessary content words are exactly there in (5.2); what is lacking is none other than the inflectional morpheme -s after the verb.

Therefore, (5.2) is wrong just syntactically: Its speaker forgot to apply some "glue" between the NP and the VP. (5.4) is another case:

(5.4) *She might come join us.*

If (5.4) is produced by a non-native speaker of English, then we can say he is successful in making himself understood. He has correctly used several content words ("she", "come", "join", "us") to express an entire meaning, with a sole failure in organizing them into a natural English sentence. What he has ignored is an infinitive particle *to* before the VP *join us*. The correction should be:

(5.5) *She might come to join us.*

Hence, there are two groups of syntactical categories: lexical categories and functional categories. All the content words, namely nouns, verbs, adjectives, and adverbs, belong to lexical categories; on the other hand, any word or morpheme which has no descriptive content and which serves an essentially grammatical function belongs to a functional category. A functional category plays a role like glue in combining content words into phrases and phrases into a sentence.

Apparently all the categories in a tree diagram similar to Fig. 5. 2 are lexical categories, with the role of any functional category unfairly concealed. Such a diagram is far from satisfactory in reflecting the structural nature of a sentence. We need a new tree which can present both the content and functional aspects of a sentence.

5.4 X-bar trees

The following is such a tree, which came into being in the early 1980's, based on a new theoretical model — the X-bar scheme.

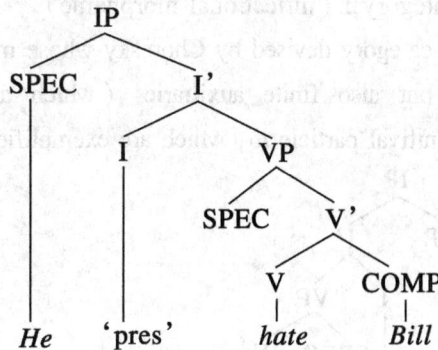

Fig. 5.4   An X-bar tree

Compare Fig. 5. 4 with Fig. 5. 2 and you will find that the tree in Fig. 5. 2 is three-layered while the tree in Fig. 5. 4 has five layers. The labels of the two additional layers in Fig. 5. 4, I' and V', both wear an apostrophe, which, incidentally, can also be replaced by a bar: Ī and V̄, called I-bar and V-bar. Now we enter into a more restrictive scheme of phrase structure known as X-bar syntax, where the symbol X is used as a variable denoting any word (or morpheme) category you care to choose. When you choose a category as X, you can insert a level between X and XP, label it X', call it X-bar and define it as the intermediate projection headed by X. Correspondingly, XP can be defined as the maximal projection headed by X, and X itself, i. e. the head, as the minimal projection.

With the introduction of the intermediate projection, a tree diagram can reflect more information about how words are combined into phrases and phrases are combined into a sentence. We used a "glue" metaphor earlier to explain the role of the inflectional morpheme -s in combining an NP with a VP. In Fig. 5.4, this -s has been taken away from the verb *hate* to which it is usually affixed, and an abbreviation within quotation marks 'pres' has been added below the label I. The 'pres' here stands for the inflectional morpheme -s, and belongs to the functional category I, whose intermediate projection I'ought to "check features" with the NP at its sister SPEC, i. e. *He* in the present example. It entails that the checked word in SPEC should be nominative, and agree with the I' in all the grammatical features, namely third person singular present-tense here. Therefore, I' reveals the glue-like role of the functional category I (inflectional morpheme).

Furthermore, I is a category devised by Chomsky whose members include not only inflectional morphemes but also finite auxiliaries (which are inflected for tense/ agreement), and the infinitival particle *to*, which are exemplified by Fig. 5.5.

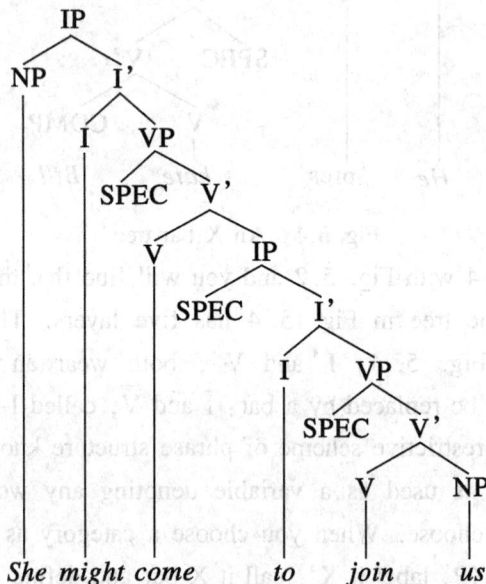

Fig. 5.5   Different IP's

In Fig. 5. 5 there are two different IP's. The one on the top is the maximal projection of a modal auxiliary *might*, whereas the one in the middle has the infinitival particle *to* as its head. Both of them are functional categories.

5.5 A universal skeleton

According to X-bar theory, head X can either be a lexical category or a functional category. It enables a tree diagram to reflect at least two syntactic dimensions: content and function. The structure of a sentence consists of both lexical phrases and functional phrases, each of them sharing the same skeleton:

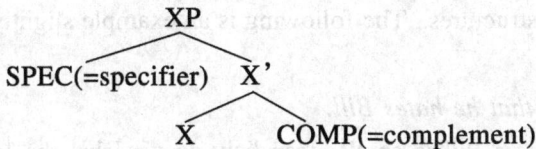

```
              XP
          ╱        ╲
SPEC(=specifier)   X'
                ╱      ╲
               X      COMP(=complement)
```

Fig. 5.6   The skeleton of phrase structure

This skeleton is arguably universal — we can use it to analyze any sentence in any language. In other words, all constituents of a sentence in any language can find its own position in an X-bar tree diagram. Take the following Chinese sentence for example:

(5.6) 他已成家。

已 in Chinese denotes perfective aspect, so it also plays a glue-like role in combining the NP 他 and VP 成家 into a sentence. Therefore, (5.6) can be analyzed with the following tree diagram:

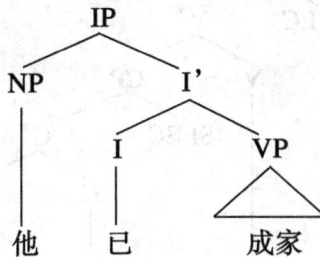

```
              IP
          ╱        ╲
        NP          I'
        │        ╱      ╲
        │       I        VP
        │       │       ╱  ╲
        他       已      成家
```

Fig. 5.7   A tree for a Chinese sentence

In Fig. 5.7 we see a Chinese IP. Some researchers argue that it is not exactly an IP because Chinese is not an inflectional language and 已 is an aspect marker, so they prefer to change the label from IP to AspP (aspect phrase). The label can be altered for one reason or another, yet the phrase structure is the same.

What is to point out is that the above discussion is focused on the aspect marker 已, so there is no need to detail the VP projection 成家. In this case a triangle can be drawn beneath the ignored VP, as shown in Fig. 5.7.

5.6 From IP to CP

The structure of a natural sentence can be far more complex. Those we deal with here are basic structures. The following is an example slightly more complicated than the previous.

(5.7) *I think that he hates Bill.*

We know *he hates Bill* is an IP; then how do we label the larger phrase *that he hates Bill*? In this phrase, *that* is known as C (complementizer) because an important use of such a functional category is to introduce a complement clause. Thus the phrase is the projection of C, called CP. In (5.7), the CP *that he hates Bill* serves as a complement clause of the V *think*. A tree diagram can be drawn accordingly as in Fig. 5.8.

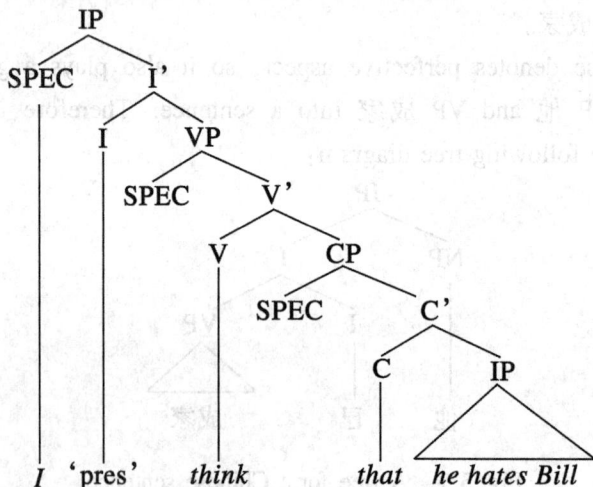

Fig. 5.8   An imbedded CP

Like IP, CP has lost its original denotation and become a mere label for any phrase which embraces an IP immediately below it. In English, for example, wh-questions, topicalized declarative sentences, etc. can also be analyzed as CPs. Fig. 5.9 is a CP diagram that can be used to illustrate the whole structure of (5.8) as well as the underlined structure of (5.9).

(5.8) *Which book does he like?*

(5.9) *This book he likes but that book he hates.*

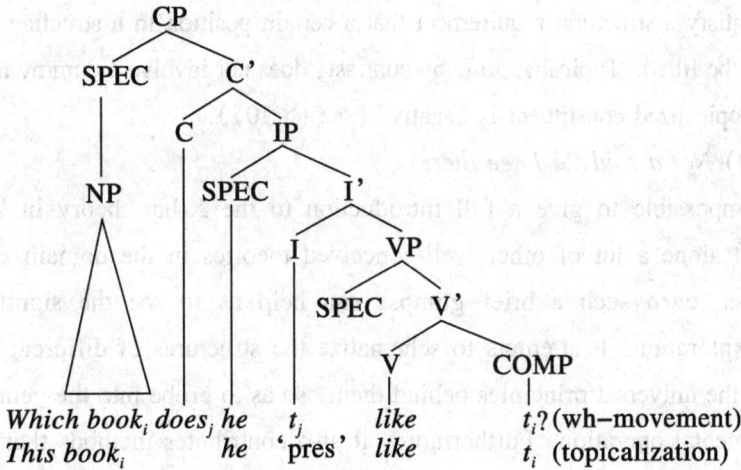

Fig. 5.9   Different CPs

Have you noticed something new below the COMP-VP in Fig. 5.9? Oh, yes. What a strange symbol — a letter "t" with a footnote "i", both italicized! This *t* refers to a trace, which is an empty category left behind in a position, out of which a constituent moves. Then where is the moved constituent? The footnote $_i$ can help you. Have you noticed another $_i$ clinging to the NP in SPEC-CP? That is the very constituent you want to chase.

Any phrase with the same footnote as that of the trace is the moved constituent. If more than one movement takes place, different pairs of footnotes such as j's will be used.

Questions with one or more wh-words (i.e. a word such as who, which, what, where, why, when, and how) are called wh-questions. An English wh-question will involve a wh-word being moved to the front of the clause. This is called wh-movement. Likewise, when a constituent is made the topic of a sentence, it may be moved into a more prominent position at the front of the sentence. This process is called topicalization. Wh-movement will involve another movement; for instance, the functional features of the morpheme 'pres' at I in (5.8) will be "packaged" into a word *does* and moved to C. Such a word is called dummy for it has no intrinsic semantic content, but is used simply to satisfy a structural requirement that a certain position in a structure (e. g. the position C) be filled. Topicalization, by contrast, does not involve a dummy movement, unless the topicalized constituent is negative (see (5.10)).

(5.10) *Not a soul did I see there.*

It is impossible to give a full introduction to the X-bar theory in so short a chapter, let alone a lot of other well-conceived theories in the domain of syntax. Nevertheless, even such a brief glimpse can help us to see the significance of syntactic exploration. It attempts to schematize the structures of different languages and reveal the universal principles behind them, so as to probe into the genetic nature of human mental operation. Furthermore, it also contributes methods that may help program computers to speak.

EXERCISES ✍

I. Translate the following statement into Chinese.

Syntax is the subfield of linguistics that studies the internal structure of sentences and the relationship among their component parts.

II. Fill in the blanks with the linguistic terms you have learned.

1) In the VP *draw a tree*, *draw* is the _____ of the phrase while *a tree* is the
_____.

2) A phrase is the _____ of the head. XP can be defined as the _____ projection headed by X, X', as the _____ projection, and X itself, i. e. the head, as the _____ projection.

3) According to X-bar theory, head X can either be a _____ category, such as nouns and verbs, or a _____ category.

4) In the skeleton of XP, SPEC stands for _____ and COMP stands for complement. SPEC and X' are _____. So are X and COMP.

5) IP refers to _____. I, a functional category, includes not only _____ _____ but also finite auxiliaries, and the _____ _____ _____ to.

6) CP refers to _____ _____ and can be found in the analysis of complex sentences as well as _____ and topicalization.

III. Answer the following questions.

1) Why should we draw a tree diagram to represent the structure of a sentence?

2) What is an X'-tree diagram?

3) How do you explain the "gluing" role of functional categories in Chinese — a non-inflectional language? Could you give some examples?

4) What is topicalization?

5) How many occasions do you know in English that auxiliary inversion takes place?

IV. Give a summary of less than 150 words to Section 5.4.

V. The following trees give different CP structures. Please sum up the similarities and differences of all these CP varieties (Not all of them are mentioned in the present chapter).

a) the root CP:

```
                    CP
                  /    \
              Spec      C'
                      /    \
                    C       IP
                          /    \
                       Spec     I'
                               /   \
                              I     VP
                                    /\
                                   /__\

              that    he    'pres'  like the book
This book_i         he    'pres'  like t_i  (topicalization)
What_i       do     you           like t_i ?(wh−movement)
Not a soul_i did     I            see t_i (negative topicalization)
```

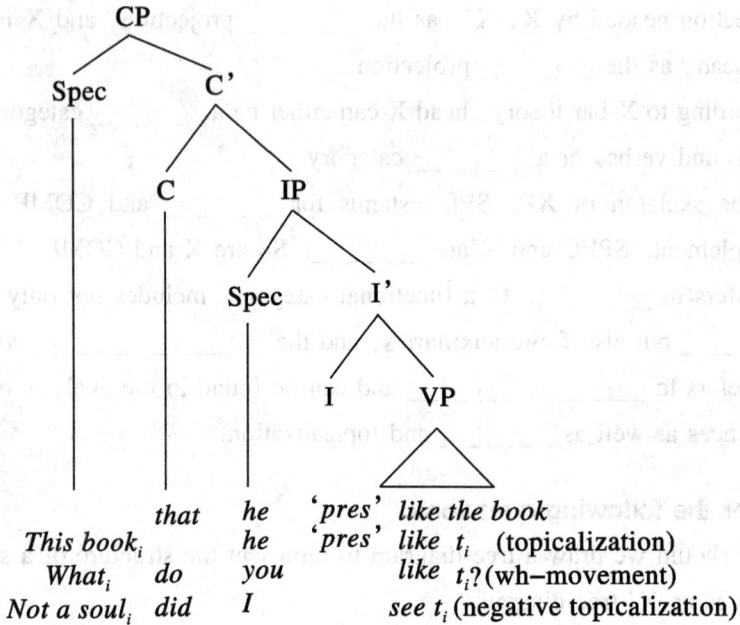

b) the adjunct CP

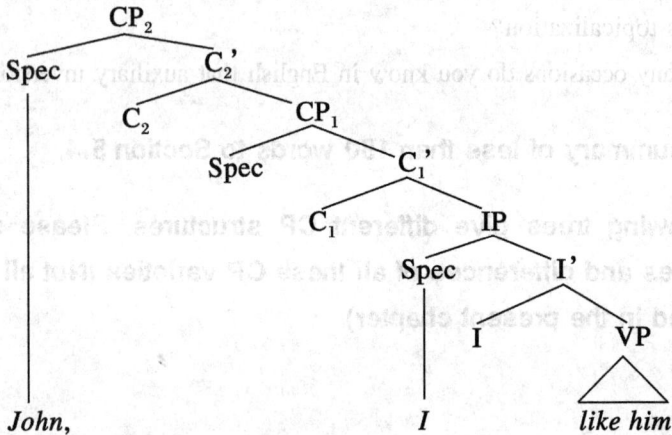

```
                    CP_2
                  /      \
              Spec        C_2'
                        /     \
                     C_2       CP_1
                             /      \
                         Spec        C_1'
                                   /     \
                                 C_1      IP
                                        /    \
                                    Spec      I'
                                             /   \
                                            I     VP
                                                  /\
                                                 /__\

          John,                       I      like him
```

VI. Challenging work.

1. Draw an X-bar tree-diagram for the following sentences.

    (1) John met Bill.

    (2) John asked whether Bill hated him.

    (3) 他买了一本书。

    (4) 他说他买了一本书。

2. Write an essay on the following topic:

The mental hierarchy of a sentence

■■

N. Chomsky (1928 —)

Avram Noam Chomsky is the Institute Professor Emeritus of linguistics at Massachusetts Institute of Technology (MIT). He is credited with the creation of the theory of generative grammar, often considered the most significant contribution to the field of theoretical linguistics of the 20th century. He also helped spark the cognitive revolution in psychology through his review of B. F. Skinner's *Verbal Behavior*, which challenged the behaviorist approach to the study of mind and language dominant in the 1950s. His naturalistic approach to the study of language has also impacted the philosophy of language and mind.

Chomsky was born on December 7, 1928 in Philadelphia, Pennsylvania, the son of Hebrew scholar William Chomsky. He was brought up in Hebrew culture and literature.

Starting from 1945, he studied philosophy and linguistics at the University of Pennsylvania, learning from Zellig Harris. During the years 1951 to 1955, Chomsky was a Junior Fellow of the Harvard University Society of Fellows. While a Junior Fellow he completed his doctoral dissertation entitled, "Transformational Analysis". According to his theory, utterances have a syntax which can be characterized by a formal grammar, in particular, a context-free grammar extended with transformational rules. Children are hypothesized to have an innate knowledge of the basic grammatical structure common to all languages. This innate knowledge is often referred to as universal grammar. The Principles and Parameters approach (1979) make strong claims regarding universal grammar: that the grammatical principles underlying languages are innate and fixed, and the differences among the world's languages can be characterized in terms of parameter settings in the brain.

Chomsky has written and lectured widely on linguistics, philosophy, intellectual history, contemporary issues, international affairs and U. S. foreign policy. He is one of America's most prominent political dissidents, authoring over 30 political books dissecting such issues as U. S. interventionism in the developing world, the political economy of human rights and the propaganda role of corporate media.

Linguistic Stars

Linguistic Stars

Reading recommendation

Beginner-friendly：

温宾利. 当代句法学导论. 外语教学与研究出版社,2002

More challenging：

A. Radford. Syntax：A Mininalist Introduction. Cambridge University Press, 1997. 外语教学与研究出版社, 2000(顾阳　导读)

V. Cook, & M. Newson. Chomsky's Universal Grammar：An Introduction, Oxford：Blackwell Publishers,1996; 外语教学与研究出版社, 2000(宁春岩　导读)

—You mean you are an agent?

—Yes.

—When did you become an agent?

—Anytime I did something.

—Who assigned you the role?

—Veeeeerb.

Chapter 6

From Form to Meaning

6.1 Proposition

On hearing its master's words "*Go for a walk?*" a dog follows him immediately out of the house. Undoubtedly the dog does not know what it has heard is a sentence, nor has it done any syntactic analysis. If the master changes the word *walk* to a word unfamiliar to the dog, for example, "*Go for a jog?*", and produces the sentence in the same intonation pattern, it will still lead the dog to expect a walk. The dog's response is a typical stimulus-reflex process, directly related to the intonation pattern, rather than the individual words. A human child will behave differently. If he has not caught the meaning of *jog*, he may ask an echo question "*Go for what?*" His behavior shows that he knows what he has heard is a string of words, representing the speaker's mental intention.

A linguist once observed that an English baby enunciated two words "*car want*", which seemed absolutely ungrammatical. Then how could the adults figure out its meaning? They might first consider the verb *want*, which usually requires two NPs to form a complete idea. In this baby's utterance, there was only one "NP" —

car. Though it appeared before the verb *want*, it seemed not like a subject but an object. The adults also noticed the baby pointing to a toy car when making the sounds. Then they understood that the baby wanted that toy.

Similar cases can be found with non-native speakers of a language. Their utterances may contain more or less syntactical errors, but they are often understood by native listeners if they use the proper content words. For instance, if a Chinese says, "*I go to London yesterday*", his English friends will guess that he means he went to London yesterday. The error of tense hardly influences the comprehension but indicates that the speaker must be a foreigner.

So, we can conclude that an information receiver usually focuses his attention on the meaning of a sentence rather than the form. We have all had such experiences: to tell others what we have just heard with our own words is usually not difficult, but if we are required to repeat someone's talk word by word, we probably would have to give in. It seems that what stays in our mind is just the meaning, not the exact words we have heard.

Furthermore, when we put a sentence in our mind by reading or listening, our mind will immediately treat it as a set of meaning units, called **propositions**. Let's observe the following example:

(6.1) A: (watching a live telecast) *Wow, a horse! My son wins a horse! A horse there... It's red... The winner is my son, my dear! Oh, what a red horse, my son's horse...*

B: *What is he saying?*

C: *His son wins a red horse.*

Here C is asked to tell B what he has heard from A. His retelling is a pithy statement, rather than copying out A's chattering word by word. But what A says and what C says are semantically the same, both with two propositions as follows:

1. the son wins a horse;

2. the horse is red

So, as a listener, one often ignores memorizing the syntactic patterns of what he has heard. Those left in his mind are not phrases (CPs, IPs, VPs...), but propositions. Any time, if required, he can retell the meaning stored in his memory with his own words, with his own CPs, IPs, or VPs. In the example above, therefore, C can also respond to B in other ways, like

(6.2) *A red horse is won by his son now.*

(6.3) *His son wins a horse, a red one*!

(6.4) *A horse, which is red, have you seen? Just there. That is his son's now. His son wins it.*

On the other hand, when a person's mind works out wrong propositions from what he has heard, misunderstanding occurs. Such a situation is reflected in the multiple-choice exercises of listening comprehension similar to the example below:

(6.5) **Voice**: The president told the secretary that a trainee fancied him.

Question: Who fancied whom according to the president?

Choices: A. The president fancied a trainee.

B. A trainee fancied the president.

C. A trainee fancied the secretary.

D. The secretary fancied a trainee.

This TOFEL-type exercise is designed to test the mental efficiency of the listener in collecting a proposition. Apparently, failure in perceiving a proposition may lead to misunderstanding or confusion.

The core of a proposition is a verb. Different verbs require different numbers of NPs in a grammatical sentence. Specifically, an intransitive verb only requires the subject, which is its external argument; a simple transitive verb requires two NPs, one as the subject (external argument) and the other as the object (internal argument); a ditransitive verb requires three NPs as its subject (external argument), direct object and indirect object (internal arguments); besides, an unusual verb in English, *rain*, requires no NPs (That's why it is always accompanied by a meaningless "dummy" subject *it*). NPs required by a verb are called its arguments. A proposition comprises a predicate V and a set of arguments, which can be represented in predicate calculus by a formula: predicate V (external argument, internal argument(s))

For instance, the two propositions in the above example can be represented as:

(6.6) I. *win (the son, horse)*

Ⅱ. *red* (*horse*)

The predicate V of proposition Ⅰ is *win*, which requires two arguments, *the son* and *horse*, as external argument and internal argument respectively; the predicate V of proposition Ⅱ is *red* (i. e. *be red*), requiring just one external argument, *horse*.

That is the process in comprehending a sentence: to figure out what propositions underlie what have been heard or read. It is a process of mental computation, rather than stimulus-reflex. What it depends on is the human's unconscious sense of predicate logic, i. e. how many arguments are required by a predicate V.

The knowledge of the number of arguments required by a verb plays an essential role as well in identifying the incompleteness of an utterance. For instance, if someone says "*Jane sent him*", we will expect to hear more because the verb *send* usually requires three arguments, but in this utterance we only hear two, the subject and the indirect object, which cannot form a complete proposition. So we do not think that is a complete sentence.

In addition to its arguments, a verb very often permits some further phrases, which are optional. These optional phrases are adjuncts, which are expressed most often as prepositional phrases or adverbial phrases in English. For example, the minimal sentence *John kissed Mary* can be expanded with some optional adjuncts to yield *John kissed Mary on the neck in the garden this morning*. There are three adjuncts in this sentence.

6.2 Theta roles

The term *argument* comes from philosophy, more particularly, from predicate calculus. The argument structure of verbs is particularly important in theta theory, which seeks to describe the thematic role that arguments fulfill in individual sentences.

Theta theory (or θ-theory) is concerned with assigning thematic roles to the arguments of verbs. "Theta" is the name of the Greek letter θ, which corresponds to *th* in English, and since *thematic* begins with *th* it has become standard to abbreviate the expression "thematic role" to "θ-role". The essential elements of the theory differ somewhat from linguist to linguist, but the following are the commonly assumed theta-roles, each with a gloss and an illustrative example, in which the underlined expression has the theta role specified.

Agent: instigator of some action. e. g. *John threw the ball.*

Theme: entity undergoing the effect of some action. Often a theme is accusative (and can be called a **patient** as well), e. g. *John hit the cat*; however, it is nominative with a few verbs like *fall*, *die*, etc. e. g. *The cat died.*

Experiencer: entity experiencing some psychological state. e. g. *John was happy.*

Benefactive: entity benefiting from some action. e. g. *Mary bought some chocolate for John.*

Recipient: entity receiving some entity. e. g. *John got Mary a present.*

Instrument: means by which something comes about. e. g. *Joanna dug the garden with a spade.*

Locative: place in which something is situated. e. g. *John put the washing in the bin.*

Goal: entity towards which something moves. e. g. *Mary passed the plate to John.*

Source: entity from which something moves. e. g. *John returned from London.*

Theta theory enables us to reveal some semantic differences that are not reflected in the syntactic structure demonstrated by X-bar tree diagrams. In the following pair of sentences, for example, the phrase *the vase* fulfils the same grammatical role, that of subject, but two distinct thematic roles:

(6.7) *The vase shattered the glass.*

(6.8) *The vase shattered.*

In (6.7), the vase is the cause of the shattering, hence it performs the role of *instrument*, whereas in (6.8), it is the entity which undergoes the effect of shattering, hence it acts as the *theme*.

Theta roles are defined according to a limited group of universal thematic functions/relations, and hence are shared by all the languages of the world. No matter what language one speaks, a sentence is generated from one's mind in the same way. This process starts from one's mental lexicon, in which is stored the mental representation of all that one knows about the lexical items of that language, such as how to pronounce them, what their meaning is, and what word class they belong to. As for verbs, the lexicon contains information about their transitivity, their argument structure, and the theta roles that can be assigned to their arguments. Metaphorically, a verb springs out of the mental lexicon with a certain number of "chairs", each for an argument to sit on. How many "chairs" a verb can take depends on its valency. For example, *like* is a divalent verb, requiring two arguments — the subject and the object. When it goes out of the lexicon, it can be represented as

(6.9) *like* (____, ____)

(6.9) indicates that the speaker must take two NPs from his mental lexicon to fill in the slots ("chairs"). Let's suppose a speaker has two NPs to fill the blanks, namely, *John* and *the book*. This forms a proposition in his mind, which can be represented as follows.

(6.10) *like* (*John, the book*)

Then it is the time for the predicate V *like* to merge with the internal argument *the book* and assign the θ-role of theme (patient) to it, resulting in V' (*like the book*). The whole V' (not the V alone) merges with the external argument *John* and assigns the θ-role of experiencer to it. The original position of the subject *John* is in SPEC-VP. Since it carries a strong nominative case-feature, it has to raise to SPEC-IP to have it checked with I'(see Fig. 6.1)

Wow, what is *case-feature*? What is meant by *checked*? Why is *raise* used as an intransitive verb? So many new concepts spring out, too technical for a layman to handle. OK, don't worry too much. We won't go deeper into this nerve-racking subject unless some day one of you decide to pursue a career in this field.

Through merger and movement operations, the grammatical system of our mind succeeds in generating a syntactically qualified sentence and further, converts it into a string of sounds pronounced by the phonetic system. (see Fig 6.2)

Fig. 6.2 tells us that the output of the grammatical system consists of two levels

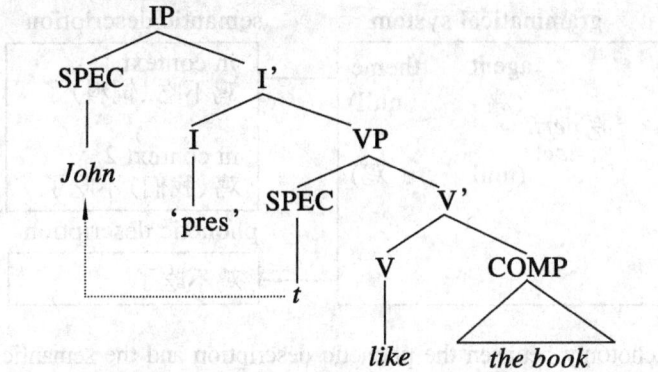

Fig. 6.1   Subject raising

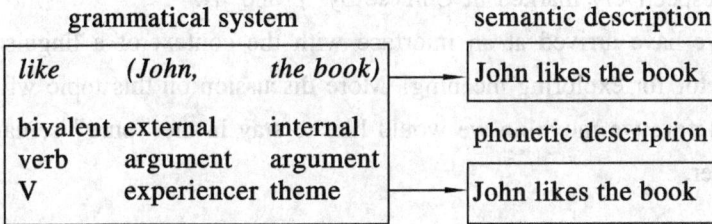

Fig. 6.2   From proposition to sentence

of description: the phonetic description for the generated sentence to be spoken out; the semantic description which logically represents the meaning the speaker would like to convey through uttering the sentence.

The Logic of the meaning must be universal, but different languages have different phonetic forms to convey it. A famous example has often been discussed among Chinese speaking linguists, that is, 鸡不吃了。Owing to the fact that Chinese as a non-inflectional language, unlike English, allows covert subject and object, this short sentence may present two widely different ways of parsing. One is to take the NP 鸡 as the subject, with the object of the verb 吃 hidden between the lines; The other is to take it as the topicalized NP with a trace in the position of the object. A proper parsing is decided by the context related to the utterance, i. e. whether it is uttered by a poultry raiser (context 1) or a banquet guest (context 2). Fig 6.3 illustrates the dichotomy between the phonetic description and the semantic description.

| grammatical system | semantic description |

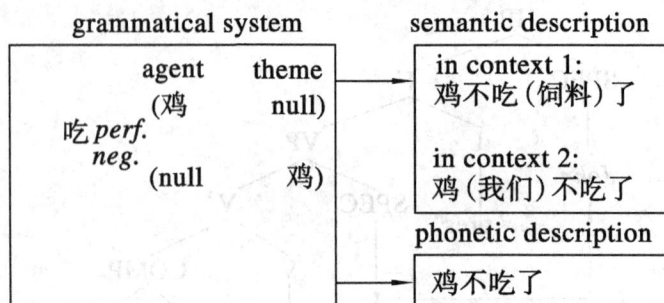

Fig. 6.3   Dichotomy between the phonetic description and the semantic description.

In Fig. 6.3, the abbreviations *perf.* and *neg.* stand for *perfect* and *negation*, which are respectively marked in Chinese by 了 and 不.

Now we have arrived at an interface with the context of a linguistic unit, an essential factor for exploring meaning. More discussion on this topic will be carried out later. Before we move on we would like to stay in the "pure" semantic domain a little longer.

EXERCISES ✍

I. Translate the following quotations into Chinese.

More interest is the fact that languages differ in inflectional systems: case systems, for example. We find that these are fairly rich in Latin, even more so in Sanskrit or Finnish, but minimal in English and invisible in Chinese.

Chinese and English, for example, may have the same case system as Latin, but the phonetic realization is different. Furthermore, it seems that much of the variety of language can be reduced to properties of inflectional systems.

(from N. Chomsky: *New Horizons in the Study of Language and Mind*)

II. Fill in the blanks with the linguistic terms you have learned.

1) Logicians have long been concerned with formulating representations for the semantic structure of sentences, or more correctly _____. NPs required by

a verb are called its _____. A proposition comprises a predicate V and a set of arguments. In addition to its arguments, a verb very often permits some optional phrases which are called _____.

2) The _____ argument of a verb has to be realized inside the maximal projection of that verb. The _____ argument of a verb is not contained in the maximal projection of that verb. For example, in *John* [VP *buys books*], *John* is the external argument and *books* is the internal argument of the verb *buy*.

3) Each verb may have _____ external argument(s). Each verb may have _____ internal argument(s).

4) Each argument is assigned one and only one _____ role. Each theta/ thematic role is assigned to one and only one _____.

III. Represent the following sentences in the form of propositions.

Example: Mary gives Bill a book. →give (Mary, Bill, a book)

1) It often rains. →

2) The table is old. →

3) The baby has slept. →

4) John likes his new teacher. →

IV. Specify the theta roles assigned to the underlined arguments by the verbs in the following sentences.

1) I work hard.

2) She was sad.

3) The atom bomb destroyed the city.

4) Mary gave a book to me.

5) Tom opened the door with his key.

6) The door opened slowly.

V. Give a summary of less than 150 words to Section 6.1 *Proposition*.

VI. Challenging work.

1) We have learned from this chapter that utterances with the same phonetic form can have disparate logic forms, like "鸡不吃了". Can you give more examples of this kind, and try to do some linguistic analysis as well? The following is such an example for you to start with.

A big-game hunter was showing a charming young lady the skin of a lion that he had shot. "One night," he explained, "I heard the roar of a lion: I jumped out of bed, raised my gun, took careful aim and shot it in my pajamas." "Good heavens," the young lady exclaimed, "How ever did it get into your pajamas?"

2) Write an essay on the following topic:

On sentence meaning

■ ■

C. Fillmore (1929 —)

Charles J Fillmore is an Emeritus Professor of Linguistics at the University of California, Berkeley. He received his Ph. D. in Linguistics from the University of Michigan in 1961. Professor Fillmore spent ten years at the Ohio State University before joining Berkeley's Department of Linguistics in 1971. He has been a Fellow at the Center for Advanced Study in the Behavioral Sciences. His research has concentrated mainly on questions of syntax and lexical semantics, and has emphasized the relationship between properties of linguistic form and matters of meaning and use.

He has been extremely influential in the areas of syntax and lexical semantics; he was one of the founders of cognitive linguistics, and developed the theories of Case Grammar (Fillmore 1968), and Frame Semantics (1976). In all of his research he has illuminated the fundamental importance of semantics, and its role in motivating syntactic and morphological phenomena. His earlier work, in collaboration with Paul Kay and George Lakoff, was generalized into the theory of Construction Grammar.

His current major project is called FrameNet（http：//framenet. icsi. berkeley. edu）. It is a wide-ranging on-line description of the English lexicon. In this project, words are described in terms of the Frames they evoke. Data is gathered from the British National Corpus, annotated for semantic and syntactic relations, and stored in a database organized by both lexical items and Frames. The project is influential — Issue 16 of the International Journal of Lexicography was devoted entirely to it. It has also inspired parallel projects, which investigate other languages, including Spanish, German, and Japanese.

Reading recommendation

Beginner-friendly：

高明乐. 题元角色的句法实现. 中国社会科学出版社,2003

More challenging：

C. J. Fillmore. The Case for Case. "格"辨（胡明扬译）商务印书馆,2002

S. Lappin. The Handbook of Contemporary Semantic Theory. Blackwell Publishers Ltd, 1997；外语教学与研究出版社,2001（方立　导读）

Male voice: Should I put more fire into my poems?

Female voice: You should put more of your poems into the fire.

Question: What does the man mean?

From the listening script of an English test

Chapter 7

From Meaning to Function

7. 1 Structurizing meaning

What is semantics? Some books and dictionaries may tell you that semantics is the study of meaning. It sounds so natural that not many of us realize that this definition is semantically improper. Semantics is a branch of linguistics, but meaning is studied by other sciences, too, such as philosophy and psychology. Language is symbolic, but not all symbols belong to language. In addition to symbols, there are icons and indexes which also convey meaning. Picasso is an icon of modernism; smoke is an index of fire. Such relationships are beyond the reach of semantics. They are the research objects of a more general field called semiotics, which investigates the types of relationships that may exist between a sign and the object it represents. Semantics can be regarded as a part of this extensive effort, with its particular emphasis on linguistic meaning. Therefore, John I. Saeed, a contemporary authority in this field, proposes a more proper definition: semantics is the study of meaning communicated through language.

It seems interesting that meaning, though having been discussed for thousands of years, is still a hot potato baffling many self-assured linguists. When language is there, meaning is there. Language is the vehicle, and meaning is the cargo. While the internal construction of the "vehicle" has been scrutinized from various perspectives, the study of the "cargo", according to another authority, G. Leech (1974), remains "a messy, largely unstructured intellectual no-man's land on the fringes of linguistics."

"Is that true?" you may ask. Maybe you would list the theta theory introduced in the last chapter to show how successful it is in exploring the internal structure of sentence meaning. Every argument has a theta role assigned from the predicate according to the theory. But the specific role an argument has is often controversial among analysts. For example, in *Jane filled the bottle with juice*, it is clear that *Jane* is an agent, but what are the *bottle* and *juice*? Location? Goal? Patient? Instrument? Because of the difficulty in answering such questions, many linguists have preferred to reject theta roles altogether in constructing their descriptions, but many others are convinced that theta roles are of fundamental importance in spite of the difficulties.

Such troubles also accompany the study of word meaning. A Chinese host and an English guest may exchange their fondness for eating leek, a common vegetable in both countries. However, not until the Chinese treats his guest to scrambled eggs with leek will the English visitor realize that the Chinese leek is totally different from the English namesake. The Chinese leek is much thinner, with deep-green chive-like leaves. After dinner, the Englishman takes out his laptop, accesses the Internet, and shows a picture of leek grown in his own country, which surprises his friend. "It looks very similar to our 大葱," he comments. Then he picks up the Chinese translation of 大葱 from an on-line dictionary — "green Chinese onion." The Englishman is more confused, because he has no image in his mind of such a vegetable. Both of them resort to Google pictures again.

Not only may the meaning of a word differ from place to place, it can also change from time to time. Decades ago children enjoyed *gay* sunny meadows, but today's children may display indifference to a *gay* bar. Words as signs of meaning are not always reliable.

Semanticists can give you lots of similar examples. They know all aspects of word meaning. Some of them are not just knowledgeable, but ambitious. They vow in their minds, "We'll uncover all the internal structures of language meaning some day." Why not? Phonetics, phonology, morphology, syntax... all these linguistic branches have made good progress. Rules discovered in these domains have found wide application in many fields. Policemen today can identify a suspect with the help of voiceprints, and a computer can communicate with people because it has been programmed to analyze morphological and syntactic rules. Linguists are also confident of breakthroughs in decoding semantic rules.

Efforts have been made in different orientations, one of which is to exhaust the semantic features of a word (or more exactly, a lexeme). Semantic features are defined as a class of theoretical constructs developed in analogy to the distinctive features of phonology — they are considered to be the smallest semantic units for the description of linguistic expressions and their semantic relations. *Man*, for example, could be analyzed as ADULT, HUMAN, and MALE. Contrasts of these semantic features can be presented in terms of + or −, and often drawn in a matrix. Below are two such matrixes.

	man	woman	boy	girl	cow
HUMAN	+	+	+	+	−
ADULT	+	+	−	−	+
MALE	+	−	+	−	−

Tab. 7.1 Matrix of semantic features for some nouns

	walk	march	run	limp
NATURAL	+	−	−	−
HURRIED	−	+	+	−
FORWARD	+	+	+	+
ONE FOOT ALWAYS ON GROUND	+	+	−	+

Tab. 7.2 Matrix of semantic features for some verbs

If someone tells you what he wants to express is "natural, not hurried, forward, and one foot always on ground", can you guess that means *walk*? Moreover, *march* has at least another feature: with firm, regular steps. To exhaust all the semantic features of a word is not an easy thing, and sometimes even impossible, because, in philosophical parlance, the whole is more than the sum of its parts, so how can the whole word be represented by its components?

Although a huge amount of fruitful work has been done by linguists of different countries in semantic feature analysis, its application in some advanced areas, such as artificial intelligence and robotics, still seems doubtful. Let's consider the word *man* again. *Man* is + ADULT, + HUMAN, and + MALE, which can be programmed into a robot without difficulty. Suppose the robot is reading a newspaper. A headline like (7.1) will plunge it into a predicament.

(7.1) She was the only man in her cabinet

How can the – MALE nominative and possessive pronouns refer to the noun *man* which should be + MALE? Our dear robot feels puzzled.

But human readers will not be puzzled at all. In fact, that headline belongs to an article in memory of the great Indian stateswoman, the late Prime Minister Indira Gandhi. Praises are quoted in the article such as " She acted like a He-Man"; "Unlike the big leaders who change their views, she was consistent about her stand and never used to waver from it". In light of the context, readers have no trouble telling that the word *man* is used as a metaphor. When a word is used as a metaphor, it will not keep all the features of its conceptual meaning, but will highlight a certain associative property of its connotative meaning, according to Leech. Obviously, the associative property of *man* used here, is the consistency of the political stand. Indira Gandhi, though a woman, was outstanding in this aspect, which led to praise from her people comparing her to *the only man*.

If robots can be made to handle such figurative usage, they should possess the same encyclopedic knowledge as human beings and be sensitive to human intentions as well. Essentially, robots should learn to understand linguistic expressions in light of context.

Nevertheless, semanticists tend to confine their work to an arena away from context. They think researches related to context pertain to another discipline — pragmatics. In their cage there is only one animal to tame, i. e. meaning.

Let's go on with more of their taming, or structurization.

7.2 Signifier vs. signified

Today's linguists still respect a century-old cornerstone standpoint called Saussurean arbitrariness, which claims that the relationship between a linguistic sign (signifier) and its content (signified) is arbitrary. In the Olympic Games the highlight for medal winners and their supporters is the flag-raising ceremony. Their national flag stands for the honor of their country, with its color(s) and patterns representing some highly-valued ideals and beliefs of their people. So the relationship between a national flag and the country it stands for is not arbitrary. In contrast, it is not necessary for the relationship between a word and what it refers to to arouse any special feeling among its users. Why is a cat called *cat*? You may say that all the English people call it that way. If an English baby calls it *miao*, he will eventually give up his creation to follow the convention. If some day he goes to China, he may find some people with a certain southern Chinese accent call a cat *miao*. Apparently *miao* imitates the cat's cry, and perhaps some other words originated in the same way. However, even such imitations vary widely. In the northern dialects of Chinese a cat is called *Mao*, which is also a sound imitation, but different from *miao*. Besides, *cuckoo*, *coucou*, *Kuckuck* , *Kakuk*, *Kokkyx*, and *bugu* are said to be the onomatopoeia of the same bird in English, French, German, Hungarian, Greek, and Chinese respectively. It seems that a natural sound can have many versions of imitation. The variation is arbitrary as well.

There is also a problem with the signified. When a child asks an adult, "What is a camel?", the adult will respond immediately, "Let me show you one. " Then he may take the child to the zoo or show him a picture of a camel, and thus the child knows the signified of the sound sign *camel*. Next month the child goes to a rural area with his parents and sees a high mountain with three towering peaks. "That mountain looks like a huge camel!" he exclaims. How can a child make such a comparison? That's because *camel* in his mind is an image, with some prominent features, such as a head always held high, and two humps behind, just like three peaks.

So, there is not a direct link between the sound of a word and the object it refers to. What is called the signified is not actually what we have been shown but an abstract concept formed in our mind.

Semanticists like to formulate such a view with a triangular diagram, and Fig. 7.1 is the earliest version.

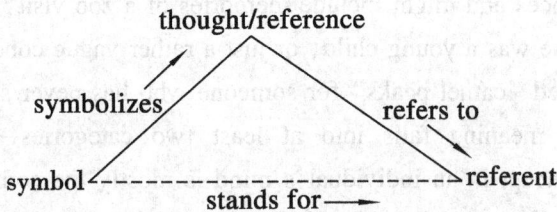

thought/reference

symbolizes   refers to

symbol ← - - - - - - - - - - - - - - - - → referent
                    stands for →

Fig. 7.1   Ogden & Richards' Semantic Triangle

According to Ogden and Richards, the "symbol" refers to the linguistic elements (word, sentence, etc.), the "referent" refers to the object in the world of experience, and the "thought" or "reference" refers to concept or notion. Thus the connection (represented with a dotted line) between symbol and referent is made possible only through "concept", by virtue of which the symbol of a word signifies "things".

7.3 Denotation vs. connotation

One main criticism of Ogden & Richards' Semantic Triangle is how to identify concepts. As has been mentioned, an Englishman's concept of *leek* may be totally different from that of a Chinese. In other words, can anyone guarantee that a concept coming to his mind when he uses a word is going to be the same as the one brought to his reader's mind? Therefore, a concept so arbitrarily produced cannot be regarded as the word's meaning.

However, most signs have at least one normal, "common sense" meaning. This meaning, called the sign's denotaion, is shared among many people and is the most widely used meaning of the sign. But signs may also have many different "subjective" meanings that arise from each individual's personal experiences. These are called the connotations of the sign.

For example, most people would agree that the sign *camel* refers to a light brown, ruminant animal that has either one or two humps on its back and is adapted to a dry climate. This is its denotation as well as the definition one can find in a dictionary. On the other hand, the connotations of *camel* depend on each person's individual experiences and might include memories of a zoo visit, or a story about a camel read when he was a young child, or just a rather vague concept like the shape of a mountain called "camel peaks" for someone who has never seen a camel.

Accordingly, meaning falls into at least two categories — denotative and connotative. A concept in an individual's mind is mostly the connotative meaning, formed through one's perception of some features of the object a sign refers to. The denotative meaning is not necessarily generated in such a process, but has long been an agreement among all the people in a community. If one of them does not know that meaning, he can ask others to tell him, or he can consult a dictionary. Meanings of this type are said to arise through social convention.

However, even conventional meanings change over time. Remember the variation on the most frequently used meaning of the word *gay*? In fact, the conventional meanings of signs in a society are under continual renegotiation as new possible meanings arise, are considered, and are accepted or rejected.

Therefore, the connection between the concept of a sign and the object it refers to is made through experience. Once you walk into a gay bar, or read an article about male homosexuals, you conceive a new meaning of the word in your mind.

The above discussion leads us to another triangular diagram — Pierce's "Semiotic Triangle". Charles S. Pierce (1839 — 1914) is generally acknowledged as an important pioneer in the study of signs.

Each of the lines in the Semiotic Triangle represents a two-way negotiation, i. e.

Perception — the ongoing group of bodily processes by which human beings

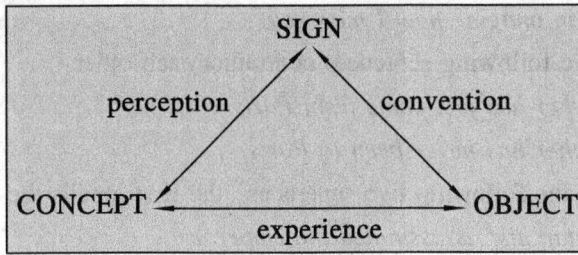

Fig. 7. 2   Pierce's Semiotic Triangle

receive data about their environments,

Experience — the memory of previous perceptions and concepts, which is constantly being altered or "updated" by new experience,

Convention — the constantly changing social "rules of meaning" that unify groups of people within their communication environments.

As a philosopher, Pierce does not confine his focus merely to language. His sign involves icons and indexes, and his model helps to explain how communication works as an interactive process. Today's philosophy attaches more importance to dynamic exploration than static description, which leads to some philosophers' deconstructing Saussurean arbitrariness, with their new proposition — floating signifier, based on such discoveries as meaning's continual renegotiation.

Are they correct? If not, then why do we occasionally ask a question like "Is that the word you use?" or "What do you mean by saying that?"

7.4 Meaning vs. function

Just as with syntactic principles, our mind also has some "talent" with meaning. It can grasp some prominent semantic features of a word without deliberate training.

Some semantic properties of the words we use to think and talk about the world are automatically captured by the resources of our human minds. English speakers, for example, have internal semantic knowledge of the following:

a) telling that the following sentences describe the same situation:

(7.2) *You can't imagine how I miss you.*

(7.3) *You can imagine how I miss you.*

b) noticing that the following sentences contradict each other:

    (7.4) *My father has just come from Paris.*

    (7.5) *My father has never been to Paris.*

c) judging that of the following two sentences, the first entails the second:

    (7.6) *The anarchist assassinated the emperor.*

    (7.7) *The emperor is dead.*

d) deciding that of the following two sentences, the first presupposes the second:

    (7.8) *The Mayor of London is a tall man.*

    (7.9) *There is a Mayor of London.*

e) finding that the sentence below has more than one possible meaning:

    (7.10) *If I'm a priest, I'll marry you.*

f) discovering that *let's* is different from *let us* in the sentence below because the latter does not involve the addressee:

    (7.11) *Let's beg the monster to let us go.*

g) understanding the metaphoric expression in the sentence below:

    (7.12) *He is a storehouse of repartee.*

h) feeling the sentence below infelicitous:

    (7.13) *I promise to forget my name.*

All these dimensions of internalized semantic knowledge, namely a) synonymy, b) contradiction, c) entailment, d) presupposition, e) ambiguity, f) inclusive-exclusive distinction, g) metaphorical interpretation, h) infelicity, can be attributed to properties of I-meaning proposed by Chomsky (2000).

Chomsky lists an interesting example to see how powerful the human mind is in dealing with I-meaning. He writes:

Suppose the library has two copies of Tolstoy's War and Peace, Peter takes out one, and John the other. Did Peter and John take out the same book, or different books?

Then Chomsky reveals that the human mind knows the answer tacitly, which can be overtly described as follows:

If we attend to the material factor of the lexical item, they took out different books; *if we focus on its abstract component*, *they took out the same book.*

So, there are at least two components of the meaning of *book*: material and abstract. If we say

(7. 14) *The book that he is planning will weigh at least five pounds if he ever writes it.*

We attend to both material and abstract factors simultaneously.

Chomsky concludes: "The semantic properties of words are used to think and talk about the world in terms of the perspectives made available by the resources of the mind".

Since these semantic properties are internalized, possessed by all humans no matter whether they are educated or not, Chomsky holds that I-meaning falls under syntax. He asserts that natural language has a "semantics" only in the sense of the study of how this instrument, whose formal structure and potentialities of expression are the subject of syntactic investigation, is actually put to use in a speech community.

Beyond I-meaning, all other categories of meaning are closely related to the use of language. In other words, I-meaning is the human genetic faculty in calculating the logic in meaning (e. g. presupposition, entailment...). It is not the specific meaning needed to be conveyed in communication. Meaning to be conveyed by language cannot be a part of language, just as a cargo cannot be regarded as a part of the vehicle. Therefore, it makes no sense to structurize meaning without considering such dynamic factors as context and culture beyond language.

Larsen-Freeman, an influential applied linguist, once cited three examples to show how meaning cannot be separated from use.

(7. 15) *That'll be John. He calls every day at this time.*

(7. 16) *You have been going all day. You must be tired.*

(7. 17) *He should be here somewhere. He said he was coming.*

Sentences above are unquestionably meaningful. But we still do not know why they are spoken. Genuine understanding comes only when we have learned (or imagined) the context associated with their use.

If John is the boyfriend of a girl, her flat-mate may give her a warning like

(7.15) when she sees a man walking towards their dormitory from the window, because their flat is still in a mess. In this context, (7.15) actually means

(7.18) *"You'll pick up your room now!"*

(7.16) is easier to be associated with a usual context, and means

(7.19) *"You must take better care of yourself."*

(7.17) is possibly used to press the hearer to hand over a hidden person. It can be interpreted as

(7.20) *"He's shy. You should ask him out."*

When meaning is conveyed like cargo, the conveying should have a certain purpose, which can only be manifested by referring to the context. The real meaning in communication is contextual meaning. Without context, a sentence conveys only literal information. However, we have to maintain a distance from context for a while again, because we still have another aspect of language to discuss in the next chapter.

EXERCISES ✍

I. Translate the following quotations into Chinese.

Normally human beings do not produce utterances for the sake of the phonetic, phonological and grammatical features. Utterances are produced because they convey meaning.

(from J. Simpson: *A First Course in Linguistics*)

Semantics as a subfield of linguistics is the study of meaning in language. Semantics deals with the meanings of words, and how the meanings of sentences are derived from them.

(from G. Tserdanelis & W. Wong: *Language files*)

II. Fill in the blanks with the linguistic terms you have learnt.

1) Words or expressions that have identical meanings are called _____.

2) Words or phrases that have opposite meanings are called _____.

3) When a word has two or more meanings that are at least vaguely related to each other, it is called a _____. For example, "leaf" can refer to "a part of a tree" and also "a sheet of paper".

4) When words have a single phonetic form but two or more entirely different meanings, they are called _____. For example, "bank" can mean "a commercial lending institution" and "a small cliff at the edge of a river".

5) Words have two kinds of meanings: denotative and connotative. _____ meaning is precise, literal, and objective. You can find a word's _____ from a dictionary.

6) _____ meaning is more variable, figurative, and subjective. It is whatever the word suggests or implies. _____ meaning includes all the feelings, associations, and emotions that a word touches off in different people.

7) The relation of _____ that holds between "chase" and "follow" is based on properties of I-meaning.

III. Tell what semantic relation holds between each of the following pairs of sentences.

1) a. The police caught the thief.
   b. The thief was caught by the police.

2) a. The shirt is red.
   b. The shirt is not white.

3) a. Tom is a bachelor.
   b. Tom is married.

4) a. When did he stop beating his wife?
   b. The husband has been beating his wife.

IV. Give a summary of less than 150 words to Section 7.1.

V. Answer the following questions.

1) What problems can be dealt with by semantics?

2) What do you think is the major difference between Ogden & Richard's Semantic

Triangle and Pierce's Semiotic Triangle?

3) What is I-meaning?

4) How does the human mind deal with the meaning of *window* in the following sentences?

    a. *He knocked at the window.*

    b. *He jumped out of the window.*

    c. *The morning light was stealing through the window.*

5) How does human mind acquire the meaning of a word? How does it deal with the denotative meaning and connotative meaning? Cite some examples to illustrate your viewpoints.

6) The following are a pair of examples cited by The American logician R. Montague. Do you feel they are equally truthful? If no, think where the problem lies?

    John seeks a unicorn.

    John finds a unicorn.

VI. Challenging work.

1) In Ogden & Richard's Semantic Triangle, the "symbol" refers to the linguistic elements (word, sentence, etc.), the "referent" refers to the object in the world of experience, and the "thought" or "reference" is actually an abstract concept formed in our mind. To distinguish "referent" from "reference", ask different people "What is a dog?" and invite them to give you a detailed description of a typical dog in their minds. Then try to analyze their responses.

2) Write an essay on the following topic:

On the floating of the signifier

▬▬

R. Montague (1930 — 1971)

Richard Montague was an American mathematician and philosopher. His research focused on the foundations of logic and set theory. Though not a professional linguist, Montague exercised a major influence on semantics in the 1970s and 1980s. He was one of the first people to systematically explore the possibilities of a completely rigorous formal analysis of both the syntax and the semantics of natural languages along the lines of logic. His seminal works on language between 1970 and 1973 founded the theory known after his death as Montague Grammar, one of the main starting points for the field of formal semantics.

Montague was born September 20, 1930 in Stockton, California and died March 7, 1971 in Los Angeles. At St. Mary's High School in Stockton he studied Latin and Ancient Greek. After a year at Stockton Junior College studying journalism, he entered the University of California, Berkeley in 1948, where he studied mathematics, philosophy, and Semitic languages, and graduated with an A. B. in philosophy in 1950. He continued graduate work at Berkeley, receiving an M. A. in mathematics in 1953 and his Ph. D. in Philosophy in 1957. Alfred Tarski, one of the pioneers in the model-theoretic semantics of logic, was Montague's main influence and directed his dissertation. Montague taught in the philosophy Department of the University of California, Los Angeles from 1955 until his death.

Montague's work constitutes a decisive breakaway from the traditional view that natural languages are too vague and too unsystematic to be treated formally, in the same way as the formal languages of logic and mathematics. From the rapid developments in generative linguistics in the 1960s and early 1970s, scholars like Montague, Donald Davidson, David Lewis, and others gained confidence that a formal syntactic theory of natural language was no pipedream, and that, therefore, a formal semantics might also prove to be a possibility.

Although the work in generative linguistics thus constituted an important impetus for the development of formal, model-theoretic semantics for natural language, this is not to say that this undertaking met with much enthusiasm in generative linguistic circles. On the contrary, whereas people like Montague and Davidson were of the opinion that not just the syntax but also the semantics of natural languages can be studied in a precise, formal fashion, this view has remained far from common among generative linguists.

Montague's work itself forms part of a development which includes the work of Davidson, Lewis, Cresswell and many others. Its characteristics, which to a greater or lesser degree distinguish it from the work of others, are, first of all, the generality and rigor with which Montague carried out his analyses; second, his ample use of whatever logical machinery he deemed necessary; and third, the way in which he combined syntax and semantics.

Reading recommendation

Beginner-friendly：

J. Saeed. Semantics. Blackwell Publishers Ltd. 1997；外语教学与研究出版社,2000(吴一安　导读)

王寅.语义理论与语言教学.上海外语教育出版社,2001

More challenging：

J. Lyons. Linguistic Semantics：An Introduction. Cambridge University Press, 1995. 外语教学与研究出版社,2000(汪榕培　导读)

E. Hatch & C. Brown. Vocabulary, Semantics and Language Education. Cambridge University Press, 1995；外语教学与研究出版社,2001(王初明　导读)

张志毅,张庆云.词汇语义学.商务印书馆,2001

石毓智.语法的认知语义基础.江西教育出版社,2000

"You see, my real shoe size is four," said Vera. "But I'm wearing sevens because fours hurt!"

— an Irish joke

Chapter 8

Functional Structures in Communication

8.1 Given and New

We have introduced the different branches of "core linguistics", specifically, phonology, morphology, syntax, and semantics. The interests of them start from the level of phoneme, and stop at the level of sentence. Researchers in these fields focus on the exploration of the internal mechanisms of language, i. e. the way the human mind structures language, instead of describing the general patterns which emerge in the use of language. The former approach is referred to by Chomsky as I-language (or internalized language), and the latter E-language (or externalized language).

Now let's go beyond I-language approaches to see how people attempt to answer other questions such as how sentences are generated to convey information, and what rules work in the process. The most systematic research in this area is guided by one of our major modern linguists, Michael Halliday, the founder of the systemic functional grammar.

To start with, let's go back to the title design of this chapter, where we see a ridiculous quotation beside the picture of a pair of shoes. It seems that the speaker, Vera, produces a grammatical utterance, but why do we still think it stupid and absurd?

The first half of Vera's utterance sounds as if she would like to talk about her *shoe size*, which is *four*—a piece of new information in this sentence. In the second half, the "size four" becomes the known (or given) information *fours* (shoes of size four), as the subject of a subordinate clause introduced by *because*, and the new information is at the end of the clause — *hurt*, which nevertheless conflicts the starting information *real* (since shoes of the real size will not hurt), as the diagram below indicates:

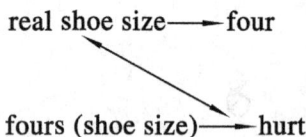

real shoe size——four

fours (shoe size)——hurt

Fig. 8.1   Conflicting information

Below is another example, in which the new information at the end of each sentence becomes the given information of the next sentence, and assumes the initial position of that sentence.

(8.1) *My friend John gave me a book. The book is about Nigeria. Nigeria is a great African country. The country hopes to play a more active role in international affairs.*

Let's have a look at its information structure. The given information and the new information together make up an information unit. (8.1) has four such units:

given information	new information
My friend John	*a book*
The book	*Nigeria*
Nigeria	*a great African country*
The country	*a more active role*

Through information units, sentences are put together to convey what a speaker intends to express.

A sentence can be very complex, including several clauses, or be as simple as just one clause. Therefore, linguists prefer to count the number of clauses in an utterance rather than the number of sentences. A clause consists of a subject and a finite verb, so it is easy to make sure how many clauses there are in an utterance —

just count the finite verbs.

Usually, a clause embraces an information unit, i. e. given information + new information. Like (8.1), the new information of a clause may become the given information of the next clause in an utterance so as to make a group of clauses cohesive in meaning.

One exception is the imperative clause, in which all the information is effectively new. Since all such clauses are addressed to the listener—*you*, *you* is the given information, which is actually hidden.

(8.2) *Stop dawdling and finish your work*!

Analysis:

(*you*)	*Stop dawdling and finish your work*!
hidden given information	new information

Another exception is the dummy *there* and *it*, which carry no information at all, but still have a role to play—to introduce new information. A famous example is the opening sentence of Jane Austen's *Pride and Prejudice*:

(8.3) *It is a truth universally acknowledged, that a single man in possession of a good fortune must be in want of a wife.*

In (8.3) *it* does not refer to any given information, but just implies that what follows is new information. Let's turn to the dummy *there*. Please compare *There comes John* with *John comes*, the former *John* is the information unexpectedly mentioned for the hearer, whereas the latter *John* at the initial position of the clause should be a shared topic between the speaker and the hearer.

Another case introduced by Larsen-Freeman, an applied linguist we have mentioned, can also be used to help understand the importance of Given-New distinction. Larsen-Freeman's example is a short dialogue between a couple.

(8.4) Wife: (in answering the phone) *I need something to write with.*

Husband: *There is a pen on the table.* / *A pen is on the table.*

Analysis:

1) The wife needs a pen or pencil to write down something from the phone.

The husband has two choices to answer with. The difference between these two English choices may not be perceived by a second language learner, but both the wife and the husband are native speakers, who are intuitively aware of it, i. e.

The structural pattern *there is...* is used to introduce some new information for the hearer;

The sentence-initial NP represents the shared information with the hearer.

2) In saying *There is a pen on the table*, the husband is to provide some new information needed by the wife.

In saying *A pen is on the table*, the husband emphasizes the shared information.

3) By saying *There is a pen on the table* the husband offers help to the wife.

By saying *A pen is on the table* the husband shows his impatience and irritates the wife.

8. 2 Theme and Rheme

In functional grammar, there are two parallel and interrelated systems of analysis that concern the structure of the clause. The first is the information structure, which is in essence listener-oriented and has been introduced in the previous section. The present section will deal with the second, called thematic structure, which is speaker-oriented. The constituents involved in the information structure are labeled Given (information) and New (information), and those in the thematic structure are labeled Theme and Rheme (We have encountered the terms *thematic* and *theme* (not initiated with the capital letter) in Section 6. 2 *Theta roles*, but they are defined differently here). Mostly (not always) Given is introduced in the Theme position, and New in the Rheme position.

According to Halliday, a Theme in English is always at the initial position of a clause, as "the point of departure" of the message carried by one clause. The rest of the clause is called Rheme. For example, in (8.5), the first NP *John* is the Theme, and the rest is the Rheme. The contrast is similar to the traditional grammar's contrast between subject and predicate.

(8.5) *John sat in the front seat.*

Analysis:

John	sat in the front seat
Theme	Rheme
subject	predicate

But in (8.6) we can see the disparity: a Theme is not necessarily an NP.

(8.6) *In the front seat sat John.*

Analysis:

In the front seat	sat	John.
Theme		Rheme
complement	verb	
predicate		subject

The Theme in (8.5) is called an unmarked Theme because it is also the subject of the clause, while the Theme in (8.6), which is not the subject but the complement, is a marked Theme. (8.7) has another kind of marked Theme, which is a circumstantial adjunct:

(8.7) *For a long time, the Spartans proved themselves invincible on land.*

Analysis:

For a long time,		the Spartans proved themselves invincible on land.
Theme		Rheme
circumstantial adjunct	subject	predicate

Some clauses have more than one Theme. They are starting points of different levels, namely, topical, interpersonal, and textual. For example,

(8.8) *Well, children, the story is about to continue.*

Analysis:

Well,	children,	the story	is about to continue.
textual	interpersonal	topical	
Theme			Rheme

(8.8) is a typical clause with multiple Themes: the textual Theme — *Well,* whose function is to signal the beginning of a new move in the exchange; the interpersonal Theme — *children,* to address listeners directly; the topical Theme, which expresses the main topic of the clause. Below are two other examples:

(8.9) *But, surely, the course doesn't start till next week.*

Analysis:

But,	surely,	the course	doesn't start till next week.
textual	interpersonal	topical	
Theme			Rheme

(8.10) *Not surprisingly, then, its operations were viewed with admiration.*

Analysis:

Not surprisingly,	then,	its operations	were viewed with admiration.
interpersonal	textual	topical	
Theme			Rheme

It is obvious that the thematic structure can help explain the speaker's efforts in maintaining the coherence of an utterance. This type of linguistic analysis originates from an influential theory known as Functional Sentence Perspective (FSP), developed by the Prague School of linguistics in the 1950s, which describes how information is distributed in sentences.

8.3 Topic-comment and end focus

Other terms outside the Prague School's tradition which refer to relationships similar to the Theme-Rheme distinction include topic and comment. Topic-comment distinction is from the perspective of discourse. In contrast, subject-predicate distinction is syntactic. (8.11) and (8.12) illustrate the difference between topic-comment and subject-predicate.

(8.11) *Jonathan has never been to America.*

Analysis:

Jonathan	has never been to America.
subject	predicate
topic	comment

(8.12) *As for food, Jonathan has never tasted anything so terrible before.*

Analysis:

As for food,	Jonathan	has never tasted anything so terrible before.
	subject	predicate
topic		comment

The topic of the clause usually represents what the clause is about, and the comment can either be a VP as in (8.11), or an NP + VP as in (8.12). Topic-comment analysis is not often used by English linguists because cases like (8.12) are very rare in inflectional languages. Such phenomena, however, are common in non-inflectional languages like Chinese:

(8.13) 要说饭量,谁也没法跟他比。

Analysis：

要说饭量,	谁	也没法跟他比。
	subject	predicate
topic	comment	

(8.14)这个人，脑子不开窍。

Analysis：

这个人,	脑子	不开窍。
	subject	predicate
topic	comment	

(8.15)这本书,我昨天就看完了。

Analysis：

这本书,	我	昨天就看完了。
	subject	predicate
topic	comment	

Therefore，topic-comment is very important in analyzing the information structure of Chinese as well as contrasting the textual structures of Chinese and English. Typologically，it is generally accepted that English is a subject-prominent language and Chinese is a topic-prominent language.

For example，(8.14) cannot be translated maintaining the original order like (8.16).

(8.16) *This guy, brain not clear.*

Analysis：

This guy,	*brain*	*not clear.*
	subject	predicate
topic	comment	

There is no such subject + predicate comment in English. A proper translation, instead, is

(8.17) *This guy is muddle-headed.*

Analysis:

This guy	*is muddle-headed.*
subject	predicate
topic	comment

(8.17) returns to a subject-predicate structure, which demonstrates that syntactic structure is emphasized more in English than in Chinese, while the information structure in Chinese is prominent.

Furthermore, Chinese has a strong psychological tendency to stress the most important new information at the end of a sentence, i. e. the position for end focus. *More and more* in (8.18), for instance, is the information focus, but it cannot be put at the end of the sentence like its equivalent (underlined) in Chinese (8.19).

(8.18) *More and more people are surfing the Internet.*

(8.19) 上网的人越来越多。

The subject-predicate framework in an English sentence rarely gives way to the emphasis of its information focus. Please look at the following English sentence and its Chinese translation:

(8.20) *A bomb cast from behind the booth blew up undamagingly in a ditch.*

(8.21) 从电话亭后面扔出一颗炸弹,炸到一条沟里了,没造成破坏。

In (8.20) *undamagingly* refers to the consequence of the bombing, and hence the focus of the new information. In this English version there is not any special effort to highlight this essential information, which stays at the usual position as an adverbial. In the Chinese version (8.21), by contrast, this essential information is turned into a verbal phrase 没造成破坏 and goes to the end of the sentence, the position of end focus.

More interestingly, English allows the same arrangement if (8.20) is reorganized into (8.22), though it sounds a bit literary.

（8. 22）*A bomb cast from behind the booth blew up in a ditch, undamagingly.*

But Chinese does not permit the same arrangement of information as in （8. 20）：

（8. 23）* 从电话亭后面扔出一颗炸弹，没造成破坏地炸到一条沟里。

（8. 23） indicates that a topic-prominent language is linear in time order: the consequence（没造成破坏） should not be presented before the event（炸到一条沟里）.

And（8. 18） indicates that a subject-prominent language is not used to putting an NP complement in the position of end focus, as in （8. 24）. Syntactic structure is prior to the information structure in such languages.

（8. 24） <u>More and more</u> people are surfing the Internet. →? People who are surfing the Internet are <u>more and more</u>.

Functional grammar arouses more interest in typological observation. Let's identify another distinction between subject-prominent language and topic-prominent language. By subject-prominence we mean that the subject of a clause should always be overt, but it can be covert in a topic-prominent language like Chinese. Please compare （8. 25） and （8. 26）.

（8. 25） A：*Where is John?*

　　　　　B：*He has gone to New York.*

（8. 26） A：约翰呢?

　　　　　B：上纽约去了。

B's answer in （8. 26） omits the subject 约翰, but B cannot do it in his English answer in （8. 25）, like "*Has gone to New York*".

So, if （8. 27） in Chinese is translated to （8. 28） in English, the "hidden" subjects of all the clauses after the first one have to be recovered.

（8. 27）约翰真忙，昨天去了纽约，今天又去费城，明天还得奔旧金山。

（8. 28） *John is really busy. Yesterday <u>he</u> went to New York, today <u>he</u> is leaving for Philadelphia, and tomorrow <u>he</u>'ll fly to San Francisco.*

The underlined words in （8. 28） are the recovered subjects, which are also topics of their clauses. These clauses form a topic chain, a way to maintain the cohesion and coherence of an utterance. In English-like languages, every topic in the chain should be overt, even though they are identical with the initial one. In Chinese-like languages, identical topics can be covert. A chain of covered topics strengthen the coherence between clauses, which makes a main characteristic of topic-prominent languages.

8. 4 A "meaning potential"

A sentence is the largest unit of grammatical organization. If someone argues that above sentences we have paragraphs, and above paragraphs we have chapters, he must have confused the concept of language with that of written texts.

Educated or not, an adult speaker has the ability to produce sentences. Sentences are generated from one's internalized syntactic knowledge, whereas paragraphs, chapters, and other levels of written texts are organized with the learned knowledge from school training. Oral utterances do not need such rhetorical organization. No matter how long one speaks, what he produces is just a set of sentences (unless he has made any previous preparation, such as a draft). Sentences are to an utterance what bricks are to a building.

If we just want to know the mechanisms of language per se, what we explore will be within the level of the sentence. That's why Chomsky focuses his fruitful work here. With the capacity to generate sentences, human beings set out to use language to do things. "What a person can do in the linguistic sense," Halliday claims, "that is what he can do as speaker/hearer, is equivalent to what he 'can mean'; hence the description of language as a 'meaning potential'". When this potential meets a trigger, that is, an intention to speak, meaning will be borne by it, not alone, but with the help of an excellent midwife — context.

EXERCISES

I. Translate the following statement into Chinese.

Functional grammar is an approach to linguistics which is concerned with language as an instrument of social interaction rather than as a system that is viewed in isolation. It considers the individual as a social being and investigates the way in which he acquires language and uses it in order to communicate with others in his social environment.

II. Fill in the blanks with the linguistic terms you have learned.

1) The constituents involved in the information structure are labeled _____ and _____, and those in the thematic structure are labeled _____ and _____.

2) According to Halliday, a _____ in English is always at the initial position of a clause, as "the point of departure" of the message carried by one clause. The rest of the clause is called _____.

3) When the Theme is also the subject of the clause, it is called a(n) _____ Theme; when it is not the subject, a(n) _____ Theme.

4) Some clauses have more than one Theme. They are starting points of different levels, namely, _____, _____, and _____ Themes.

5) In topic-comment analysis, the _____ is the thing being talked about and the _____ is what is said about the topic.

III. Fill in the blanks to complete the analyses of the sentences below.

1) 这棵树，叶子很大。

这棵树	叶子　　很大
Theme	

2) 张三我已经见过了。

张三	我　　已经见过了
	Rheme

3) 老师站在讲台上。

老师	站在讲台上
Theme	

4）讲台上站着老师。

讲台上	站着老师

5）*Have some bread and butter.*

（*you*）	*Have*	*Some bread and butter*
		Rheme

6）*Please, don't touch the cucumber sandwiches.*

Please	*don't*	*touch the cucumber sandwiches*
interpersonal Theme		Rheme

7）*Now at first sight this might seem to be contradictory.*

Now	*at first sight*	*this might seem to be contradictory*
textual Theme	topical Theme	

8）*Surprisingly, however, this tendency has declined in the mid-1970s.*

Surprisingly	*however*	*this tendency has declined in the mid-1970s*
	textual Theme	Rheme

IV. Identify the Themes in the following sentences. If any are multiple Themes, label the thematic elements as interpersonal, textual or topical.

1）哎呀,孙悟空,月光宝石怎么能乱扔呢?

2）好大一会儿,这伙人谁也没说话。

3）And no doubt he'll deny everything.

4）Well, perhaps he simply isn't interested in the same kind of things.

5）The first three letters, of course, were his mother's initials.

6）Oh, Alice, you are all right, aren't you?

V. Give a summary of less than 150 words to Section 8.3.

VI. Challenging work.

1) Analyze the information structure of the following extract from an American counting-out game for children, which could go on indefinitely, or could be terminated by an end-of-rhyme formula, such as "Minnie and a Minnie and a ha-ha-ha".

> *I went downtown*
> *To see Mrs. Brown.*
> *She gave me a nickel,*
> *To buy me a pickle.*
> *The pickle was sour,*
> *She gave me a flower.*
> *The flower was dead,*
> *She gave me a thread.*
> *The thread was thin,*
> *She gave me a pin.*
> *The pin was sharp,*
> *She gave me a harp.*
> *...*

2) Recall any similar verbal games in Chinese you enjoyed when you were very young. Analyze the information structure of them. Then discuss the role of such verbal play in children's linguistic development.

M. Halliday (1925 —)

Michael Alexander Kirkwood Halliday is a linguist who developed an internationally influential grammar model, the systemic functional grammar (which also goes by the name of systemic functional linguistics (SFL)). In addition to English, the model has been applied to other languages, both Indo-European and non-Indo-European.

Michael Halliday was born in Yorkshire, England in 1925. He was trained in Chinese for war service with the British army. Meanwhile he took a BA Honors degree in Modern Chinese Language and Literature (Mandarin) at the University of London, then studied for three years at Peking University and Lingnan University in China, and returned to take a PhD in Chinese Linguistics at Cambridge. Having taught Chinese for a number of years, he changed his field of specialization to linguistics, and developed systemic functional grammar, elaborating on the foundations laid by his British teacher J. R. Firth and a group of influential European linguists of the early 20th century, the Prague School. His seminal paper on this model was published in 1961. He became Professor of General Linguistics at the University College London in 1965. In 1976 he moved to Australia as Foundation Professor of Linguistics at the University of Sydney, where he remained until he retired. He has worked in various regions of language study, both theoretical and applied, and has been especially concerned with applying the understanding of the basic principles of language to the theory and practice of education. He received the status of Emeritus Professor of the University of Sydney and Macquarie University, Sydney, in 1987, and is currently Distinguished Visiting Professor in the Faculty of Education, University of Hong Kong.

Ever since Halliday started thinking about language, his main interest has always been in "meaning". For him, meaning is not a closed stable product which is ready-made or given in the human mind and is simply waiting for a linguist to describe

Linguistic Stars

it；but rather, meaning is an open dynamic process both as text and as system. He has made enormously important theoretical and applicational contribution to linguistics and other related fields of study.

Reading recommendation

Beginner-friendly：

G. Thompson. Introducing Functional Grammar. Edward Arnold（Publishers）Ltd, 1996；外语教学与研究出版社,2000（黄国文　导读）

T. Bloor & M Bloor. The Functional Analysis of English：A Hallidayan Approach. Edward Arnold（Publishers）Ltd, 1995；外语教学与研究出版社,2001（黄国文　导读）

曹逢甫. 主题在汉语中的功能研究. 语文出版社,1995（谢天蔚译）

More challenging：

M. A. K. Halliday. An Introduction to Functional Grammar. Edward Arnold（Publishers）Ltd, 1994；外语教学与研究出版社,2000（胡壮麟　导读）

胡壮麟. 功能主义纵横谈. 外语教学与研究出版社,2000

朱永生,严世清. 系统功能语言学多维思考. 上海外语教育出版社,2001

彭宣维. 语言过程与维度. 清华大学出版社,2002

徐烈炯,刘丹青. 话题与焦点新论. 上海教育出版社,2003

As Mrs. McGinty entered the house she looked up to see a ceiling 15 feet high.

" Begod," she said to husband Seamus, "when you said you were going to knock two rooms into one I didn't think you meant upwards!!"

an Irish joke

Chapter 9

Meaning and Use

9.1 Language games

People may think that any sentence ought to be grammatical as well as meaningful, but linguists can list some sentences as grammatical but not meaningful.

The following example is from a British joke showing how a grammatical sentence can be illogically funny:

(9.1) *You three are a right pair if ever I saw one*!

Some mentally deranged people can create lots of senseless sentences like this one, but a sane person always rejects such grammatical nonsense.

Now we would like to invite you — our readers — to participate in an interesting game, called "Senseless or Meaningful".

At first, please judge whether each of the following sentences is grammatical.

(9.2) *Little green frogs sleep quietly.*

(9.3) *Colorless green ideas sleep furiously.*

Then, please judge whether or not each of them is meaningful.

You may regard (9.3) as grammatical but not meaningful. Chomsky (1957) held the same opinion. As a matter of fact, this sentence was composed by him to illustrate that the notion "grammatical" cannot be identified with "meaningful" or "significant" in any semantic sense.

OK, let's read a story, in which *green* means "not quite ripe", and to *sleep on something* is an informal expression which means "to delay making a decision on something until the following day so as to have more time to consider it".

(9.4) *I have got some immature ideas recently. So they are green ideas. Some of them are colorful, some are colorless. I don't want to publish my colorless green ideas immediately. I would rather sleep on them, or, to put it in my favorite way, let them sleep. Unfortunately, these colorless green ideas contradict each other, and fight each other furiously, turning the sleep into a nightmare. So I would like to complain to my friends that I've never expected that* <u>colorless green ideas sleep furiously</u>.

Now tell me how you think about the underlined part in the above story, senseless or meaningful?

This funny story is an adaptation from Chao Yuen Ren's *The Story of My Friend, Whose Colorless Green Ideas Sleep Furiously*. We have introduced Chao Yuen Ren (1892 — 1982), the famous American Chinese linguist, and his wonderful story in Pinyin *shíshì shíshì* in Chapter 3. The present story evidences his talent again. With delicate conception, he successfully turned the "typical" senseless sentence cited by Chomsky into a meaningful one. What was his secret in doing this? The answer is simple: adding an appropriate context.

Here is another game for you: Contextualize the short sentence below.

(9.5) *Time flies!*

You may think the first word *Time* is a noun and this sentence is a two-word exclamation, metaphorically referring to the quick passage of time. But the sentence can also be an imperative, where *Time* serves as a verb. The following is a way to justify this opinion:

(9.6) *Suppose insects also hold their Olympic Games, and one game is for flies to "run" a race (with their wings, not legs, of course). Once before a race starts, the Chairman of the Games reminds an absent-minded timer loudly, "Time flies!"*

If you are a school teacher in America or another English-speaking country, try to assign your pupils a composition with the title *Time flies*. You may find some contexts imagined by those little authors very surprising and unexpected. Maybe a little boy will write, "*Time is the name of a baby angel in my dream. She has two wings but she is too fragile to fly... I hope I'll encounter my angel again tonight, and this time I'll see her fluttering her wings in the sky. Then I'll quickly awake and tell my mother: 'Time flies!'*"

Isn't the use of language like a game?

Now, please rethink the relationship between language and meaning. It seems that the actual meaning of a sentence is not decided by its syntactic structure but by the context it is associated with. Even the syntactic role of a word in a sentence (e. g. whether it is a noun or a verb) has to be determined by the context. Only in the various and multiform activities of human life do words and sentences have meaning. Conversely, the same utterance can be interpreted in different ways if we imbed it in different contexts. This fact was first revealed by Ludwig Wittgenstein (1889 — 1951), a great philosopher, who found that our daily speech can play countless roles if it is woven into actions. He pointed out, "... the speaking of language is part of an activity, or a form of life". He defined such activities as *language games*, which are played by all human beings every day, just as we have done now.

9.2 Act in words

What we have just mentioned is referred to as *later Wittgenstein's model*, according to which, language should not be viewed as an abstract calculus but as a tool, and the proper characterization of a linguistic expression must include an account of how it is used, and what it is used for. "Meaning is use", he proposed, pertinently.

Immediately after the Second World War, a new generation of philosophers at Oxford University enlightened by this idea formed a school named Ordinary Language Philosophy. One of its highest achievements was made by the notable figure J. L. Austin (1911 — 1960). He postulated the exquisite theory of speech acts, the aim of which is to explore how to do things with words, an effort to reveal the "game rules".

Austin identified three classes of human activities with language, namely, locutionary act, illocutionary act, and perlocutionary act. A locutionary act is the saying of something which is meaningful and can be understood; an illocutionary act is using a sentence to perform a function; a perlocutionary act is the results that are produced by means of saying something. A good translation of these three acts in Chinese was done by He Ziran, a master of pragmatics in China, as 以言指事, 以言行事, 以言成事 respectively.

For example, the utterance "Shoot the snake!" will be analyzed as

1) a locutionary act if the hearer understands all the words and the sentence structure, and can identify the particular snake referred to;

2) an illocutionary act if the sentence is intended as an order or a piece of advice;

3) a perlocutionary act if the snake is shot by the addressee.

Unlike logic-based theories of meanings, Austin's Speech Act Theory reveals the functions performed by utterances in communication, especially the illocutionary act, i.e. "the act performed in saying something", which corroborates Wittgenstein's argument that language is a tool.

The intended effect of a speech act is called its illocutionary force. Even a simple, plain statement will have strong illocutionary force. "I've got a gun." is such a statement. If it is spoken by someone in a mask to a bank cashier, its illocutionary force is *threatening*. Similarly, "It's cold in here" could either be a request to close the window or an offer to do the same thing according to different contexts. A sentence, even though it is grammatically perfect, only appears in a proper context with a reasonable intention. If someone exclaims "Shoot the snake!"

in his office but there is no snake around, and afterwards explains to his puzzled colleagues that he has just uttered a grammatical sentence, he must be thought to be behaving oddly instead of having performed a locutionary act. So J. Searle, the brilliant student and successor of Austin, developed Speech Act Theory to a new phase by emphasizing that all utterances are sayings and doings at the same time. According to Searle, no sentence can only perform a locutionary act. Think of the extreme case "*Colorless green ideas sleep furiously*", which is sheer nonsense when it is not embedded in a proper context, therefore failing to meet the criterion of a locutionary act. But it will sound quite acceptable by being imbedded in a proper context. Besides, a perlocutionary act, as "the act performed by or as a result of saying" according to Austin, is actually beyond the control of the speaker. Think of a person who has heard and understood the order "*Shoot the snake!*" but refuses to perform the task, which will undoubtedly fail the expected perlocutionary act. That's why the term perlocutionary act is rarely mentioned today. Influenced by Searle and other researchers' work, the term *speech act* is often used to denote specifically an illocutionary act. Where the result of a saying is concerned, discussions are mostly around the expected effects such as commanding, offering, promising, thanking, apologizing, requesting, warning, threatening, all called illocutionary forces.

The theory of speech acts was originally the brainchild of several philosophers, whose work gradually opened up a new field in linguistics — pragmatics.

9.3 What does the speaker mean by saying that?

Pragmatics is concerned with the study of meaning as communicated by a speaker (or writer) and interpreted by a listener (or reader). Unlike semantics, it involves the interpretation of what people mean in a particular context and how the context influences what is said. Its objects are all kinds of people — language users, instead of sentences isolated from any environment of language use.

People in communication alternate their roles between communicators and addressees. Speech Act Theory mainly concerns the communicators — speakers or writers, who use language to do things but are not always sure whether they are skillful enough to achieve their purposes. On the other hand, listeners or readers (both are addressees) may misunderstand the received information. The following dialogue is an illustration:

(9.7) Man: *Does your dog bite?*

Woman: *No.*

(The man reaches down to pet the dog beside the woman. The dog bites the man's hand.)

Man: *Ouch! Hey! You said your dog doesn't bite.*

Woman: *He doesn't. But that's not my dog.*

In (9.7), either the woman has not noticed that a dog is nearby, or she gives less information to misguide the man. The latter possibility is generally thought of as improper, because the woman's response only relates to the literal meaning of the man's question, but not to its implicature, i. e. some unstated meaning which makes the question sensible in their shared context. The man feels the implicature of his question must be clearly relevant to the dog near the woman, so he derives a sense of safety from the woman's answer, and starts to touch the dog, incurring the bite.

The case above is relatively rare. Usually people know that any communication is intentional, in which the audience will make inferences about what is said in order to arrive at an interpretation of the communicator's intended meaning. Intentional communication and conversational implicature are two important propositions made by H. P. Grice, another British philosopher and founder of pragmatics, whose contribution, different from Austin's, is not only from the speaker's perspective but also from the hearer's.

So, usually, someone who hears a question "*Does your dog bite?*" will set out to seek the intention of the asker through analyzing the physical environment. If a dog is found nearby and apparently arouses the speaker's interest, the hearer may infer that the question means "Does your dog bite if I would like to pet it?". Then the response will not be "*No*" but "*No, he doesn't. But this dog is not mine.*" Only by unraveling more than what is said can people carry on their conversation smoothly.

There is always more communicated than is said, waiting for the hearer to infer. If a teacher overhears a student commenting on his lessons to another student by saying (9.8),

(9.8) *They're sometimes really interesting.*

then he knows the comment implies that he needs to improve his teaching, because *sometimes* means *not always*, *not often*.

Context plays an essential role in fathoming the conversational implicature. Sometimes the hearer may arrive at different implicatures in different situations, e. g.

(9.9) A: *What's with your boss?*

B: *Let's go upstairs.*

A proper inference made by A in (9.9) requires some particular knowledge shared by A and B. If they know the topic is sensitive in the place where they are talking, then A will infer that B's response implies that upstairs is a safer place, preventing eavesdropping. If they do not think so much of the topic itself, A may deduce that B would like to show him something upstairs related to his boss' problem.

In (9.9), the shared knowledge for one specific inference is different from that for another. An additional unstated meaning deduced in this way is called a particularized conversational implicature. On the other hand, an additional unstated meaning that does not depend on any special knowledge like the case in (9.8) and (9.10) is called a generalized conversational implicature.

(9.10) A: *Did you manage to fix the leak?*

B: *I tried to.*

In (9.10) B's implicature comes from the general knowledge of the word *try*. B does not use the same verb *manage* in his answer, and *manage* means "try and succeed (in doing something)", so A can infer that B tried but failed to fix the leak. A's inference requires no particular, local knowledge.

Moreover, not all inferences are implicatures. Look at (9.11) below.

(9.11) A: *It works now.*

B: *When did Eric fix it?*

A: *Oh, you're wrong. That's not done by Eric.*

What A infers from B's question is a presupposition: Eric fixed it. And A's response is not directly to B's question but to its presupposition — to deny it.

Leech points out that "What does X mean?" is a question in semantics, and "What did you mean by X..." is a question in pragmatics. Why is there the difference? Because when a sentence is not used, it only has the literal meaning. When it is used, it will involve factors like the intention of the speaker, the intended audience, the specific time, location, and circumstances of its production, and anything else related to the context, which may add certain unstated meaning to the sentence for the hearer to figure out. As G. Yule observes, pragmatics is the study of how more gets communicated than is said.

9.4 Flouting maxims enjoyably

The most significant contribution of Grice to pragmatics is the cooperative principle, by which conversational exchanges are governed. This principle holds that people in a conversation normally cooperate with one another, and that they assume that the others are cooperating to a maximum extent. Grice breaks this principle down into four basic maxims.

1. Maxim of Quality: Do not say what you believe to be false. Do not say that for which you lack adequate evidence.

Examples: People may say (9.12) but they never say (9.13).

(9.12) *I've stopped smoking, although I've been smoking for many years.*

(9.13) *I've stopped smoking, although I've never smoked.*

Comment: (9.13) is not a qualified sentence because it has two contradictory propositions.

2. Maxim of Quantity: Make sure your contribution is as informative as is required for the current purposes of the exchange (i. e. not more or less informative).

Examples: People may say (9.14) but they never say (9.15).

(9.14) *I found an old bicycle on the ground. The chain was rusted, and the tires were flat.*

(9.15) *I found an old bicycle. A bicycle has a chain. The chain was rusted. A bicycle also has tires. The tires were flat.*

Comment: The underlined parts in (9.15) are additional, unnecessary information.

3. Maxim of Relevance: Make your contribution relevant to the aims of the ongoing conversation. (It is also termed Maxim of Relation)

Examples: People may say (9.16) but they never say (9.17).

(9.16) A: *Can I borrow $5?*

B: *My purse is over there.*

(9.17) A: *Can I borrow $5?*

B: *My pipe is over there.*

Comment: Since a reply to a request is usually either an acceptance or a refusal, and A in (9.16) assumes that B's reply must be relevant to the question, A can reasonably infer that B means "Please take it yourself. My purse is over there". In (9.17) A cannot find any possibility that B's reply is relevant to his request.

4. Maxim of Manner: Be clear. Try to avoid obscurity, ambiguity, wordiness, and disorderliness in your use of language.

Examples: People may say (9.18) but they never say (9.19).

(9.18) *He got on the bus, carrying a briefcase under his arm.*

(9.19) *He carried a briefcase under his arm, getting on the bus.*

Comment: *Get on the bus* is a dynamic, immediate action, whereas *carry a brief case* is a static, accompanying action. We cannot force a dynamic, immediate action to accompany a static action.

The four maxims are susceptible to violation and flouting. (9.13), (9.15), (9.17), and (9.19) above are examples of real violation, which occurs rarely. Flouting, however, is apparent rather than real violation, and preferred by many people in that it is actually a vivid way of communication.

A lady standing in the middle of a busy street asked a policeman, "*Could you tell me how to get to the hospital, officer?*" The policeman, very worried about her safety, answered, "*Just stand where you are.*"

Indeed, the policeman showed the lady how to get to the hospital. But that was not the way the lady hoped to know, for she wanted to get there following a route, rather than being sent there as an accident victim. The policeman's answer flouted the Maxim of Relevance. By doing so he solved a more urgent problem: warning the lady that standing in the middle of a heavy-traveled street was very dangerous.

Another conversation between a man and a reporter goes like this:

"*Where is Washington?*"

"*He is dead.*"

"*I mean the capital of the United States.*"

"*They loaned it all to Europe.*"

"*Now, do you promise to support the Constitution?*"

"*Me? How can I? I've got a wife and six children to support.*"

There are three ambiguous words in this conversation. *Washington* can be the first president as well as the capital of USA. *Capital* has another meaning — "fund". *Support* means "stand by" or "sustain somebody financially". The interviewee caught these polysemants and gave irrelevant answers in order to avoid head-on conflicts. His skill was flouting the Maxim of Manner.

Flouting cooperative maxims is also a common skill in literary and artistic creations, especially in creating humorous effects.

There is a very cool comic dialogue in China called "Talk Big", a topic of which is "whose concocted sausage-making machine sounds more powerful".

"*We put a pig on one side of the machine, and then swing the handle, and then sausage is going out from the other side.*"

"*It's just a piece of cake. Our machine can do all of that. And if we are not satisfied with the sausage, what we should do is just swing the handle back so that the whole pig will return alive.*"

Obviously, both parts flout the Maxim of Quality: Although technology nowadays is highly developed, no one can make sausage directly from a pig with a single machine, let alone make the sausage back into the pig. However, this preposterous talk can make the audience die of laughing.

Alice's Adventures in Wonderland is a famous fairy tale written by Lewis Carroll. The following is a dialogue between Alice and the Mouse as they were swimming in a pool.

"*Not like cats!*" cried the Mouse, in a shrill, passionate voice, "*Would YOU like cats if you were me?"*

"Well, perhaps not," said Alice in a soothing tone: "don't be angry about it. And yet I wish I could show you our cat Dinah: I think you'd take a fancy to cats if you could only see her. She is such a dear quiet thing," Alice went on, half to herself, as she swam lazily about in the pool, "and she sits purring so nicely by the fire, licking her paws and washing her face — and she is such a nice soft thing to nurse — and she's such a capital one for catching mice — oh, I beg your pardon!" cried Alice again, for this time the Mouse was bristling all over, and she felt certain it must be really offended. "We won't talk about her any more if you'd rather not."

In this excerpt, Alice, an innocent and lovely girl, gave a wordy answer which made the Mouse shake all over. Carroll deliberately designed this rambling talk, which has brought laughs to generations of readers by flouting the Maxims of Quantity, Relevance and Manner.

Language is full of creation. Language is creative only when it is used by people. Let's conclude this chapter by quoting Wittgenstein's famous aphorism "The meaning of a word is its use in a language".

EXERCISES

I. Translate the following statement into Chinese.

Pragmatics is the branch of linguistics which studies how utterances communicate meaning in context.

II. Fill in the blanks with the linguistic terms you have learned.

1) According to Austin, _____ act refers to the basic literal meaning of the utterance which is conveyed by particular words and structures which the utterance contains.

2) J. _____, the brilliant student and successor of Austin, developed Speech Act Theory to a new phase by emphasizing that all utterances are sayings and doings at the same time.

3) According to Searle, the sentence "*I'll return the book to you tomorrow*" is "a proposition + a _____".

4) The _____ principle holds that people in a conversation normally cooperate with one another, and that they assume that the others are cooperating to a maximum extent.

5) The four conversational maxims proposed by Grice are of quantity, quality, relevance, and _____. The use of conversational maxims to imply meaning during conversation is called conversational _____.

III. Try to interpret the underlined utterances below referring to their context.

1) A: *Where are my glasses?*
   B: *I am too busy.*
2) A: *Where's my box of chocolates?*
   B: *Where's your diet sheet?*
3) *Look at this room. Steve's a pig.*
4) A: *Do you like my new hat?*
   B: *It's pink.*
5) (on the signboard of an American seafood restaurant)
   We serve shrimps and crabs
   And tall people and nice people too

IV. Give a summary of less than 150 words to Section 9.3.

V. Challenging work.

1) Grice's work is one of the foundations of the modern study of pragmatics. He proposed an intention-based theory of meaning. Go to the library to search for information about Grice and write an essay on his contribution to pragmatics.

2) In 1980s, the British linguist Deirdre Wilson and the French philosopher Dan Sperber proposed Relevance Theory based on Grice's Maxim of Relevance. This influential but controversial theory holds that utterances are interpreted in such a way that they combine with the context to produce the maximum amount of new information with the minimum amount of processing effort. Go on the

internet to search for the basic arguments, core terminology, and recent developments of Relevance Theory and prepare a ppt-aided presentation to introduce what you have found to your classmates.

▪▪

L. Wittgenstein (1889 — 1951)

Ludwig Wittgenstein was one of the most original and influential philosophers of the 20th century. He was by birth an Austrian of Jewish descent. He received most of his early education at home before studying engineering at Berlin and Manchester, which led to an interest in pure mathematics and the philosophy of mathematics. In 1912 he moved to Cambridge to become a pupil of Bertrand Russell. His work from 1914-18 led to the writing of the *Tractatus Logico-Philosophicus*, which was published in Germany in 1921 and in London in 1922. Wittgenstein served in the Austrian army in World War I and was captured in Italy. Upon his release after the war he gave away a considerable fortune he had inherited. From 1920-26 he went to work as an elementary schoolmaster in Austria, then returned to Cambridge in 1929. During the next few years he came to a new position in philosophy, which was first stated in the *Blue and Brown Books*, a set of lecture notes from 1933-35 and published posthumously in 1958, and later in his *Philosophical Investigations* (published in 1953). He became Professor of Philosophy at Cambridge in 1939, succeeding G. E. Moore. In 1947 he resigned to devote himself to research, but his health soon deteriorated and he died of cancer in 1951.

The *Tractatus*, the definitive account of his earlier views, is a modern classic of philosophy. He states that the world consists entirely of independent, simple facts out of which complex ones are constructed. Language has as its purpose the stating of facts by picturing these facts. Wittgenstein's later philosophy is given in the *Blue and Brown Books* and *Philosophical Investigations*. The basis of the new approach is a new view of language; the old view in the *Tractatus* that there is in principle a perfect language is abandoned and language is seen as a set of social activities, each serving a different kind of purpose. Each different way of using language is a "language game" which we learn by training in childhood.

Wittgenstein has had a great influence on modern philosophy and linguistics. His earlier views had great influence on logical positivism, and from his later views grew a new branch of language study — pragmatics.

Linguistic Stars

Linguistic Stars

==

Reading recommendation

Beginner-friendly：

G. Yule. Pragmatics. Oxford University Press 1996；上海外语教育出版社，2000

何自然，陈新仁. 当代语用学. 外语教学与研究出版社，2004

J. S. Peccei. Pragmatics. Routledge, 1999；外语教学与研究出版社，2000（蓝纯　导读）

More challenging：

J. L. Mey. Pragmatics. An Introduction 2nd edition. Blackwell Publishers Ltd, 2001；外语教学与研究出版社，2001（徐盛桓　导读）

D. Sperber et al. Relevance：Communication and Cognition 2nd edition. Blackwell Publishers Ltd, 1995；外语教学与研究出版社，2001（何自然，冉永平　导读）

J. R. Searle. Expression and Meaning：Studies in the Theory of Speech Acts. Cambridge University Press, 2001；外语教学与研究出版社，2001（何自然，冉永平　导读）

陈嘉映. 语言哲学. 北京大学出版社，2005

In German, a young lady has no sex, while a turnip has... a tree is male, its buds are female, its leaves are neuter; horses are sexless, dogs are male, cats are female — tomcats included.

— *Mark Twain*

Chapter 10

Language Instinct

10.1 The modularity of language

Not everyone has the chance to go to school; not every student has the talent to master a subject perfectly; but every normal person can speak effortlessly in his mother tongue. One's capacity to acquire language is endowed genetically, like the spider's capacity to spin webs. If a student misses a class, he will probably not know how to solve certain problems related to the content of that class. If a man encounters any basic problem related to his mother tongue, he does not need to ask for help from his teachers or friends. Just by asking his own mind he can get an answer similar to most of his compatriots. According to an excellent contemporary psycholinguist in America, Steven Pinker, what they rely on is the language instinct.

Here are some observations.

1) If your mother tongue is Chinese, please tell which of the following is a better verse?

(10.1) A. 春眠不觉晓

B. 春眠不觉晨

Verse A in (10.1) is from a famous Chinese poem and known to many people in China. It was translated by an American sinologist Witter Bynner as *I awake light-hearted this morning of spring*. The only difference between verses A and B is the last word：晓 or 晨, both referring to *morning*. Does your mind accept that verse B is as nice as verse A? If not, why?

As a student, you may attempt to explain the difference with your knowledge of Chinese tones：晓 is of falling rising tone, while 晨 is of rising tone; therefore, verse A sounds more rhythmic and sonorous. Though many Chinese people may not know such theories, they still have a preference for verse A, without any explanation. This unconscious perception of rhythmic beauty is the phonological endowment described by Chomsky as I-sound.

If your mother tongue is English, you also have certain phonological intuitions. For example, you can tell whether the letter combinations *slip*, *slib*, *spill*, *sbill* are possible English words. The prevailing response may be：

(10.2) *slip*   yes

slib   possible

spill   yes

sbill   impossible

Actually, both *slib* and *sbill* are not English words. In comparison, the former is phonologically acceptable if some day it becomes an English word, but the latter can never be an English word because its pronunciation will tend to be confused with that of *spill* for *p* is unaspirated after *s*. Average native speakers know little about such academic analysis, but their minds still lead them toward the same judgment.

A further observation is that all native speakers make such judgments without considering the syntactic structure and semantic features of their language. Resorting to their mental phonological knowledge is enough. Thus we arrive at a conclusion：*The intuitive phonological knowledge of a lexical item is self-governed*. It makes no reference to its syntactical or semantic information.

2) If your mother tongue is German, you will have no hesitation accepting the first utterance and rejecting the second in (10.3).

(10.3) A. *Ich habe einen Füller. Er ist rot.*

B. **Ich habe einen Füller. Es ist rot.*

The word-for-word translation of A is *I have a pen. He is red.* And that of B is *I have a pen. It is red.* Both the English and the Chinese mind will prefer B, but native speakers of German all hold that *Füller* (pen) is masculine, so its pronoun should be masculine, too. Does it sound strange? No. Many ancient cultures have their own presuppositions of the gender of all the inanimate objects of the world. Ancient Chinese people, for instance, also had an inclination to divide things into *yang* and *yin*, that is, masculinity and femininity. But such a cultural phenomenon did not permeate the forms of Chinese language. It did in German and some other ancient cultures. This fact does not make these languages more difficult to acquire for small children. Today even the German children know the gender of everything. They use *er* (= he) to refer to a pen (*Füller*), a foot (*Fuβ*), or a stool (*Stuhl*), which are all masculine; they use *sie* (= she) to refer to a lamp (*Lampe*), a banana (*Banane*), or a machine (*Maschine*), all feminine; moreover, *es* (= it) is reserved for a bed (*Bett*), a ship (*Schiff*), or a girl (*Mädchen* or *Fräulein*), since such nouns are neuter. Undoubtedly, few in Germany today can tell any reason for their gender division. They just speak this way.

Besides, if your mother tongue is English, you will surely accept the first utterance and reject the second in (10.4).

(10.4) A. *I want to have a big breakfast.*

B. **I want having a big breakfast.*

When a German makes a judgment between A and B in (10.3), or an Englishman does the same thing in (10.4), what he depends on is his tacit knowledge of the syntactic form of a lexical item. No reference is made to its meaning or its pronunciation. Therefore, it is concluded that *the intuitive syntactic knowledge of a lexical item is self-governed.* "No syntactic rule can make reference to pragmatic, phonological, or semantic information." — a finding of Chomsky known as *Autonomous Syntax Principle.*

3) A native speaker of English will find the second sentence of (10.5) inappropriate:

（10.5） A. *The girls left.*

            B： *?The fog left.*

He thinks that he would prefer to say *The fog went away* instead. Is it that the verb *leave* is only reserved for human beings? Probably no. English also allows saying：

（10.6） *The train left.*

（10.7） *The mail left.*

So a better description can be that "to leave" refers to a movement routinely controlled by human beings.

Then please have a look at the Chinese equivalents：

姑娘们走了。

雾散了。

火车开走了。

信寄走了。

It is probable that non-native speakers of Chinese will take great pains trying to grasp all these semantic differences, but native Chinese people will scarcely confuse them.

Conclusion： *The intuitive semantic knowledge of a lexical item is self-governed.* It makes no reference to its syntactic features.

4）"*What time is it in the kitchen?*" is an understandable question to English ears. It does not mean the time in the kitchen is different but implies that the clock in the kitchen may give its own time. Similarly, a natural inference of the Chinese utterance "先割我的肉！"is not a request for a Chinese butcher to cut the speaker's flesh first but an urge to cut off a piece of meat and sell it to him. So, *the pragmatic inference is also self-governed.*

All in all, we come to a general conclusion that one's mental knowledge of language is modular, and each linguistic module is governed by its particular set of general principles. These principles are much more similar to the mental principles for a person to judge the distance of anything seen or heard, than to the learned principles guiding our driving in the street. These modular principles exist in different parts of our brain, making it possible for every one of us to acquire a language as mother tongue, no matter how complicated a specific language is in a certain aspect（e.g. gender in German）. They also allow us to develop very complex skills in oral communication without any necessary school training. That's why an uneducated fishmonger can persuade a customer with a doctorate diploma to buy his average staples at a handsome price!

10.2 Clinical evidence

Language is modular. The superficial complexity of language is a consequence of the interaction of such modules in the brain. This argument has been supported by neurobiological observations. Revealed by cerebrology, there are several identified speech areas in the human brain.

One's phonological, morphological, and syntactical endowments seem to be inseparable from an area discovered by the French surgeon Paul Broca in the 1860s. This area is technically described as the anterior speech cortex, but usually called Broca's area. Its impairment will lead to extreme difficulty in producing speech, described clinically as Broca's aphasia. The patient has to make great efforts to produce a sentence. He uses distorted articulation, and most typically, fails to use functional morphemes such as articles, prepositions and inflections, and, if his impairment is very serious, fails to remember word sequence. For example, a not very severe patient of this disease once described the breakfast he had by saying *I eggs and eat and drink coffee breakfast*. Another patient, whose aphasia was more serious, wanted to describe a ship he had been on. What he intended to express was a simple idea that he had been on a steamship. But what he produced was *a stail... you know what I mean... tal stail...* .

The area that directly decides whether one can speak a language is the motor cortex which generally controls the muscular movement of different physical organs. A part of the motor cortex close to Broca's area controls the articulatory muscles of the face, jaw, tongue and larynx. Imaginably, any damage there may destroy a person's ability to coordinate speech organs to articulate anything.

We have talked about how terrible it is to suffer from a certain modular failure. Maybe you have noticed that patients of Broca's aphasia still know what they want to say. Their tragedy is their difficulty to articulate what they mean. That's why such a

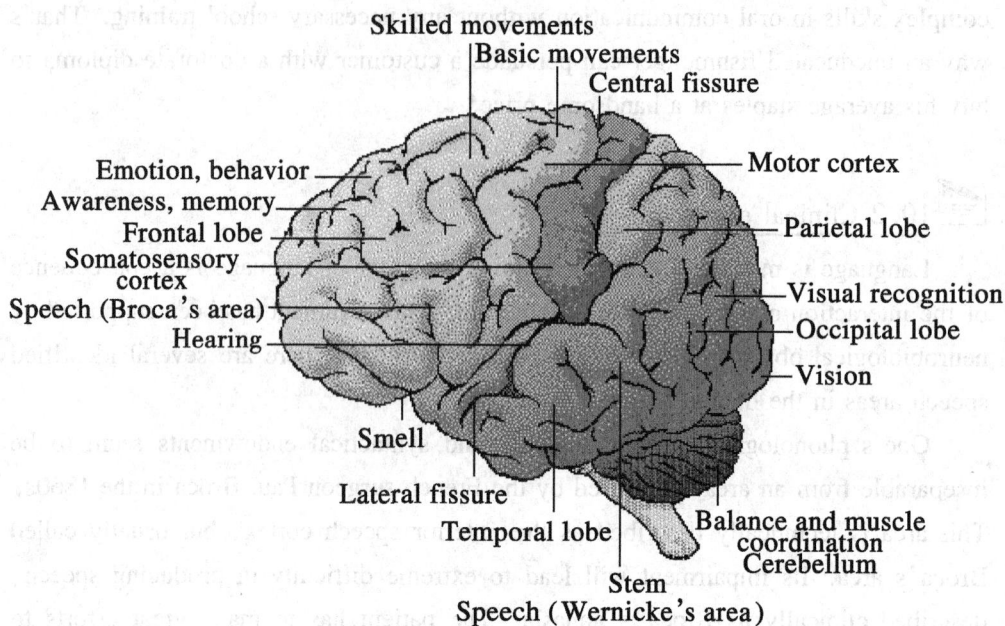

Fig. 10.1   The human brain and its functional areas

Labels in figure: Skilled movements; Basic movements; Central fissure; Emotion, behavior; Awareness, memory; Frontal lobe; Somatosensory cortex; Speech (Broca's area); Hearing; Motor cortex; Parietal lobe; Visual recognition; Occipital lobe; Vision; Smell; Lateral fissure; Temporal lobe; Stem; Speech (Wernicke's area); Balance and muscle coordination; Cerebellum

malady is described as "motor aphasia". If one suffers from another kind of language disorder called Wernicke's aphasia or "sensory aphasia", his semantic and pragmatic capacity will be robbed.

Wernicke's area was identified by Carl Wernicke, a German doctor in the 1870s. This area is involved in the comprehension and the selection of words when producing sentences. Any large destruction in this area results in the loss of understanding and making meaningful speech but not the loss of sound production. Some patients of Wernicke's aphasia speak fluently, but what they say is often difficult to understand, with very general terms conveying little specific meaning, such as *I don't know what's happened to that, but it's taken that out. That is mm there without doing it, the thing that are being done...* As for word selection, such patients behave very ineffectively, as in the case of a patient answering the question "What's ink for?" with a circumlocution: *to do with a pen.*

Wernicke also discovered a bundle of nerve fibers called the arcuate fasciculus, which forms a crucial connection between Wernicke's area and Broca's area.

Damage to it will cause a less common type of aphasia. Its victims can both speak and listen, but they find it difficult to repeat a word or phrase spoken by someone else. In one research report, a patient repeated the words "base" and "wash" with the sounds *vaysse* and *fosh*. Such impairment of language function is called "conduction aphasia", for the patient cannot transfer what he has heard and understood to the speech production area.

If you hope to read well and write well, your angular gyrus should be healthy. It is an area between Wernicke's area and the visual cortex, in charge of converting visual stimuli into auditory stimuli and vice versa. With it we can match the spoken form of a word with the object it describes, as well as with the written form of the word.

All these language centers are located on the left hemisphere of the human brain, as neurologists have found that damage to the corresponding areas on the right hemisphere does not lead to any aphasia. Within the left hemisphere, there are separate areas which involve certain specific aspects of language ability respectively. Successful linguistic performance depends on the healthy operation and interaction of these brain areas. Linguistic failures, on the other hand, can be attributed to certain modular impediments.

10.3 Species uniqueness

Different animals have different instincts. A silkworm spins silk; a bee dances to inform other bees of the direction and distance of the nectar source it has found; a wild European rock dove flies over hundreds of kilometers to feed its baby birds using the sun as a compass... All such instincts are not for showy display but are essential for the species' survival.

Language is a human instinct, vital for this superior but highly social species to survive. An instinct is different from a learned skill in that it is shared by all its members with unimpaired brains, but inaccessible to any individual of other species. In recent decades some attempts have been made to train animals to speak human language, or rather, to use an artificially adapted language considering their physical limitations (e. g. the vocal organs of all kinds of apes are too curving to produce many sounds, so an adapted sign language is designed for them to learn). All such efforts have turned out to be no more fruitful than a chimpanzee's achievement in producing gesture sentences like *Me banana you banana me you give.* There has been no negation, nor question produced by any subjects. This does not mean that animals are awkward trainees — they are often marvelous learners of some circus skills, for example. The cause lies in the fact that any animal cannot learn another species' instincts. A human being would be similarly inept if someone tried to train him to imitate a chimpanzee's hoot and shriek, or a silkworm's spinning.

An instinct must have its material foundation. The outer layer of the brain, about 1/4 inch thick, is the cortex, which is multiply fissured or enfolded, containing about ten billion nerves. The vocalizations made by some primates trained to imitate the sound of simple words are found to be primarily under the control of centers in the limbic system, rather than the cortex which is much smoother than a human being's. Destruction of the cortical speech centers in humans, however, either destroys speech or affects it critically, whereas destruction of similar areas of the cortex in monkeys and primates does not affect their vocalization. Thus the human brain appears to be uniquely adapted for speech. How can other animals acquire the human language with their cerebral cortex underdeveloped and any linguistic modules non-existing?

With the language instinct, human babies can acquire a natural language as their mother tongue, no matter how peculiar a certain aspect of this language is. (Think of the "horrible" gender system of German!) With the language instinct, mankind can talk about matters not "here and now", persons and places not present, and even about hypothetical things, like "flying rabbits". This ability is called displacement, which marks the beginning of abstract thinking, an impassable chasm for any other species. With the language instinct, man can also obtain a complete description of an event far displaced by combining a lot of small pieces of information, which is called reconstitution, the superstructure of abstract thought.

As humans we "can shape events in each other's brains with exquisite precision", Pinker remarks passionately. "The ability comes so naturally that we are apt to forget what a miracle it is."

EXERCISES ✍

I. Translate the following statements into Chinese.

Psycholinguistics is the study of the interrelationship of language and the mind (i. e. cognitive structures) which encompasses the acquisition of language.

Neurolinguistics is the study of the brain and how it functions in the production, perception, and acquisition of language.

II. Fill in the blanks with the linguistic terms you have learned.

1) _____ allows man to construct events far displaced in time and is the superstructure of abstract thought.

2) _____ is mainly the posterior part of the left temporal lobe, with parts of the parietal area; any large destruction of this area results in the loss of the capacity for meaningful speech but not the loss of sound production.

3) Every speaker knows a set of principles which apply to all languages and also a set of _____ that can vary from one language to another, but only within certain limits.

4) _____ as an important feature of language marks the beginning of abstract thinking.

5) _____ lower down at the back of the left frontal lobe of human brain appears to involve functions of articulation, vocabulary, inflection, and word sequence.

6) According to _____, different animals have different instincts. Any animal cannot learn another species' instincts.

7) The outer layer of the brain, about 1/4 inch thick, is the cortex, which is multiply fissured or enfolded, containing about ten _____ nerves. Destruction of the cortical speech centers in humans, however, either destroys speech or affects it critically.

III. One's mental knowledge of language is modular, and each linguistic module is governed by its particular set of general principles. If your mother tongue is Chinese, give your intuitive response to the following questions.

1）Which of the underlined vowels in the following English words are never encountered in spoken Chinese?

b<u>e</u>d　　h<u>a</u>d　bi<u>k</u>e　date　m<u>ou</u>th　t<u>oi</u>l　b<u>oo</u>k　t<u>ee</u>th

2）Which of the underlined consonants in the following English words may appear in spoken Chinese（putonghua）? If yes, may they appear in the same position within the syllable?

<u>t</u>ie　<u>c</u>o<u>m</u>e　<u>n</u>eed　<u>r</u>eply　<u>j</u>eep　<u>b</u>oss　<u>l</u>ike　corre<u>c</u>t

3）Which of the following sentences sound strange and may possibly be made by a non-native speaker of Chinese?

　　a. 我的房间干净和舒服。

　　b. 我家饲养了好多动物,有一匹羊,二个猪,三头兔子,几只鸭,和一些鱼。

　　c. 那天乡下马蜂扎了手,痛了好几天。

　　d. 我认为他们夫妻生活不是幸福。

　　e. 你们屋子是大不大?

　　f. 啤酒勉强,烈性酒不奉陪。

Now, think which module in your mind you have resorted to when answering each of the above questions.

IV. Give a summary of less than 150 words to Section 10. 2.

V. Challenging Work.

1）Aphasia is the loss or partial loss of normal language abilities as a result of damage to cortical and/or sub-cortical brain tissue. The following are excerpts from the research report of two aphasic patients. Can you guess who of them may suffer from impairment to the Wernicke's area and who to the Broca's area? And why do you think so?

　　Case No.1: The patient has to make great efforts to utter short halting phrases, without function words in between. Bound morphemes such as tense, plural, and comparative markers are frequently missing. Although he takes great pains to produce even a few words, he is painfully aware of the mistakes he has made.

The following is a talk between him and an examiner:

Examiner: *Tell me, what did you do before you retired?*

Aphasic: *Uh, uh, uh, puh, par, partender, no.*

Examiner: *Carpenter?*

Aphasic: (shaking head yes) *Carpenter, tuh, tuh, tuh tenty* [20] *years.*

Examiner: *Tell me about this picture.*

Aphasic: *Boy... cook... cookie... took... cookie.*

Case No. 2: Fluency is usually not a problem, although interruptions in the flow of speech occur when the patient cannot retrieve a specific word. He often speaks very rapidly, the content of what he says ranging from mildly inappropriate to complete nonsense, as in the following conversation:

Examiner: *Do you like it here in Kansas City?*

Aphasic: *Yes, I am.*

Examiner: *I'd like to have you tell me something about your problem.*

Aphasic: *Yes. I ugh can't hill all of my way. I can't talk all of the things I do, and part of the part I can go alright, but I can't tell from the other people. I usually most of my things. I know what can I talk and know what they are but I can't always come back even though I know they should be in, and I know should something eely I should know what I'm doing...*

2) Write an essay on the following topic:

Language is uniquely human

■ ■

S. Pinker (1954 —)

Steven Pinker is one of the world's leading experts on language and the mind. He is the Johnstone Family Professor in the Department of Psychology at Harvard University. Until 2003, he taught in the Department of Brain and Cognitive Sciences at MIT as Peter de Florez Professor of Psychology.

Pinker was born in Montreal, Canada. He studied experimental psychology at McGill University and Harvard University, where he earned his PhD in psychology.

Pinker serves on numerous editorial and advisory boards, writes for publications such as the *New York Times*, *Time*, and *Slate*, and is the author of six books, including *The Language Instinct*, *How the Mind Works*, *Words and Rules*, and *The Blank Slate*. His research on visual cognition and on the psychology of language has received the Troland Award from the National Academy of Sciences, the Early Career Award, and another prize from the American Psychological Association.

When Pinker was in MIT, he once introduced his own work on a webpage to net surfers. He said, "My research includes both empirical studies of linguistic behavior and theoretical analyses of the nature of language and its relation to mind and brain."

"On the empirical side, I study specific modules of grammar from a variety of disciplines, much as biologists direct focus on a few 'model organisms'. Currently, our group is studying inflectional morphology: the ability to derive *walked* from *walk* or *mice* from *mouse*. We are aiming for a unified theory and an extensive database of how the system works computationally, how it is learned, how it varies across languages, how it is used in language production and comprehension, and how it is represented in the brain... We study people with neurological and genetic language and memory disorders (aphasia, Alzheimer's, specific language impairment), gathering evidence on how the different cognitive and linguistic modules underlying morphology might dissociate."

"On the theoretical side, I have used linguistic and psycholinguistic data to develop a comprehensive model of the acquisition of grammar and lexicon, and to analyze issues such as the role of symbolic and connectionist computational architectures in language, the evolution of human language, and the nature of conceptual categories."

Reading recommendation

Beginner-friendly：

T Scovel. Psycholinguistics. Oxford University Press, 1998；上海外语教育出版社, 2000

桂诗春. 新编心理语言学. 上海外语教育出版社, 2000

S. Pinker. The Language Instinct. Penguin Books, 1994（连续数年为美国畅销书, 已由台湾学者洪兰译成中文, 平克本人写了中文版序。中文书名为：语言本能. 探索人类语言进化的奥秘. 汕头大学出版社, 2004）

More challenging：

J. Aitchison. The Articulate Mammal：An Introduction to Psycholinguistics（4th edition）Routledge, 1998；外语教学与研究出版社, 2000（董燕萍　导读）

D. W. Carroll. Psychology of Language（3rd edition）. Brooks/Cole Publishing Company, 1999；　外语教学与研究出版社, 2000（桂诗春, 董燕萍　导读）

A critic once castigated Winston Churchill for composing a sentence which ended with a preposition. Churchill replied with a mocking note: "This is the sort of English up with which I will not put."

Churchill later won the Nobel Prize for Literature (in 1953).

Chapter 11

Language Convention

All humans are born with a capacity to master a language, but the actual language a human baby is going to master is different from place to place, from race to race, from time to time. If you were born to an Arabic family, you would be an expert in making a special sound—pharyngeal with your pharynx; if you were born in Guangdong, China, your nose would be very active in speech. Some southern African languages are referred to as "click languages", featured by using clicks — sharp, suction noises made by the tongue or lips without using a stream of air from the lungs—as consonants. All such widely different speech sounds can be learned successfully by any human baby, but a baby with linguistic instinct never knows what kind of language is waiting for him to learn. Many particular aspects of a language are totally conventional.

11.1 Noah Webster's oath

Imagine a huge mass of people speaking different languages flooding into a colony. What a hopeless oral communication mess it would be. America faced such a situation more than two hundred years ago. Its citizens from different corners of the world spoke multifariously. Settling down in that ex-English colony, they had to learn English, the lingua franca of the land. Anyone could reasonably envisage how inaccurate and varied their English might be.

However, a wonder emerged soon after the United States of America was founded: Yankees suddenly spoke English more clearly than the typical John Bull! John Hay, an American statesman at that time, once wrote down his witness in London excitedly: "How our Ambassador does go it when he gets a roomful of bovine Britons in front of him... I never so clearly appreciated the power of the unhesitating orotundity of the Yankee speech, as in listening—after an hour or two of hum-ha of tongue-tied British men — to the long wash of our Ambassador's sonority."

What Hay praised was not the ambassador's personal charm but the power of the Yankee speech, a new variety of English at that time. How could the Yankee speech be orotund and sonorous and outshine the British officers' "hum-ha" performance? It was the contribution of a great American scholar — Noah Webster.

Today most of us associate Webster's name with his great work *An American Dictionary of the English Language* (referred to today simply as *Webster's*). But his earlier success was a more popular publication in 1783 known as the "Blue-Backed" *American Speller*, with over eighty million copies sold in his lifetime.

What is the content of this book? Let's have a look at one of the tables inside the book:

TABLE XIX   *Words of Three Syllables, accented on the Second.*

a-ch*iev*e-ment	ac-qua*i*nt-ance	ab-do-men
ad[-]ven-tur*e*	al-le-gro	ap-pren[-]tice
ap-pr*ais*[-]er	ar-r*ea*r-ag*e*	bis-sex-til*e*
blas-phe-mer	com-pen-sate	com[-]pul-sive
con-jec-tur*e*	con-sis[-]cate	con[-]ta-g*i*on
con-ta-g*i*ous	con-vul-siv*e*	cur-mud-ge*o*n
con-tem-plate	cor-ro-siv*e*	con-*sis*[-]cate

The major information of the above table includes spelling, syllable division and accented syllable, the essential factors of correct pronunciation. How did people use the book? We can get a picture from the following record:

> It was the custom for all such pupils [those who were sufficiently advanced to pronounce distinctly words of more than one syllable] to stand together as one class, and with one voice to read a column or two of the tables for spelling. The master gave the signal to begin, and all united to read, letter by letter, pronouncing each syllable by itself, and adding to it the preceding one till the word was complete. Thus a-d ad, m-i mi, admi, r-a ra, admira, t-i-o-n, shun, admiration. This mode of reading was exceedingly exciting, and in my humble judgment, exceedingly useful; as it required and taught deliberate and distinct articulation.

The collective activity described in the above quotation was called *spelling bees* (here *bee* means *meeting*), which reflected how the early generations of American citizens were eager to speak "with one voice". It was a movement to popularize American English pronunciation. The ambassador admired by Hay surely benefited from such exercises. Webster's intention was "to introduce uniformity and accuracy of pronunciation into common schools." His maxim was "a good articulation consists in giving every letter in a syllable its due proportion of sound". The word *secretary*, for instance, was advocated to be pronounced as *sec-ret-ary* instead of the British *secret'ry*.

It was Noah Webster's oath to "break with British English and its eighteenth-century classical traditions." He said to his fellows of their new country, "Our honor requires us to have a system of our own, in language as well as government." Today the majority of American people (especially in the middle and western states of the country) can communicate smoothly with each other in American English, whose uniformly featured pronunciation starting from *spelling bees* is a typical product of the power of convention.

11.2 Stretching the grammar

The establishment of a criterion for such phonological aspects as spelling and syllable pronunciation is welcomed because it is essential for the physical quality of a specific language as a tool of communication. After all, a mere mistake in stress, e. g. mispronouncing the word *uni'versity* as *univer'sity*, will spoil the understanding of a whole sentence. A uniform standard at the phonological level relies on some artificial effort like Webster's movement of spelling bees. These aspects, though a solid foundation for the effective conveyance of meaning, have nothing to do with meaning themselves.

Meaning is the interface between language and the world. From morphology we begin to find the attachment of meanings to linguistic structures. For example, the word *irregularly* contains two meaningful units: a prefix *ir*-which means "not", a root *reg* which means *rule*. When meaning is involved, no artificial effort can impose any "rules" upon the language. That is why prescriptive doctrines are bound to be mocked. Two prescriptive rules are:

Don't start a sentence with "and";

Don't end a sentence with a preposition.

With such arbitrary rules, some self-important teachers always have reason to disdain their students' performances in composition and examination, regardless of the fact that no one actually remembers the "rules" in language use. In literary works, such prescriptive "rules" are even being broken quite deliberately, as in the following extract from Angela Carter's novel *Wise Children* (1991).

You spent your childhood on the road, here today, gone tomorrow; you grew up a restless man. You loved change. And fornication. And trouble. And, funnily enough, towards the end, you loved butterflies. Peregrine Hazard, lost among the butterflies, lost in the jungle, vanished away as neatly and completely as if you had become the object of one of those conjuring tricks you were so fond of.

In the above extract, three *and's* are sentence-initial, and one preposition *of* is at the end of the last sentence. Undoubtedly, these sentences are brilliant and appreciated by readers. In literary language, therefore, the structures of grammar can be "stretched" or disrupted in various ways to produce different effects, while still being recognizable as a version of English.

Webster was a real sage after all. When he set out to compile his American English dictionary, a tough and thankless task in his time sponsored solely by the fortune he had made from selling his popular spelling book, he took a descriptive stance to the variation and development of English in his motherland, that is, to respect, follow, and record them instead of repelling them. Today Webster's dictionary still enjoys a tremendous popularity, partly due to the publisher's practice of constantly updating editions.

11.3 Social imprint

Compared with Webster's spelling bees, today's people are more familiar with George Bernard Shaw's play *Pygmalion* which was adapted into a splendid film *My Fair Lady*. The synopsis is that a flower girl with a strong Cockney accent is trained by a linguist to talk and behave like an upper-class lady. It is a biting satirical example of the hypocrisy behind the social varieties of language.

One's speech is one's identity card. Labov, a famous American sociolinguist, conducted a cleverly conceived investigation in early 1970s. He went to three department stores — Saks, Macy's, and S. Klein — in New York, which were usually patronized by people from high, middle, and low classes respectively. He pretended that he was new to the place and asked one after another customer about the location of a department that he knew was on the fourth floor. When he got the answer which contained "fourth floor", he would pretend not to have heard it clearly and ask for a careful repetition. He recorded the responses as his data of the pronunciation [r] in these two words in casual and careful type of speech. Then he told them that he was conducting a survey and invited them to read aloud a sentence with words like "fourth floor" in it, a word list also containing some [r]-words, and finally a pair of words with the sole difference of the involvement of [r], e. g. *pa* and *par* (called "minimal pairs" in linguistics). The reading performance of his informants was recorded, too. The statistical analysis of his recorded data supported his hypotheses before investigation that the [r] pronunciation after vowels (e. g. *guard*, *ear*) was more attended to in New York 1) by people with higher status, 2) by younger people, 3) as the formality level in speech increased, and 4) when [r] was at the end of a word (e. g. *floor*) rather than before a consonant (e. g. *fourth*).

But there was one noticeable exception: Labov's lower-middle-class speakers pronounced [r] more clearly than his upper middle-class speakers on word lists and minimal pairs. Labov explained that it was an instance of hypercorrection: unconsciously, these lower-middle-class speakers stuck to their conventional negligence of [r] production, while consciously they pronounced this sound with special care to assert their identity of "middle class". Labov concluded that overt [r]-pronunciation in New York City served as a class imprint in the use of language.

There are different social imprints. New students from the same city or county tend to form a circle of their own, with its access available only to those with the local accent. Only native ears can tell the subtle differences between the accent developed from childhood and that picked up by a person from another place. British middle class parents used to send their children to expensive public schools where they could acquire RP (= received pronunciation), the prestigious accent of England which would mean a pass to upper society. But those parents hesitate to send their children there today because pure RP may widen their distance from the average people, causing their children not to be accepted by a populace-oriented era when even a prime minister will try to behave like a common citizen.

Therefore, successful people today will not only just pride themselves on a prestigious accent as depicted by Shaw, but will be skilled at switching from one sociolect to another in different situations. A lawyer, for example, may talk to a group of working class clients around a café table in America with sentences like *I done it yesterday*; *He ain't got it*; *It was her what said it*. In this way they feel closer to each other. When he later has to speak to the jury in the court, he may alter his tone and use sentences like *I did it yesterday*; *He hasn't got it*; *It was she that said it*, because that situation is much formal.

A sociolect is the language spoken by a social group, social class or subculture. As long as the demarcation lines exist between people of different statuses and different subcultures, sociolects will not be erased by the standardization of a language. One's sociolects usually fall into two distinct varieties: one used only on formal and public occasions; the other used under normal, everyday circumstances. They are normally called "high" and "low", or "standard" and "vernacular" varieties, and the relatively stable language situation with these two varieties in parallel is called diglossia by Ferguson. Though not many people can speak two languages fluently and be regarded as bilingual, most people are actually diglossic.

11.4 Tongue and face

Human sensibility is so perceptive that the brain not only has to manipulate the tongue to speak, but it has also to be aware of the listener's "face". One's face, in pragmatics, is one's public self-image, or the emotional and social sense of self that one has and expects others to recognize. Not every person is very tactful but no one dares to entirely ignore the conventional principles of different cultures related to politeness. Politeness is the means employed to show awareness of another person's face. There are different kinds of politeness associated with the assumption of relative social distance or closeness. The participants in an interaction often have to determine the relative social distance between them.

If an English girl is to give a negative response to a boy's comment *Clinton's a fool*, she will exhibit different attitudes by making different utterances in accordance with the distance between them.

If they are close friends, the girl will reject the boy bluntly by saying *He is not*! If they are not very familiar with each other, this response will threaten the boy's face because it implies that the speaker does not value the hearer's beliefs. So the girl may possibly express her disagreement indirectly by emphasizing a partial agreement by saying *Well, he has done some foolish things*. A direct repartee with an apology for it like *I'm sorry, I have to disagree with you* would be appropriate between acquaintances.

One has two kinds of faces — positive face and negative face. The former is one's need to be connected, accepted, and treated as a member of the same group; the latter is the need to be independent, to have freedom of action, and not to be imposed on by others. Correspondingly, people have positive politeness strategies and negative politeness strategies. The former draws attention to a common goal and appeals to solidarity by using such patterns as *You and I have the same problem, so...*; *How about letting me...?* The latter shows concern about imposition (e. g. *I'm sorry to bother you...*) and typically uses a modal verb in a question (e. g. 1) *Could you...?* 2) *I know you are busy, but might I ask you if...?*) .

In practice, most people use language in various ways depending on who is being addressed, where they are, and what kind of effect they want to produce. This is an essential aspect of pragmatic competence and goes beyond the scope of Grice's cooperative principles. Therefore, Robin Lakoff, an American linguist, believes that two rules are enough behind pragmatic strategies: 1) be clear; 2) be polite. One rule for tongue and one rule for face, as we see.

11.5 Magic kaleidoscopes

A kaleidoscope is a tubular toy. Do you remember holding it in your hands and looking through it in your childhood? What did you see? Colorful patterns changing constantly. Were you so curious that you dismantled it at once? What did you see inside? Nothing exciting but small loose pieces of colored glass or plastic between two flat plates in the bottom, and long panes of glass. Its working principle is that the glass panes reflect the colored pieces and produce changing patterns when the tube is turned.

Language functions were compared to the mechanism of kaleidoscopes by the famous linguist Bolinger (1907 — 1992), who regards morphemes and words as "entities that keep their shapes no matter what kaleidoscopic patterns they take whenever they are shaken up", and sentences as "the patterns themselves". He believes that a sentence — a particular sentence, not a sentence type — does not mean in the same way that a word means. He says, "The meaning of a sentence is something in the outside world at a given time and in relationship to given persons, qualities, and objects. The meaning of a word is potential, like that of a dollar bill before it is involved in a transaction. The statement *X word means* 'Y' carries a prediction of how a speaker will use *X* word. To make it refer to a real event we must turn it into a sentence—an exclamation like *John*! when we unexpectedly see a friend or *Run*! when danger threatens. "

According to Bolinger, morphemes and words are similar to colored glass pieces in a kaleidoscope and their meanings are unchangeable. Their comprehension relies on the accurate mastery of their meaning, e. g.

(11.1) *He turned angry and gave her a short answer.*

Here the meaning of *short* is not only "brief" but also "curt". Similarly, if one is impatient or angry with someone else, we can say he is *short* with that person, i. e. rude to the guy.

Moreover, sentence (11.2) below could be hard to comprehend if one does not know the shade of meaning of the noun *madam*—a girl or young woman who likes to get her own way.

(11.2) *She's a real little madam*!

The following are the Chinese versions of these two sentences:

(11.3) 他怒火顿起,给了她一个简单、生硬的回答。

(11.4) 她可真是个我行我素的小姐!

Applied to sentence translation, Bolinger's metaphor is quite enlightening. Sentences are compared to kaleidoscopic patterns, and do not develop meaning the same way that words do. Like a pattern, a sentence has its own specific effects in a specific circumstance. A qualified translator never deals with the words of a sentence respectively but tries to reproduce the effect of that sentence with the necessary rearrangement of the words and morphemes.

Let's attempt to translate the following well-known Chinese verses into English.

(11.5) 少年不识愁滋味

(11.6) 十年一觉扬州梦

(11.7) 衣带渐宽终不悔,为伊消得人憔悴

The literal translation of (11.5) can be

(11. 8) *I didn't know the taste of gloom when I was young.*

Such a "correct" translation fails to retain the heroic spirit of the original verse. A pattern of words can be changed, but the effect of the original sentence should not be destroyed. What a translator has to do is seek for words in the target language which can form a pattern to yield a similar effect.

In English there is an excellent idiomatic expression *one's salad days* referring to the time when one is young and inexperienced. If we use this phrase, we will quite desirably retain the original effect for English readers:

(11. 9) *Gloom captured none of my salad days.*

Similarly, we can translate (11. 6) and (11. 7) into English as in the attempts below.

(11. 10) *Ten years in Yangzhou, my fool's paradise*!

(11. 11) *For you I'm pining myself away without regret.*

(11. 10) reveals the exclamatory nature of the original verse, and (11. 11) merges the overlapping "pieces of colored glass" —— 衣带渐宽 and 憔悴 with a vivid expression *pine oneself away.*

One's salad days, *fool's paradise*, and *pine oneself away* are called Shakespeare quotes in English, since they were all created by that great dramatist in his famous plays. Shakespeare greatly enriched English. He had an extraordinary ability to spin off memorable combinations of words. Scores of his phrases have entered the language and many new words from his time have survived owing to his enthusiasm in experimenting with them in his literary creations.

Not every culture has its own Shakespeare, so it seems that not every language enjoys the same conventional richness as English does. On the other hand, English has been the most widely used international language, not only owing to the powerful influence of major English-speaking countries but also its open attitude to new concepts which made other languages borrow terms from its ever-enriched vocabulary. Every language has its own conventions, some richer and some poorer. It seems, therefore, that some babies with the same gifted UG are not as lucky as others if the data they are exposed to happen to belong to a language with a less enriched convention.

EXERCISES

I. Translate the following statements into Chinese.

Sociolinguistics is the study of the interrelationships of language and social structure, of linguistic variation, and of attitudes toward language.

Stylistics is a branch of linguistics which studies the characteristics of situationally-distinctive uses of language, with particular reference to literary language, and tries to establish principles capable of accounting for the particular choices made by individuals and social groups in their use of language.

II. Fill in the blanks with the linguistic terms you have learned.

1) _____ was a movement to popularize American English pronunciation more than two hundred years ago initiated by Noah Webster.

2) In many speech communities two or more varieties of the same language are used by some speakers under different conditions. The most familiar pattern is the standard language (known as the H variety) and the regional dialect (known as the L variety). This is known as _____.

3) The methods developed by Labov, now known as "variation studies", have proved to be very significant for the study of _____ and accents.

4) One's _____ face is one's need to be connected, accepted, and treated as a member of the same group; one's _____ face is the need to be independent, to have freedom of action, and not to be imposed on by others.

5) _____ holds that a sentence — a particular sentence, not a sentence type — does not mean in the same way that a word means.

III. An American medicine advertisement says that *it helps your pain while you sleep.* Most people would rather have their pain hindered than helped; explain the apparent anomaly. Is there something similar in the following question-and-answer pair? " *How's your headache?*" " *Its better now.*"

IV. Give a summary of less than 150 words to Section 11.3.

V. Challenging work.

1) Stylistics tells us that in literary language, the structures of grammar can be "stretched" or disrupted in various ways to produce different effects, while still being recognizable as a version of English. List an excerpt from an English short story to illustrate this idea.

2) Write an essay on the following topic:

Tongue, ears and face

W. Labov (1927 —)

William Labov is a professor in the Linguistics Department of the University of Pennsylvania. He is widely regarded as the founder of the discipline of quantitative sociolinguistics and pursues research in sociolinguistics and dialectology.

Born in Rutherford, New Jersey, he studied at Harvard (1948) and worked as an industrial chemist (1949 — 1961) before turning to linguistics and taking his PhD at Columbia University (1963). He taught at Columbia (1964 — 1970) before becoming a professor of linguistics at the University of Pennsylvania (1971), and then became director of the university's Linguistics Laboratory (1977). The methods he used to collect data for his study of the varieties of English spoken in New York City, published as *The Social Stratification of English in New York City* (1966), have been influential in social dialectology. In the late 1960s and early 1970s, his studies of the linguistic features of African American Vernacular English (AAVE) were also influential: he argued that AAVE should not be stigmatized as substandard but respected as a variety of English with its own grammatical rules, although speakers of AAVE should be encouraged to learn standard American English for interactions in society at large.

In his article *How I got into linguistics, and what I got out of it* William Labov pondered：" 'What is success?' That's one of the questions that I asked people in the first linguistic interviews I put together. One man told me that it's figuring out what you want to do, and then getting someone to pay you to do it. Another man said it's making use of everything that ever happened to you. I like both ways of defining it, but I usually look at it another way：if you get to be 70 years old, and you can look back without feeling that you've wasted your time, you've been successful. Reflecting on how I got into the field of linguistics, and what I've been doing since, I seem to have been following all three ideas the same time, so they may turn out to be the same idea after all."

Reading recommendation

Beginner-friendly：

B. Spolsky. Sociolinguistics. Oxford University Press, 1998；上海外语教育出版社,2000

D. Bolinger. Aspects of Language. （已由方立等人译成中文。中文书名为：语言要略,外语教学与研究出版社,1993）

More challenging：

L. Wright & J. Hope. Stylistics：A Practical Coursebook. Routledge, 1996；外语教学与研究出版社,2000（秦秀白　导读）

秦秀白. 英语语体和文体要略. 上海外语教育出版社,2002

R. Scollon & S. W. Scollon. Intercultural Communication：A Discourse Approach. Blackwell Publishers Ltd. 1995；外语教学与研究出版社,2000（贾玉新　导读）

Child: *My teacher holded the baby rabbits and we patted them.*

Mother: *Did you say your teacher held the baby rabbits?*

Child: *Yes.*

Mother: *What did you say she did?*

Child: *She holded the baby rabbits and we patted them.*

Mother: *Did you say she held them tightly?*

Child: *No, she holded them loosely.*

from a research report by Cazden(1972)

Chapter 12

Language Acquisition

Specific languages develop as a function of the development of the respective cultures, but human language by nature is not the result of cultural development. Von Humboldt (1767 — 1835), an influential German philosopher, argued that language was a creative act of the individual and that humans had an innate capacity for language, which was by no means endowed by culture. Chomsky developed his theory by arguing that the individual's potential for language acquisition was universal. The emergence of language marks the emergence of human beings. No evidence has been found that a man from the most primitive society we have known has a less developed linguistic faculty. Every human being has a head, two hands, two legs, and the ability to speak a language, no matter whether they are civilized or not. Such ideas are evident everywhere: Chinese takes root in the Chinese culture, Russian takes root in the Russian culture and English takes root in the British, American, and many other cultures. However different these languages are from one another, any of them can be efficiently acquired by the same child as his mother tongue, if he happens to be born in the environment of that specific language. This individual's capacity for acquiring any language, called "Language Acquisition Device" by Chomsky, is irrelevant to cultural differences, or race differences, and determines that a baby's first language acquisition is a spontaneous process.

12.1 Babbling

Psychological studies have demonstrated that babies at the age of four months can already distinguish between the vowels [a] and [i]. Researchers show the mouths of two adult faces to an infant, one with the shape when saying [a], the other with the shape when saying [i]. Simultaneously, a tape-recorder plays either [a] or [i]. When the baby subjects hear an [a], they tend to look at the face saying [a]; when they hear an [i], they tend to look at the face saying [i]. These findings suggest that infants of about four months of age can already distinguish different vowel qualities and use visual cues to determine the kind of articulation involved in producing them.

At the age of four to six months or so, babies begin to babble, producing sequences of vowels and consonants, which may not belong to the speech sounds of their prospective mother tongue. According to Roman Jakobson's Discontinuity Hypothesis, once a child produces meaningful words and starts pairing sounds with meaning, he will abruptly stop producing all kinds of non-native speech sounds. It is postulated that children babble because they must go through a process of biological maturation during language development.

12.2 Prosodic boot strapping

A German legendary hero was said to be able to lift himself out of the sea by pulling his own bootstraps. This allusion gives rise to the term *bootstrapping*. In computer science, this term (often simplified as *booting*) refers to any process where a simple system activates a more complicated system. In language acquisition, the process for a baby to decode adults' utterances and acquire their meaning and form for the first time is also called *bootstrapping*.

Some researchers have found that children often use some words before they apparently understand their concepts. For example, when a child imitates some adults saying *Mom giggles*, he may not know the meaning of *giggle* but since there is not any noun phrase after *giggles*, he may grasp that giggling is something Mom can do by herself. If he also learns to say *Arnold smacks Gloria*, he can work out that *smacking* involves acting on something or someone else. Therefore, children may use the syntactic knowledge they have developed to help learn what words mean. This is termed syntactic bootstrapping by Leila Gleitman, which means that semantics builds on top of syntax.

Steven Pinker later advocated the reverse position — semantic bootstrapping: when children understand the meaning of some words, they can discover their syntactic behavior by observing in which positions in sentences adults use the words, i. e. , syntax builds on top of semantics.

Syntax or semantics, which comes first? Though there is no verdict yet, it is apparent that this dispute has nothing to do with the initial stage of linguistic exposure for a little baby. What a new baby perceives is neither words nor sentence structures but a string of sounds from an adult's mouth—a string possibly with pausing, vowel lengthening, stressing, and a certain pattern of intonation. A baby is quite sensitive to such prosodic features. If a baby gets familiar with such features of an adult's pronunciation of *milk*, the next time that adult says *Want milk*, he may infer that this string of sounds consists of two segments—*Want* and *milk*. This inference marks the beginning of dissecting a continuous string of speech into individual components, a milestone called prosodic bootstrapping. Then, infants may guess that some segments refer to things and others refer to actions or events. In this way they gradually become capable of telling nouns from verbs or adjectives and of telling the topic from the comment in a sentence. If the baby has a pet companion which has the equal opportunity of exposure to human adult language performance, the pet, whether a cat or a gorilla, will have no hope to "bootstrap", i. e. , to break down a string of speech sounds and identify different words from it spontaneously.

The following is a conversation in Chinese between a mother and a baby.

(12.1) Mother：宝宝乖。

Baby：嘿嘿！

Mother：宝宝不乖。

Baby：哇！！！！！

The contrastive responses of the baby reveal that the mother's utterances in her child's ears are no longer an integral string of sounds but a combination of two segments — 宝宝 and 乖, and the baby even knows the function of these two segments — the former as the topic and the latter as the comment, because the inserted element 不 has been successfully parsed as a negative particle which changes the tone of the comment.

Let's continue our observation：

(12.2) Mother：宝宝可乖了。

Baby：唔……

Mother：宝宝可坏了。

Baby：哇！！！！！

How can the baby tell the depreciatory implication of the comment 可坏了? Has he mastered the meaning contrast between the words 乖 and 坏? Not yet. He may be unable to isolate them as individual words, because it seems too early for a small baby to analyze the roles played by 可 and 了; therefore, he just treats the three sounds 可坏了 as a whole comment. He gives an unsatisfactory response to it only because he has noticed some uncomplimentary hints from the mother's articulation and expression. If the mother enunciated 可坏了 with the same sweet tone as she said 可乖了, the baby would probably take it as a positive comment and respond merrily instead.

Prosodic as well as non-verbal factors, then, play a key role in infants' earliest processing of speech meaning. Only some while later may we notice the infant progress in identifying individual words and fathoming their syntactic and semantic information.

12. 3 Error-marked creation

All children make mistakes before they master the phonological system of their native language. When an eighteen-month-old child attempts to pronounce the word *water*, he might say [wawa]. When he wants to say *that*, his pronunciation might sound like [dæt]. A Chinese child might call his uncle [houhou] instead of *shushu*. Such errors vary from person to person and may persist for some time, despite correction by the child's parents or caretakers and even despite the child's own realization that his pronunciation does not quite match the adult's.

Such deviation is strong evidence that language acquisition is not mere imitation but a creative process. A baby has his own way: when he finds the pronunciation of *water* is rather "boring" for him, he chooses to reduplicate the stressed syllable *wa* instead, hence the creative pronunciation [wawa]; similarly *bottle* is pronounced [baba]. Besides, more interestingly, a Chinese baby may reduplicate single-syllable words, e. g. *qiu* (ball) becomes *qiuqiu*, and *deng* (lamp) becomes *dengdeng*.

Small children have their own ways to develop their lexicon as well. For instance, they often overextend a word's meaning. When a baby learns the word *daddy*, he may first use it only for his own father and then extends its meaning to all male adults. And when he uses the word *dog*, he may mean any four-legged creature. Babies also like to name their things before they develop the enthusiasm to ask adults for the conventional names of objects. A twenty-month-old Chinese child was observed to open the refrigerator and throw some eggs on the ground while murmuring *guoguogaga*, which seemed to be the name he gave to eggs. More to his parents' annoyance, the next time he threw his father's watch downstairs while murmuring *guoguogaga* as well. Apparently the "word" coined by him had a wider denotation — something with a hard crust, perhaps.

Word creation as such appears to be fairly random, but as a matter of fact, it is rule-governed. Overextensions, for example, are usually based on physical attributes such as size, shape, and texture. Ball may refer to all round things, sock may refer to all undergarments, and so on. The self-made word *guoguogaga* refers to all crusted things, but not a part of the object, such as the crust, nor just an attribute, such as being crusty. Morphologically, children all undergo a period of overgeneralization, e. g. , attaching the regular past-tense morpheme to all verbs — *played*, *smiled*, as well as *comed*, *goed*, *bringed*. These systematic errors give us clues to the process for children to acquire their native language. Children do not just soak in what goes on around them, but actively try to make sense of the language they are exposed to.

Error-marked periods like that of *ed*-overgeneralization are predictable and unavoidable. Adults cannot force children to give up their own erroneous creation. The following is a record of such vain efforts:

(12.3) Child: *Nobody don't like me.*

Mother: *No, say "nobody likes me."*

Child: *Nobody don't like me.*

(Eight repetitions of this dialogue)

Mother: *No, now listen carefully! Say "nobody likes me."*

Child: *Oh! Nobody don't likes me.* (McNeill, 1966)

Notice that the child's way of forming negative sentences involving *nobody* is completely regular: every such sentence contains *nobody* + a negative verb. The child must possess a rule that defines this pattern, though the rule is not the same as that in adults' grammar. Eight repetitions of the mother's correction only result in a partial imitation of her utterance — *likes*. The self-created rule remains intact. It seems that the rule will stay with the child some time until later self-regularization. The process of L1 acquisition can be better described as "growth" than "learning".

Would children behave better if language learning were simply imitating? Good imitation might be error-free. But that means there would be sufficient examples available for children to follow. However, not every child is so lucky. Think of those unattended children. How could they get enough exposure to adult linguistic performance? But they acquire their first language as efficiently as well-attended children. Even the latter might hardly be able to focus their attention on adults' "coaching" for a long time. Evidence of what the language should be remains limited for them. Therefore, language acquisition cannot be mere imitation but a creative, self-regularized process with predictable error types as landmarks.

12.4 Triggering and choosing

Children are often exposed to adult-adult interactions. These utterances include slips of the tongue, ungrammatical and incomplete sentences, and other ill forms. Below is an example of such adult speech (Clark, 1994):

(12.4) June: *yes*

     Daphie: *thanks very much*

     June: *OK?*

     Daphie: *right, I'll see you this*

     June: *because there how did you beat him?*

     Daphie: *no, he beat me, four one* (laughs)

     June: *four one*

     Daphie: *yes, I was doing quite well in one game, and then then I I...*

         I lost

     June: *oh, how disgusting*

If adult utterances like (12.4) are the main source of linguistic data for a child, how can he develop the systematic knowledge of his L1 grammar? In this sense, the data the children are exposed to is thought of as impoverished. Such insufficient data cannot provide exemplification of all aspects of grammar. But all grown-ups end up with a sound mastery of their L1 grammar.

One asks his friend, "*Who did you see when you went into the hall?*" His friend answers, "*I saw John and Mary there.*" If the question asker fails to catch the second name, he may ask an echo question, "*You saw John and whom?*" But he (no matter how young he is) will never ask, "*Who(m) did you see John and?*" or "*And whom did you see John?*" Linguists have investigated a great number of languages, and found none allows a *wh*-phrase as part of a coordinate structure to be moved to the initial position of a question. It is called coordinate structure constraint.

The question is: how can a common person know this grammatical rule? Who has taught him? Has his exposure to his L1 environment given him any hint that he should observe it? Is it because the asterisked questions above are ineffective? No, they are actually understandable. How can all the people of all the languages investigated, including children, never accept or produce them?

Many linguists have made a bold guess: children are equipped with an innate "blueprint" for language, which aids children in the task of constructing a grammar for their language. This "blueprint" is usually called UG (universal grammar), and some linguists, e. g. Chomsky, sometimes also call it LAD (language acquisition device).

According to this theory, UG is not the grammar of any particular language. Rather, it is a propensity for acquiring language which is a set of representations of linguistic knowledge with options built into them. The options are known as parameters, and the information that tells the system which option to choose is known as a trigger.

For example, the knowledge of inflection in English serves as a trigger for children to expect English is a subject-overt language, i. e. every English sentence must have a voiced subject, because the verb of any sentence needs to be checked with the subject, to see whether they agree in tense, gender, number and case. Subject-overtness represents a set of parameter values, while subject-covertness is a feature of another parameter set.

When all the open options within UG have been set by input triggers, we say that a "core" grammar of the language being acquired has been established. Unlike UG, a core grammar is the grammar of a particular language (English, French, German, etc.), consisting of a combination of invariant principles of language together with the parameter settings.

If a child is born in America, he may set the parameter of head-left for his mother tongue as he has been exposed to such PPs as *in the garden*, *on the wall* for some time. And a Japanese child may set the parameter of head-right for his mother tongue if he has been exposed to those frequently used phrases like

(12.5) きょうしつ

　　　教　　室　　に

　　　classroom　　in

In the Japanese phrase above, the head is に (= in), which is located on the right side. Both options (head-left and head-right) exist in UG and what a child needs to do is choose one through input-triggering. Their tree diagrams are as follows.

(12.6) head-left option:

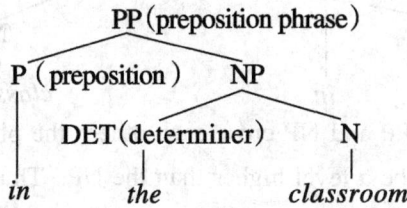

PP (preposition phrase)

P (preposition) — NP

DET (determiner) — N

in   *the*   *classroom*

(12.7) head-right option:

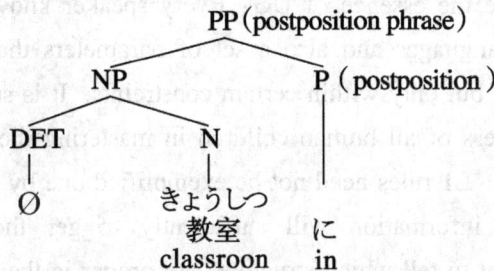

PP (postposition phrase)

NP — P (postposition)

DET — N

Ø   きょうしつ 教室   に

classroon   in

Apparently, such abstract knowledge represented by the tree diagrams above has never been taught to any baby, but all the babies are able to learn about the relative order of heads and complements in their language and in this way to set a specific parameter for their language. This process is called triggering and choosing, which presupposes that a child unconsciously observes a principle called structural dependency, namely, a knowledge of language relies on knowing structural relationships in a sentence rather than looking at it as a sequence of words. Children never treat other sequences of sounds (such as a melody) as non-linear but they only spontaneously treat a sentence as hierarchical. This special propensity must be innate.

Furthermore, UG tells the child what cannot be an option. For example, no child will choose the structure of the "phrase" * *the in classroom* as a parameter. (12.8) is the analysis of the "phrase".

(12.8) crossing branches:

```
                            PP
                   P              NP
          DET                              N

         *the        in              classroom
```

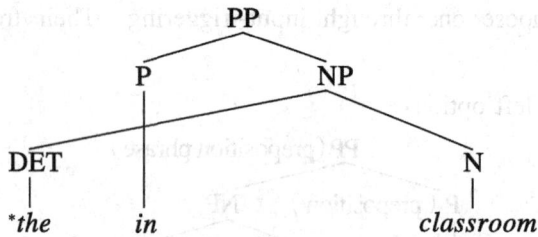

When the branches PP and NP cross each other, the phrase hierarchy fails: the PP in (12.8) can never be a level higher than the NP. Thus we see a constraint for human language grammar, namely *no crossing branches*.

Now we can see the essence of UG: Every speaker knows a set of principles which apply to all languages and also a set of parameters that can vary from one language to another, but only within certain constraints. It is such innate knowledge that decides the success of all human children in mastering the abstract grammar of their native language. L1 rules need not be exemplified one by one in the input. The exposure to certain information will sufficiently trigger the parameter setting, enabling an individual to tell which structures are proper in their language and which are unacceptable. To sum up, it is UG that helps the child to acquire a complex grammar quickly and easily.

However, not all the linguists agree to this nativist conclusion. The opposite camp is called empiricism (Both nativism and empiricism have been mentioned in Chapter 1). They deny any specific mechanism in charge of language acquisition: children can learn a language because they have general cognitive facility such as imitating, modeling, abstracting, analogy drawing. They hold that language rules can be derived from experience. The reason why all people reject questions like "*And whom did you see John?*" is that they have never heard and summarized such sentence patterns. Recently some researchers called connectionists have done a series of fruitful studies in modeling the language learning process with computers.

If language learning only relied on the child's own efforts, it would be logical that bilingual children would need to double their efforts, and it would be impossible for them to acquire both their languages within the same amount of time as other children use to acquire just one language. However, the results of a number of longitudinal studies are to the contrary. Virginia Yip, a Chinese linguist in Hong Kong whose husband, also a linguist, is British, reported her own study of the bilingual development of her three children in Yip (2002) and a forthcoming book. Through regular observation, diary keeping, video recording, and longitudinal corpus construction, she concluded that her children had experienced the same stages of language acquisition and had developed competence of two languages — English from their father and Cantonese from their mother — comparable to their monolingual counterparts with the similar speed though taking a different developmental path.

Specifically, their phonological acquisition of both languages was a parallel success. They had never confused the Cantonese [sapl] (湿 "wet"), [satl] (失 "lose"), [sakl] (塞 "squeeze in") with English [sap], [sat], [sak], for example. Yet their syntactic development involved some cases of bilingual interaction, such as null object (e. g. *You get, I eat...*), pseudo-passive (e. g. *Schoolbag put here, put at the door.*), wh-in-situ (e. g. *I know, I know, I know, I know, I know it's where.*) Like developmental errors in monolingual acquisition, these bilingual errors had also been gradually unlearned as milestones of certain acquisition stages. Yip attributed her research results in part to the child's "bilingual instinct" with UG underlying the bilingual development, and argued that the early syntactic development in Cantonese-English bilingual children shows evidence of bidirectional transfer and interaction between two languages in contact.

12.5 Critical period

The nativist camp has another strong reason to argue that language acquisition is a spontaneous maturational development (in other words, growth rather than learning), that is, the critical period hypothesis.

This hypothesis was first proposed by Eric Lenneberg. He said that the ability to learn a native language develops within a fixed period, from birth to puberty. During this period, language acquisition proceeds easily, swiftly, and without external intervention. After this period, the acquisition of grammar is difficult and for some individuals never fully achieved.

Here are two famous cases frequently cited to support the hypothesis.

1. A girl called Genie was found in 1970 when she was nearly fourteen years old. She had been abused and isolated since the age of twenty months. When first discovered, Genie was completely silent. Thereafter her language development was extremely slow, and although she did learn to speak, her speech was quite abnormal. Below are some *wh*-questions made by the girl.

(12.9) *_Where is tomorrow Mrs L. ?_

(12.10) *_Where is May I have ten pennies?_

(12.11) *_When is stop spitting?_

These "ill-formed" *wh*-questions serve as evidence that grammatical structures are not learned through imitation and memorization but "preprogrammed" and triggered in childhood. Genie was not bad at imitation and she was an avid communicator with her teacher. Since she began to learn a language after the critical age, however, she could not rely on UG to develop normal grammatical capability.

2. Isabelle was discovered in 1937 at the age of six and a half. Her mother, who was deaf and could not speak, had kept her isolated but had not otherwise mistreated her. Isabelle then began training lessons at The Ohio State University, and although her progress was at first slow, it soon accelerated. Two years later her intelligence and her language use were completely normal for a child of her age. Obviously, Isabelle was luckier than Genie because her exposure to a language started still within the critical period for language acquisition.

As further support, zoology tells us the notion of a critical period is true of many species, whose innate faculty should also be triggered within a finite period of time after birth.

Darwin observed, "... man has an instinctive tendency to speak, as we see in the babble of our young children; while no child has an instinctive tendency to brew, bake, or write." Undoubtedly language is our species-specific endowment.

EXERCISES

I. Translate the following statement into Chinese.

Research in first-language acquisition and development addresses the central question of why and how children succeed in acquiring language. To establish this, researchers focus on the acquisition of rules and structures, including grammar, vocabulary and the sound system, and also on how children gain knowledge about how to use language appropriately in different situations.

II. Fill in the blanks with the linguistic terms you have learned.

1) Many linguists have made a bold guess: children are equipped with an innate "blueprint" for language, which aids children in the task of constructing a grammar for their language. This "blueprint" is usually called _____.

2) Chomsky's UG hypothesis originates from _____'s idea that language is a creative act of the individual and that humans have an innate capacity for language, which is by no means endowed by culture.

3) A knowledge of language relies on knowing structural relationships in a sentence rather than looking at it as a sequence of words. This is called the _____ principle.

4) Babies begin to produce _____ sounds like /dæ/, /mæ/, /næ/, /bæ/ at the age of about three or four months. At around 9-12 months, real words begin to be produced.

5) In language acquisition, the process for a baby to decode adults' utterances and acquire their meaning and form for the first time is also called _____.

6) The fact that bilingual children acquire both their languages within nearly the same amount of time as other children use to acquire just one language demonstrates that children's early syntactic development should be a process of _____ and _____, instead of learning.

III. Give a summary of less than 150 words to Section 12.5.

IV. Challenging work.

The UG theory holds that the establishment of core grammar completes the work of UG in language acquisition. It does not, however, complete the work of language acquisition itself. There's a lot more to be done. For example, all the vocabulary of the language will be learned from the input.

A child does not acquire the meanings of words or expressions from the formal definition, but instead from the way they are used by the people around him, and through other people's response to his own use of them.

The following is an example from Bolinger:

*A primary school teacher asked a second-year pupil what she feared. The little girl answered, "**It**." The teacher wanted to know about that **it**. The girl explained that **it** made her frightened but she didn't know what **it** was—perhaps a punishment, a disease, or a huge animal which would eat her if she behaved badly. The teacher was very worried. So she went to visit the girl's mother and finally found out the reason: The mother often scolded her daughter with "You'll get it!"*

Analyze this particular case and think of how children build up their own vocabulary. Write an essay on your reflection.

■ ■

EH Lenneberg (1921 — 1975)

Eric Heinz Lenneberg was a linguist who pioneered ideas on language acquisition and cognitive psychology more generally about innateness. His book *Biological Foundations of Language* (1967) was a major landmark. This book collected the biological literature to support the pivotal claim that language is founded on species-specific anatomical and neurophysiological capabilities for language, and that those elements are found only in humans. Lenneberg pointed out that language is an example of maturationally controlled behavior, which is preprogrammed to emerge at a particular stage, i. e. a critical period, in an individual's life, provided the surrounding environment is normal, such as seals walking. His book has been widely accepted because of its clear explanation for difficulties in second language learning after puberty. It explains well our experience of seeing small children speak foreign languages quite naturally.

Lennerberg was born in Düsseldorf, Germany. Son of a physician, he grew up in an intellectual and artistic atmosphere. As a Jew, he left Germany for Brazil at the age of 12 because of Nazi terrorism. He worked at the Harvard Medical School and at the University of Michigan in Ann Harbor as a professor in psychology.

His 1964 paper *The Capacity of Language Acquisition* sets forth the seminal arguments picked up later by Noam Chomsky and popularized by Steven Pinker in his book, *The Language Instinct*.

His work reveals that between the ages of two and three years language emerges by an interaction of maturation and self-programmed learning. Between the ages of three and the early teens the possibility for primary language acquisition constitutes to be good; the individual appears to be most sensitive to stimuli at this time and to preserve some innate flexibility for the organization of brain functions to carry out the complex integration of sub-processes necessary for the smooth elaboration of speech and language. After puberty, the ability for self-organization and adjustment to the physiological demands of verbal behavior quickly declines. The brain behaves as if it had set it its ways and primary, basic skills not acquired by that time usually remain deficient for life.

Reading recommendation

Beginner-friendly:

J. S. Peccei. Child Language. 2nd edition. Routledge, 1999; 外语教学与研究出版社,2000 (李宇明　导读)**More challenging**:

J. B. Gleason. The Development of Language. 6th edition. Pearson Education, Inc. 2005; 世界图书出版公司,2005

H. Goodluck. Language Acquisition: A Linguistic Introduction. Blackwell Publishers Ltd. 1991; 外语教学与研究出版社,2000（李行德　导读）

S. H. Foster-Cohen. An Introduction to Child Language Development. 外语教学与研究出版社,2000（李行德　导读）

NNS: I have a favor to ask you.

NS: Sure, what can I do for you?

NNS: You need to write a recommendation for me.

(NS = native speaker

NNS = nonnative speaker)

from Goldschmidt (1996)

Chapter 13

Second Language

Though the proper time for man to learn a language is childhood, today's world requires more and more people to learn another language after puberty. Knowing another language may mean attaining a desirable position, a chance to study abroad, an opportunity to immigrate to a richer country, an expansion of one's literary and cultural horizons, etc. The goals are splendid, but the learning is extremely demanding, quite different from those effortless experiences of one's first language acquisition.

13. 1 Defining L2 acquisition

Most researchers today do not differentiate *foreign language* from *second language*. For them, the term *second language* (= L2) refers to any language that is learned subsequent to the mother tongue. It is not applicable to the case of a child learning two languages simultaneously during a bilingual upbringing. Besides, as

Rod Ellis, an authority in this field, notes, "second" is not intended to contrast with "foreign". The L2 acquisition process includes learning a non-native language in the environment where that language is spoken, e. g. Chinese speakers learning English in America, as well as learning a new language in a foreign language context, e. g. Chinese speakers learning English in China. Accordingly, while a bilingual child has two L1s, any adult can learn one or more L2s. An L2 can be one's first, second, third, fourth... or x-th non-native language.

Second language acquisition is a separate field of research. Its interest does not overlap that of first language acquisition, because L2 learners are cognitively more mature. Unlike children, they have developed skills for general knowledge learning and problem solving, and, in particular, have already established a language system— L1—for communication. Undoubtedly, these learners will not approach an L2 in the same manner as their L1 acquisition.

Stephen Krashen, a famous researcher in this field, makes a strong distinction between L2 learning and L2 acquisition. He defines the term *learning* as a deliberate, conscious attempt to master a language. In contrast, the term *acquisition* is defined as a less deliberate, subconscious process of mastering a language, similar to the manner in which children acquire an L1. Many researchers today do not underline this distinction but use the two terms interchangeably. The present chapter takes the latter stance and considers second language acquisition a concept involving both conscious and subconscious processes regardless of the language learning environment.

13.2 Fundamentally different?

To native speakers' ears, an L2 learner's performance usually sounds peculiar. This does not always mean the latter is inevitably a poor learner. Phonetically, for example, an average native speaks with at least a touch of local accent, from which other natives can guess which place he comes from. How can an L2 learner acquire such an accent associated with a local region? There is an English play which introduces its leading character by saying: *He speaks perfect English; so perfect in enunciation that some might be suspicious that he is foreign.* This character turns out to be a Nazi murderer who has hidden in England for more than 40 years — a proficient L2-English speaker indeed! However, the play reveals a paradox faced by the murderer—*it is his excellent L2 enunciation that gives him away.* This perfect L2 speaker still fails to identify himself with the native speakers perfectly!

Therefore, when Robert Bley-Vroman, an American linguist, affirms that L2 learning is universally unsuccessful, you will not be surprised. If you learn English in China, for example, you will have no hope of speaking exactly the same way as native citizens in England or America. Phonologically, you will bear some L1 influence in pronouncing some phonemes. Morphologically, you may not know some subtle differences such as that between *phenomenons* and *phenomena*. Syntactically, you may create a sentence like ** John told Mary to shave himself* without noticing anything wrong with its structure. Semantically, you may not recognize the nuance of the word *madam* in the sentence *She's a real little madam*! Pragmatically, you may as well imagine being enrolled in an American university as a postgraduate. One day you have a talk with a faculty advisor. The advisor says, *"OK, let's talk about next semester."* Then you respond to him, *"I will take syntax."* If there is a native student beside you, he may respond in a fairly different way — *"I was thinking of taking syntax."*

Bley-Vroman claims that adult foreign language learning should be fundamentally different from child language development. He uses UG theory to demonstrate that a child's first language acquisition is a process of internally driven growth, while learning another language in the classroom should be similar to general knowledge learning, a process of conscious memorization of rules and problem solving.

Is Bley-Vroman right? Is the difference between L1 and L2 acquisition really fundamental? Since the children's L1 acquisition is universally successful, why can't most of adult learners ultimately succeed in L2 acquisition?

Let's start our discussion from the perspective of you — L2 learners.

13.3 Are you fed up?

Learning a language entails knowing a set of rules with which we can produce an infinite set of sentences. How much time should a human child spend on this process? Since a child is exposed to L1 environment from morning till evening every day, the actual time for him to master his mother tongue is 6,000 to 8,000 hours, according to Strevens' estimation (1977). In contrast, in a total of 100 or 300 or 500 hours — rarely more — a teacher helps the L2 learner achieve a command of his target language's structural rules.

However, children's L1 acquisition is a process of UG driven growth. Through triggering and choosing, children can set the parameters of their L1 spontaneously. L2 learners, however, are not so lucky. Learning an L2 requires motives and efforts.

"Have I got the makings of a language learner?" L1 learners never ask themselves such a question, but L2 learners do. Some researchers have revealed that those high school students who make quicker progress in phonetic training show more confidence in L2 study than other classmates, and will probably turn out to be better L2 learners in their class in subsequent years. Such findings show that a prerequisite of L2 achievement is a good self-concept.

Those with less self-confidence begin to worry: *Am I an oaf with foreign language studies*? When they find they are not among the best L2 learners in their class, they become anxious that their L2 performance might seem comical to the teacher and advanced students, or their efforts might miss the mark. Such anxieties may not be easy to overcome because L2 learners do vary in talents or degrees of aptitude.

As we have seen, children's L1 acquisition is motivation-free, partly because it can be regarded as a natural development from an innate initial state, and partly because it is an urgent demand of human life. On the other hand, an adult's foreign language learning should be motivation-driven. Without a definite goal, no one could be expected to have a lasting desire to learn another language.

Some learners start to forget their L2 knowledge immediately after they have passed an important examination or obtained a desirable job, which is their sole reason to learn that language. What they have is instrumental motivation. Other learners have the desire to acculturate and become a member of a target language community, which forms an integrative motivation. Some learners waver between the two purposes.

Motivation, anxiety, self-concept are a few of the affective factors, which strongly influence one's L2 achievement positively or negatively. For example, low-level anxiety will strengthen one's motivation to achieve more, while high motivation with little subjective hope of achievement will increase anxiety and hinder one's progress. Some learners feel fed up with L2 studies and stop their effort at a level far from the target language norms.

In addition, L2 achievement to some extent can be predicted by certain personality factors. For example, some learners have the capacity to participate in another's feelings or ideas. Their sensitivity to others makes them better L2 learners in a natural environment where communication is the focus. They may more easily emulate a native-like pronunciation, and behave better at picking up nuances of word meaning and their implications in different linguistic contexts. Other learners have a highly rational, analytical personality, which ensures that they will do well in the traditional classroom setting where the focus is usually on analytical oral and written activities.

13.4 Lado and Corder

Anytime when seeing L2 learners having difficulties in making progress, good-natured teachers are eager to lend a hand.

Early researchers of teaching methodology believed that the potential errors of the learners could be predicted by comparing and contrasting the learner's native language with the second language. It was claimed that those similar structures would be easy to learn, while those different structures would be difficult. This approach is known as contrastive analysis (CA), proposed by the famous linguist and textbook editor Robert Lado in 1957.

The proposition of such a hypothesis aroused SLA researchers' interest in L2 learners' errors. They soon found that things were no so simple. Very often, L2 learners were observed making fewer errors with those structures strikingly different from their L1 equivalents, but making more with those structures subtly dissimilar. Besides, some errors were not influenced by either the L1 or the L2.

Many researchers gradually changed their attitudes to errors. They no longer took errors as something to be eradicated but rather used them as evidence of the state of a learner's knowledge of the L2. In 1967, Pit Corder published an article titled *The Significance of Learners' Errors*, which marked a turnabout from contrastive analysis to error analysis (EA).

According to Corder, errors are not mistakes. Mistakes are generally one-time-only events. The speaker who makes a mistake is able to recognize it as a mistake and correct it if necessary. An error, on the other hand, is systematic. That is, it is likely to occur repeatedly and is not recognized by the learner as an error. Errors indicate a learner's attempt to figure out an L2 system. For example, similar to children's L1 acquisition, adults' L2 acquisition also has a period of *ed*-overgeneralization. Therefore, errors are evidence of an underlying rule-governed system created by L2 learners themselves.

In the first month of a Japanese-speaking child learning English in an English speaking country, she formed questions like:

Do you know?

How do you do it?

Do you have coffee?

Do you want this one?

During her second month of residence, the following questions were uttered by the same child:

What do you doing, this boy?

What do you do it, this froggie?

What do you doing?

What do you drinking, her?

Obviously, the English this small girl acquired in the first month of learning was very limited. Though the questions she made were free of errors, she could only use the second person in them. In the second month she attempted to use third-person in her questions, but she did not know the way to change person. So she changed in her own way — with the third person reference as a tag of the second person question. This self-created error type marks a progress in L2 question acquisition.

From Lado to Corder, L2 teachers' attitudes towards learners' errors dramatically changed. Similar to L1 acquisition, L2 learners impose structure on the available linguistic data and formulate an internalized system themselves. Teachers cannot wipe out the learner's errors, but can ascertain the stage their students are currently at by observing the errors they have recently made. Then how can teachers speed up L2 acquisition? Clever teachers will concentrate their efforts on promoting the interaction of L2 input and output. Krashen and Swain are experts in this area.

13.5 Krashen and Swain

Input consists of what learners hear and read. According to Krashen (1982, 1985), second languages are acquired "by understanding messages, or by receiving *comprehensible input*," which is that bit of language slightly ahead of a learner's current state of grammatical knowledge. Krashen defines a learner's current state of knowledge as i and the next stage as $i + 1$. Thus the input a learner is exposed to must be at the $i + 1$ level in order for it to be of use in terms of acquisition. Ensuring that students receive comprehensible input becomes the main role of the teacher.

Then, how about output? Output consists of speaking and writing, and has traditionally been viewed as a way of practicing what has previously been learned. Krashen regards output as a result of acquisition and not its cause. It cannot be taught directly but "emerges" on its own as a result of building competence via comprehensible input.

Swain's opinion is different. By observing Canadian children learning French in immersion schools, she finds input alone is not sufficient for acquisition. Those children had enough comprehensible input of their L2 — French, but made very slow progress. She suggested that what the students lacked was the opportunity to use the

L2 productively as opposed to using the L2 merely for comprehension. Swain proposed the notion of *comprehensible output* or "pushed" output. That is, learners are "pushed" or "stretched" in their production as a necessary part of making themselves understood.

According to Swain (1985), comprehensible output refers to the need for a learner to be "pushed toward the delivery of a message that is not only conveyed, but that is conveyed precisely, coherently, and appropriately." If output is not emphasized, learners will focus their attention just on the meaning of the input, without noticing the language form in it. If learners are required to speak and write often, they will be more sensitive to the syntactic forms in what they hear and read, so that they can use them in their own speaking and writing. "Output, thus," Swain (1995) claimed, "would seem to have a potentially significant role in the development of syntax and morphology."

Both Krashen and Swain have made great contributions to L2 teaching methodology. Today, more and more L2 teachers attach importance to the interaction between input and output.

13.6 Interlanguage

Having visited some prominent teachers, let's go back to the learners. This time, we will not discuss their emotion and attributes, but their mental state.

Second language acquisition is a complex field whose focus is the attempt to understand the process underlying the learning of a second language. The basic assumption in this field is that learners create a language system known as an interlanguage (IL).

This concept was first formulated by Larry Selinker (1972). As a transitional system, interlanguage is constructed by the learner out of the linguistic input to which he has been exposed. It refers to the developing competence of L2 learners, from an initial stage of very limited knowledge about the new language to a final stage of almost complete fluency in the target structures. Selinker also hypothesized that errors were best understood as part of the learner's IL. Like in L1 acquisition, errors serve as marks of a stage of IL development. For example, elementary English learners in China may make errors like *I' ll happy if I can get your paper*; advanced learners may make errors like *This house is easy to catch fire.*

Such "stage marks" include interlingual errors or interference errors, which result from negative L1 transfer. The two examples above belong to this category. Another category of errors are intralingual errors or developmental errors, like *He comed yesterday.* Learners who have made such errors may speak different L1s, indicating that the development of IL must be universal.

Moreover, L2 learners employ various learning strategies to develop their interlanguages. The different kinds of errors learners produce reflect different learning strategies. For example, learners may leave out the articles *a* and *the* and leave the *-s* off plural nouns. Such omission errors suggest that learners are in some way simplifying the learning task by ignoring grammatical features that they are not yet ready to process.

Central to the concept of IL is the concept of fossilization. Most adult learners have a more or less fossilized L1 influence on their L2 pronunciation, for example, and even an advanced learner may unknowingly retain a fossilized structure. As Corder suggests, once the L2 learner's IL grammar is sufficiently developed to enable the learner to communicate adequately for his purposes, the motivation to improve wanes.

13.7 Is UG still awake?

Another focus of SLA research is whether UG is actually involved in L2 learning. Obviously Bley-Vroman's answer is *no*: L2 is learned in the same way as any other aspect of knowledge — cookery, physics, or whatever. This is called the *no-access* position. Opposite to it are two positions — *direct-access* position and *indirect-access* position. The former holds that L2 learners learn in exactly the same way as L1 learners; the latter argues that L2 learners have access to UG through what they know of the L1. Moreover, a revisionist position of direct access is called *partial-access* position which implies that some but not all principles of UG can be accessed directly, i. e. not via the L1 grammar, during L2 acquisition.

Though Bley-Vroman believes that UG is unavailable in adults' foreign language learning, he finds that a foreign language learner can in a sense reconstruct much of the original scheme of UG by "observing" his mother tongue. He notes, "The native language must be sifted: That which is likely to be universal must be separated from that which is an accidental property of the native language." But he fails to recognize that such "restructuring" and "sifting" can only occur subconsciously — unrecognized by the learner himself. For example, in Chinese you can say both

(13.1) 在她来之前,……

and

(13.2) 在她没来之前,……

Then, you can do an experiment like this: Go to an elementary English class and write the following pair of phrases on the blackboard with the permission of the teacher:

(13.3) *Before she comes,...*

(13.4) **Before she does not come,...*

Then ask the students to judge whether they are acceptable in English. You will find that all the students strongly reject (13.4) as acceptable. At this time, you can as well write (13.1) and (13.2) on the blackboard, and ask the students why they have not thought of (13.2) when they reject (13.4).

Apparently, your informants — those elementary English learners will make their judgment without referring to their L1 knowledge but resorting to their tacit feel for what English should be. They subconsciously presume that the syntactic structure of (13.1) is universal, and that of (13.2) is accidental and probably not expected to appear in another language. This example demonstrates that subconsciousness plays an indispensable role in second language acquisition, which distinguishes itself from general knowledge learning, because the latter is basically a conscious process.

There can be subconscious "selectivity" by learners in what is transferred and what is not transferred.

Now we come to see that L2 acquisition, contrary to Bley-Vroman's opinion, resembles UG-driven L1 acquisition in some aspects. Like L1, according to Krashen, L2 competence is subconsciously acquired. He observes,

We are generally not consciously aware of the rules of the languages we have acquired. Instead, we have a "feel" for correctness. Grammatical sentences "sound" right, or "feel" right, and errors feel wrong, even if we do not consciously know what rule was violated.

Such subconscious feel for language rules, if shared by L2 speakers, should as well be attributed to none other than UG. It seems that UG still has a role to play in adult's L2 acquisition. Syntactically, we can even find evidence of triggering and choosing. Yuan Boping, a Chinese expert on second language acquisition research who teaches in Cambridge University, has published a series of studies on this topic. For example, Yuan discovered in 1995 that though both the subject and the object of a sentence can be omitted in Chinese (termed *null subject* and *null object*), L1-Chinese learners will scarcely omit the subject of an English sentence. It seems as if their Chinese knowledge of null subject had been totally forgotten.

For example, in Chinese we can say,

(13.5) 我曾经见过约翰的女朋友,长得非常漂亮。

Apparently the subject of the second clause has been omitted. It should be 她. Yuan found a significant majority of his 159 subjects—Chinese-speaking learners of English of 7 different levels—rejected the word-to-word translation (13.6) of this sentence.

(13.6) ** I once met John's girlfriend. Was very beautiful.*

Yuan speculated that it was the acquisition of inflection in English that triggered the learners' unlearning of the L1-Chinese null subject in their IL: Since an inflectional morpheme needed to be checked with the subject, a null subject should not be allowed in an English sentence. Yuan's discovery indicated that parameter setting could also be triggered in L2 acquisition.

As for null object, Yuan found that Chinese learners were unable to detect its ungrammaticality in English, owing to lack of triggering evidence. Even an advanced learner may fail to see such an error in the sentence below.

(13.7) ** John said those students were in the library, but I told him I didn't* find there.

Comparing (13.7) with its word-for-word translation (13.8), we can see null object is an error of L1 transfer.

(13.8) 约翰说那些学生在图书馆里,但是我告诉他我在那儿没见着。

Yuan's findings imply that UG, though inaccessible in L1 acquisition after the critical age, still plays a certain part in L2 acquisition. More evidence has been provided by other studies in recent years.

As a discipline, second language acquisition has two orientations. One is to explore the rules and methods of L2 learning and teaching; the other is to study how learners create a new language system (i. e. IL) with only limited exposure to a second language. With more and more people learning another language nowadays, SLA becomes one of the most active fields in linguistics.

EXERCISES ✍

I. Translate the following statements into Chinese.

Second language acquisition (SLA) is the learning of another language after the first language has been learned. The use of this term does not differentiate among learning situations. It can occur in a classroom situation, as well as in more "natural" exposure situations.

A person's second language (L2) as a general term is frequently used to refer to any language learning or use after the first language has been learned.

II. Fill in the blanks with the linguistic terms you have learned.

1) Language transfer is the effect of one language on the learning of another. Two types of language transfer may occur. _____ transfer, also known as L1 interference, is the use of a native-language pattern or rule which leads to an error or inappropriate form in the target language.

2) Motivation, anxiety, self-concept are a few of the _____ factors, which strongly influence one's L2 achievement positively or negatively.

3) Unlike _____ errors which result from language transfer, _____

errors result from faulty or partial learning of the target language.

4) The basic assumption in SLA research is that learners create a language system — _____. In other words, the L2 learners themselves impose structures on the available L2 data and formulate an internalized system.

5) _____ is a process which sometimes occurs in which incorrect linguistic features become a permanent part of the way a person speaks or writes a second language.

III. Give a summary of less than 150 words to Section 13.7.

IV. Challenging work.

1) Some L1 features seem to be "initially" unlearned in L2 acquisition. For example, almost all the English learners in China never use or accept the structure of the sentence *I this book have read*. But Chinese people are used to saying 我这本书读过了. Try to explain this spontaneous rejection to the transfer of this L1 structure.

2) Observe a native English speaker and a non-native English learner conversing, taking careful notes on how you think their speech differs from what you would expect in a conversation between non-native speakers. Pay attention to all aspects of the native speaker's speech, including pronunciation, grammar, vocabulary, rate of speech, and so on. Are they different from his/her usual talk because the addressee is a foreigner?

■ ■

S. Krashen

Stephen D. Krashen is Professor Emeritus of Learning and Instruction at the University of Southern California. He is an expert in the field of linguistics, specializing in theories of language acquisition and development. Much of his research has involved the study of non-English and bilingual language acquisition. Recently Dr. Krashen's research has focused on reading and its effects on language acquisition and academic success. In the late 1970s, Stephen Krashen began promoting the "natural approach" to language teaching, which he laid out in a landmark text he co-wrote with Tracy Terrell. His ideas about the difference between learning and acquisition have strongly influenced the field of English as a second language (ESL) for several decades. He has published hundreds of books and articles and has been invited to deliver over 500 lectures at universities throughout the United States and the rest of the world. In the past five years, Stephen Krashen has fought to save whole language and bilingual education in the United States and, more recently, has been lobbying for "recreational reading" and better stocked school libraries because of research relating both to higher achievement.

Reading recommendation

Beginner-friendly:

R. Ellis. Second Language Acquisition. Oxford University Press 1997；上海外语教育出版社,2000

More challenging:

V. Cook. Linguistics and Second Language Acquisition. Macmillan Publishers Ltd, 1993；外语教学与研究出版社,2000（王初明　导读）

D. Larson-Freeman & M. H. Long. An Introduction to Second Language Acquisition Research. 外语教学与研究出版社,2000（蒋祖康　导读）

P. M. Lightbown & N. Spada. How Languages are Learned. Oxford University Press 1999；上海外语教育出版社,2002

J. Arnold. Affect in Language Learning. Cambridge University Press, 1999；外语教学与研究出版社,2000（程晓堂　导读）

We scarcely ask *How light is the bag*?
We use *How heavy...* instead.
We scarcely ask *How short is the boy*?
We use *How tall...* instead.
We scarcely ask *How young are you*?
We use *How old...* instead.

Chapter 14

Universals and Diversities

Human intelligence has been highlighted by two fields of activities — science and arts. Both science and arts help people to get closer to the world. Is linguistics a science or an art, or both? Recall the Galilean thesis "nature is perfect", and you will see both science and arts share the same foundation — the eternal aesthetic principles of the universe.

Like all other branches of science, linguistics cherishes a desire to explain the perfection of the world. Like her bounty for every branch of arts, the world displays all her beauty to the eyes of linguists.

14.1 Language universals

Arrived!

With a knapsack on his back, a young American trudged along a meandering streamside path in a Brazilian Indian reserve toward a village hidden amidst a series of awe-inspiring waterfalls in the middle of a lush rainforest. There he would live in a hut, neighboring with native residents, talking and dancing together with them. What he planned to do was capture phonological and syntactical features of their language — a tribal tongue with only a few hundred speakers, by transcribing their daily speech in IPA.

"When I put on my climbing boots, nothing can stop me," he talked to a journalist before he set off. "I like to explore the unknown, hear the unheard and see the unseen. I can adapt to and endure almost anything, because I'm simply amazed by the archeological wonders lost in the dark jungle for generations. I like Brazil, where Indian people speak a huge number of tribal tongues from a variety of language families. I don't know what the tribal folks will treat me to when I get there. Last year I ate king parrots in an Australian corroboree…"

This young man is a typologist. His major — typology — is a branch of linguistics which concerns itself with comparing the properties of languages, disregarding their genetic relationships. Most typologists are genuine linguists, who can speak half dozen or more languages fluently.

The investigative approach to language typology was pioneered by the American linguist Joseph Greenberg. Though what typologists seek are features of different languages, their main purpose is to reveal structural similarities among them. They call properties found in the analysis of all languages *universals* (before the emergence of the concept UG). Greenberg himself, for instance, has revealed 45 such universals. There are different types of universals: absolute, relative, implicational and so on. Absolute universals are seemingly always true without exception; relative universals are just tendencies, generally true but with a few exceptions; implicational universals refer to features which are present only if some other feature is present.

An apparent case of absolute universals is that all languages have nouns and verbs, with nouns functioning as subjects and objects of verbs, forming plurals, taking determiners, etc., and verbs expressing tense, aspect and modality, etc.

An important universal syntactic tendency concerns word order. Among subject (S), verb (V), and object (O) there are six possibilities of word order: SOV, SVO, VSO, VOS, OSV, and OVS. Approximately, 44% of languages are SOV (e. g. Japanese; Korean), 33% are SVO (e. g. Chinese; English), 18% are VSO (e. g. Standard Arabic; Irish), and only 5% are VOS (e. g. Malagasy, an African language), or OSV (e. g. Haida, a Northern American Indian language), or OVS (e. g. Päri, a Western Nilotic language). Thus the tendency is that in 95% of all the human languages we know, subjects precede objects.

An example of implicational universals is that if a language has gender categories in the noun, it has gender categories in the pronoun.

An interesting group of non-implicational universals are called markedness universals. By markedness is meant the presence/absence of a particular contrastive feature in a language or languages. For example, singular is unmarked, while plural is marked; present tense is unmarked, while past tense is marked. On the whole, the unmarked form is more general in sense or has a wider distribution and higher frequency than the marked form. Specifically, to the knowledge of typologists, in all languages masculine is less marked than feminine. People will use *man* to refer to any person regardless of gender. They will say "*One man, one vote*", instead of "*One woman, one vote*". In the same way, the adjective *deep* has a wider distribution and is less marked than *shallow*. People all ask "*How deep is the water?*" rather than "*How shallow is the water?*" Another similar case can be shown with *good* and *bad*. All languages accept the use of *good* in "*What is the good of doing it?*" and reject using *bad* to replace *good* in the same question. Markedness is a universal linguistic feature.

Typologists study a wide range of languages as part of their enquiry, and tend to make generalizations that deal with the more observable aspects of structure, such as word order, word classes, and types of sound. In contrast, generativists led by Chomsky argue that the exploration of the universals should go beyond the study of individual languages and into the human mind. They typically rely on in-depth studies of single languages, in particular, English, as a common language of exemplification, and tend to make generalizations about the more abstract, underlying properties of language.

For Greenberg, language universals are a presumption. He believes that it is essential to investigate the range of variation found across languages and the limits placed on the variations if we want to reveal language universals. Therefore, he holds that it would be a serious methodological error to base our study on a single language.

For Chomsky, language universals are a premise. He responds that since language is species-specific, the universality of language can be studied by looking closely at one's mother tongue.

Greenberg's criticism against Chomsky: There are certain language universals that simply cannot be predicted by scrutinizing an individual language. In English, for example, the determiner precedes its noun (*that book*), but in Malay determiners follow their nouns (*surat itu*).

Chomskyan criticism against Greenberg: Many languages have become extinct without ever having been recorded, and many languages will arise in the future. These two sets of languages are unavailable to us, and therefore a large number of languages are not amenable to investigation.

A Joke:

A typologist met a generativist in a conference. The typologist described his adventure in the Pamirs.

"Why did you trek all the way down there?" asked the generativist.

"To investigate a rare language," answered the typologist.

"What have you found?"

"A spectrum of new features. But none of them violate Greenberg's universals."

"How can that be?"

"I don't know at the moment. That'll be my further research."

"Let me tell you. Those universals are genetic endowments for human beings. You do not need to search over the roof of the world, but just probe your own mind, in an armchair under the roof of your house like Noam Chomsky and me."

14.2 Language diversities

At first sight, typologist and generativist studies seem to be conflicting. Yet, in practice, the two approaches proceed in parallel. Greenberg's effort is inductive; Chomsky's effort is deductive. Their achievements are mutually compensatory.

However, they have a common opponent, namely, linguistic relativism.

How does a language depict a vast crowd of people in a square? A Chinese metaphoric idiom is 人山人海, while a British English metaphoric expression is a *sea of people*. It seems that Chinese people are more impressed by the expanse of both mountains and the sea than British islanders, who attach magnificence to the sea solely. What does the difference imply? That is a common assumption — language reflects culture.

Can culture be determined by language? Let's think it over. Western alphabetic words, unlike Chinese words, generally lack implicative information for their definitions. For example, the definition of the word *create* can be found in a dictionary as *to make something exist that did not exist before*. The pronunciation of the word provides no hint for this definition. But for Chinese people, its equivalent 创新 leaks much literal information for its understanding. Therefore, Western people attach more importance to definition. Then it is easy to understand such phenomena as western feminists appealing to "*redefining ourselves and saying who we are*". By contrast, Chinese feminists may ignore this "roundabout" strategy and proceed straight to struggle to safeguard all women's rights, because *definition* is a vague word to Chinese ears. What does this phenomenon imply? Isn't it that language conditions culture? If you think so, you are a supporter of the Whorfian hypothesis.

Like typologists, Benjamin Lee Whorf (1897 — 1941) also had an interest in studying rare languages, but he never went to tropical rain forests or any other remote corners of the earth. Instead, he made friends with an Indian living in New York City, whose native language was Hopi, a tribal tongue spoken in Arizona. In their daily communication, Whorf elicited data on that language and then analyzed them systematically.

Whorf's work was concentrated on the interrelationship between the language and worldview of this non-Western speech group, and its comparison with the "Standard Average European" (SAE) worldview and linguistic categories.

For example, a Hopi cannot say *they stayed ten days* because *ten days* is not viewed as a collection like *ten men* but as successive appearances of the same day. Similar to *ten steps forward*, or *ten strokes on a bell*, *ten days* is cyclical, expressed by an adverb rather than a countable noun in Hopi. The Hopi sentence with this adverb can be translated literally as *they left after the tenth day*. But SAE predisposes the speakers to place *ten days* in an imaginary objective group in their mind.

Therefore, Whorf concluded that the worldview of a culture is subtly conditioned by the structure of its language. He said, "Formulation of ideas is not an independent process, strictly rational in the old sense, but is part of a particular grammar and differs, from slightly to greatly, among different grammars. We dissect nature along lines laid down by our native languages." His idea is referred to as linguistic relativism.

Phenomena in languages other than English seemingly imply the same conclusion as well. For instance, the SAE tense system is single-focused, with the speaker on an unmarked point, the present, which extends indefinitely into the past and future, both marked. The Chinese tense system, however, is multi-focused. Please compare the following sentences.

（14.1）昨天你上街,忘记带钥匙。

（14.2）今天你上街,又忘记带钥匙。

（14.3）明天你上街,别再忘记带钥匙。

In (14.1), the reference point is yesterday; in (14.2), it alters to today; in (14.3), tomorrow. These three sentences can be spoken successively in an utterance, which is temporarily multi-focused. Since the reference point has been changed, there is no need for tense marks. Interestingly, the Chinese culture is also multi-focused. For example, 不打不成器 is a typical Chinese philosophy, in which 打 relates to the present cruelty while 成器 refers to the future focus. It has an English equivalent *spare the rod and spoil the child*, in which both *spare* and *spoil* refer to the present focus. Besides, Chinese artists can paint the scenery along a whole river in a long scroll, by constantly changing visual focuses. Classical Western art lacks such horizontal magnificence because almost all their masters stick to a single perspective (except some ancient works like the Bayeux Tapestry).

However, we have no persuasive evidence yet to show that such subtle diversities can be attributed to the conditioning of a language. Perhaps it is still language that reflects the distinctiveness of the culture. The Whorf Hypothesis remains difficult to test. Perhaps culture and language are not in any true sense causally related, nor does language determine thought and behavior patterns in the least.

The concept of language universals arose from the debate concerning the Whorfian hypothesis, which focused on language diversities. Half a century since then has witnessed the rapid advance of the study of language universals. Nevertheless, language diversities still call for further exploration and explanation. When you notice diversities you will find how flexible and splendid the linguistic world is. One example is native speakers' love of nuance, rhythm, word-play and innovation which lead to the persistent rule-breaking in some elements of slang grammar. Some phrases simply *sound* better when the grammar sounds wrong. "*That ain't got nothing to do with it*" is much more preferred than the Standard English "*That has nothing to do with it*" for street-goers.

Much awaits our study if we hope to reveal the essence of language from all perspectives.

14.3 Implications in Translation

Languages are different from each other partly because they bear different cultural imprints. People of some ancient Western nations, for instance, believed that it was dangerous to speak the name of the devil because he might hear that and emerge to curse the speaker. So in today's English there is a proverb with the Latin origin "Speak of the devil and he appears", in which the devil no longer refers to a terrible spirit but an ordinary person who has just been mentioned. It will be associated with embarrassment or nice surprise that a guy being mentioned turns up unexpectedly.

However, there is no reason that all the cultures will compare this guy to a devil. In French a similar proverb goes "Talk of the wolf and you see his tail." "Devil" and "wolf" with the same role alternatively appear in various Western cultures. Interestingly, a well-known Chinese equivalent to them is neither a fiend nor a beast but a warlord named 曹操, in the proverb "说曹操,曹操到".

Language diversities make translation a popular profession, in which all kinds of research fruits in different branches of linguistics will find application.

Morphologically, most words in one language can be translated with an equivalent in another language. For example, *water* in English can be translated as 水 in Chinese. Sometimes the equivalence is conditioned, such as the Chinese noun 山, which equals the word *hill* in English if the height is quite limited, or *mountain* if the height is great, and the English verb *ride*, which matches 骑 in Chinese when its object is a horse or a bicycle, or 乘 when its object is a bus or an airplane. Such equivalence and matching can be understood in the light of Sausurean arbitrariness.

If lexical translation only involves Sausurean arbitrariness, then this admirable job will soon be grabbed by robots. But, human translators are fortunately more knowledgeable about those cultural factors involved in this trade, so they will not be replaced by robots in the foreseeable future.

Human translators know 毛笔 is *writing brush*, *moonlighting* is 兼职 or 炒更, and *once in a blue moon* can be 千载难逢. They also know 犯红眼病 is *be green-eyed*, 早睡早起 can be *keep early hours*, and 热锅上的蚂蚁 should be *a cat on hot bricks*. If all these knacks are programmed into an electronic brain, human intelligence still outshines robots in stylistic harmonization. Specifically, it is up to man to decide whether *romantic* is translated as 浪漫 or 罗曼蒂克 in a particular text. Similarly, a human translator would be more effective in choosing between 雷达屏幕 and 公众视野 as a proper equivalent to *radar screen* in light of the topic of the passage he has perceived.

Syntactically, a translator should be sensitive to structural covertness and other typological features. Let's examine the following examples:

(14.4) *I was, and remain, grateful for the part he played in my release.*
我的获释是他成全的,对此我过去很感激,现在仍然是感激。

In English, tense is overtly marked by the inflection of the verb; in Chinese, tense has to be manifested by adding adverbs.

(14.5) 我的言辞,竟至于读熟了一般,能够滔滔背诵。(by Lu Xun)
She could recite all that I said nonstop, as if she had learnt it by heart.

The Chinese original of (14.5) is a typical sentence with null subject and null object in it. Since neither the subject nor the object can be covert in an English sentence, they have to be recovered as each underlined addition shows.

（14.6）这几个学生他最聪明。

Among these students, he is the cleverest.

A syntactic principle called Case Filter tells us that in any language an (overtly realized) NP argument should be case marked, or be associated with a case position. In English, the case assigners such as verb and preposition cannot be omitted so that the case positions can be overt. Nevertheless, case positions in Chinese can be covert, with case assigners being dropped. That's why in the English version of （14.6）, the translator adds the underlined words so as to recover the case assigners.

Semantically, a good translator should consider how to handle each of the propositions in the original. In （14.7）, all the propositions of the original remain in its translation through rearranging the word order and adjusting the use of functional words (underlined), whereas in （14.8）, the underlined proposition in the English original has been ignored in a pithier Chinese version, and in （14.9）some covert propositions in the English original are recovered to make the Chinese version more vivid.

（14.7）*A few of the pictures are worth mentioning both for their technical excellence and interesting content.*

有些照片技术高超,内容有趣,值得一提。

（14.8）*And he took the cloak and the amber chain from the closet where they lay, and showed them to her.*

他从柜子里拿出斗篷和琥珀项链来,给她看。

（14.9）*I was extremely worried about her. But this was neither the place nor the time for a lecture or an argument.*

我真替他万分担忧,但此时此地,即不宜教训他一番,也不宜与他争论一通。

Pragmatically, a good translation should be appropriate for the given context and reflect the original intension. A dramatic example is the translation of conversation routines. The host of a Chinese family banquet likes to express welcome to his guests by saying 没有什么好菜,别见笑. It would lead to great confusion if his words were translated as *I haven't got any nice dishes, but don't laugh at me, please.* A proper, pragmatic translation is *Help yourself*, a usual English expression in the situation with the same illocutionary force.

Sociolinguistically, sometimes a good translation should reproduce the register features of the original effectively (as in (14.10)) and sometimes a good translation should not sound like a translation (as in (14.11)).

(14.10) *We are very sorry to disappoint you, but hope you will understand that stock offers are a touch-and-go kind of things.*

令贵方失望,实感抱歉。现货销售情势难测,若得买主则即脱手,尚祈理解。

(14.11) *And the marvelous rose became crimson, like the rose of the eastern sky.*

这朵奇异的蔷薇变成了深红色,就像东方天空的朝霞。(translated by Ba Jin)

Psycholinguistically, translators need not rack his brains about such aspects as I-meaning, which are linguistically universal and in no need of special rendering. Let's consider the Chinese translation of Chomsky's example (7.16) (repeated as below).

(14.12) *The book that he is planning will weigh at least five pounds if he ever writes it.*

他筹划的那本书,要是写好的话,至少会有五磅重。

Both the original and the translation reflect the material and abstract components of the concept *book/*书 simultaneously.

If there are no similarities between languages, how can speakers of different tongues express the same meaning? If there are no diversities between languages, how can the same meaning "enjoy" the immense variety of structural or pragmatic splendors in different versions?

Translation study is a branch of applied linguistics, and it is linguistics that lays a solid foundation for successful translators, whose brilliance is none other than seeking a best balance between language universals and diversities.

EXERCISES

I. Translate the following statements into Chinese.

Typology is the study of language universals by the empirical method of induction from a sample of diverse languages.

Anthropological linguistics is a branch of linguistics which studies the relationship between language and culture in a community, e. g. its traditions, beliefs, and family structure.

II. Fill in the blanks with the linguistic terms you have learned.

1) The concept of language universals arose in the debate about the Whorfian hypothesis which focused on language _____.

2) Language universals can be classified into absolute universals and relative universals; the latter exists as _____ possibly with exceptions.

3) Greenberg found that if the basic order of a language is VSO, it must have a preposition. He cited it as an example of _____ universals.

4) The distinction between "marked" and "unmarked" parameters seems to be a universal across all languages. In general, the _____ form is more general in sense or has a wider distribution than the other.

5) Linguistic _____ hypothesis holds that the worldview of a culture is subtly conditioned by the structure of its language.

III. Discuss the similarities and differences between English and Chinese based on your practice of translating the following paragraphs.

1) 我家门前有些摆摊儿的,都是生意人。大凡生意人都懂得"一步差三市"这个道理。就是说,别看你的店只和人家差了三步,但景气的程度要差了很多,也许人家的铺子红火热闹,你的铺子却开不了张。

2) *What the New Yorker would find missing is what many outsiders find oppressive and distasteful about New York — its rawness, tension, urgency; its bracing competitiveness; the rigor of its judgments; and the congested, democratic presence of so many other New Yorkers encased in their own world.*

IV. Give a summary of less than 150 words to Section 14.2.

V. Challenging work.

1) Language universal is a language pattern or phenomenon which occurs in all known languages. For example, it has been suggested that there is a high probability that the word referring to female parent will start with a nasal consonant, e. g. /m/ in English *mother*, in German *Mutter*, in Swahili *mama*, in Chinese *muqin* or *mama*,

Could you list other examples?

2) Linguistic relativism is a hypothesis that states that the worldview of a culture is conditioned by the structure of its language. Do you agree to it? Cite some examples to support your viewpoints.

■■

JH Greenberg (1915—2001)

Joseph Harold Greenberg's study of both the structure of language and the similarities between different languages gained him worldwide recognition. In the first part of his career, Greenberg focused on understanding how languages are organized, doing pioneering work in the field of typology. In the 1960s, he established certain universal principles of language structure that excited the entire world.

Greenberg was born in Brooklyn, into a German-speaking Polish family. He was a gifted boy who considered becoming a classical pianist. According to his wife, he played a concert at Carnegie Hall's annex when he was only 15 years old.

Greenberg did his PhD in anthropology at Northwestern University under the Africanist Melville Herskovits, and he served in the US Army Signal Corps in WWII, decoding Italian armed forces communications. This may have inspired him too, for after the war he moved into linguistics. He was in the Anthropology

Department at Columbia for many years, then moved to Stanford. He garnered many awards and was one of the few linguists granted membership in the National Academy of Sciences.

Greenberg cataloged similarities and differences in tongues on other continents, investigating whether, as he suspected, all languages might be descendents of a mother tongue spoken tens of thousands of years ago. In some ways it was like reverse-engineering the Genesis story of the Tower of Babel. It is a moving story, which answers a basic human question about the world: why should there be different languages? It also helps explain why Greenberg's project should seem so audacious and important, and so impossible.

Greenberg's method was to compare languages multilaterally — painstaking comparisons based on phonology, the way words sound; semantics, what words mean; grammar, the way words are put together to form meaningful messages; all in the light of information extrinsic to language — archaeology, genetics, and history. His most important tool was a list of 300 words which he felt constituted a sort of core to any language. This included words like pronouns, nouns for body parts, family members, and the like. The theory is that such words are less prone to change than others. Since they change less often, they are a good way to tell whether languages are related.

In 1966 he published *Some Universals of Grammar with Particular Reference to the Order of Meaningful Elements*. In this article he offered 45 universals of word order and inflectional categories based on data from some 30 languages. He was among the first to deal with "implicational" universals (of the form "If A, then B"). He also edited *Universals of Language* (1963) and the four-volume *Universals of Human Language* (1978).

Greenberg dreamed of deep unity, and he spent an extremely long career pursuing evidence for it. Always a hard worker and prodigious publisher, his ambition seemed only to grow after retirement. He was still publishing highly technical evidence when he died, at age 85. On his deathbed he told a colleague that his biggest regret was that he had never gotten around to studying the languages of Southeast Asia.

Reading recommendation

Beginner-friendly：

J. Aitchison. Language Change：Progress or Decay? Cambridge University Press, 1981, 1991, 2001 (1991 年出的第 2 版已由徐家桢译成中文，简·爱切生本人写了中文版序。中文书名为：语言的变化. 进步还是退化? 语文出版社，1997)

More challenging：

W. Croft. Typology and Universals. Cambridge University Press, 1990；外语教学与研究出版社,2000（沈家煊 导读）

E. Sapir. Language. An Introduction to the Study of Speech. 外语教学与研究出版社,2001（杨信彰 导读）

王逢鑫. 英汉比较语义学. 外文出版社,2001

潘文国. 汉英语对比纲要. 北京语言大学出版社,1997

English has a few rivals, but no equals. Neither Spanish nor Arabic, both international languages, has this global sway.

———— Robert Mccrum et al

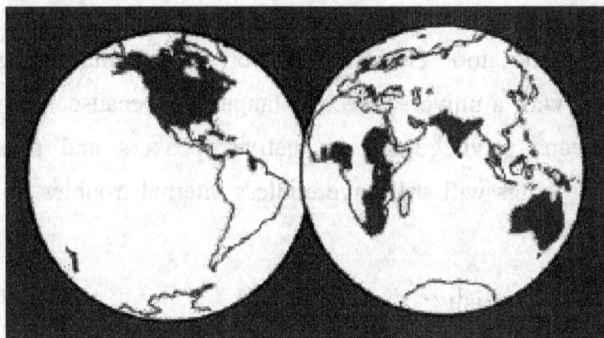

The English-speaking world（as first language or official language）

Chapter 15

Global Language

15. 1 Rebuilding the Babel

Since all the human languages share a species-specific mental foundation, people of the world have never given up their desire to rebuild the Tower of Babel, that is, to establish a global language.

God has been constantly happy since the Babel collapsed. People of the world have never united as one because they lack a common language. However, this situation is changing nowadays. More and more people from all corners of the world share a common language — English.

But God remains carefree. The luckiest future for English is to become a universal second language. It will never replace the first language of all its non-native speakers. And the attitude for people to accept it as a global language is uncertain. Widdowson says, "Control of language is, to a considerable degree, control of power." To give up one's first language means to give up one's own power. Besides, even the sense of pride and identity will leave everyone clinging to their own mother tongue, too. God will not worry that human beings will challenge his Almighty status with a universal second language, because such a global tool of communication means privilege for its native speakers and thus leads to new inequality. Human beings will still have endless internal troubles to handle.

15.2 Why is it English?

Why is it English that becomes the second language of more and more people? Is English entitled to become a global second language?

Afrikaans, a language derived from 17th century Dutch settlers, is a lingua franka in South Africa. Black people there disgust this language because of its association with bloody colonialism. They prefer learning and using English as an alternative to Afrikaans, a means of self-determination, and a window on to the free world. In the 1980s, English was more than ever discouraged by the white rulers, but cherished by the oppressed Black majority, and the struggle against racism involved a trial of strength between two languages, Afrikaans and English. More and more Blacks are choosing to write in English as a way of reaching an international audience. Nowadays, when we hear their heroic leader Nelson Mandela, the first South African president after racial discrimination was banned, speak to the world calling for a movement to *make poverty history*, we do feel the power of an international language — the inspiring and shocking power of democracy invoked by this eloquent English speaker.

English indeed possesses many characteristics that are favored by L2 learners. As the great 19th century American writer Ralph W. Emerson observed, English "is the sea which receives tributaries from every region under heaven." Of all the world's languages, it is arguably the richest in vocabulary, and relatively simple in grammatical structures; scattered across every continent, about one-tenth of the world's population uses English as a mother tongue.

English is a continuum of speech, encompassing such varieties as are found in the United Kingdom and Ireland, in North America, in Australia, in the Caribbean, in India, and in Africa, as well as in the mouths of sailors, cowboys, preachers, doctors, salesmen, pop singers, DJs, etc.

The Indian scholar Braj Kachru describes English as existing in three concentric circles: the inner circle of the predominantly English-speaking countries, the outer circle of the former colonies where English is an official language, and the expanding circle where, although English is neither an official nor a former colonial language, it is increasingly part of many people's daily lives.

On the other hand, teaching English as a foreign language (TEFL) has created a flourishing industry for English-speaking countries and encourages the study of the principles and methodology in foreign language teaching and learning, which has developed into an independent discipline named *applied linguistics* (as the micro view).

15.3 Teaching English as a foreign language

Teaching a foreign language is an intricate art. The global spread of English has generated intense interest in how to teach the language and whether it is possible to improve the results of its teaching, making it the most active area of applied linguistic enquiry.

If we examine TEFL from centuries ago until now, we see that it has progressed through four stages.

Stage one: the grammar-translation method: The traditional academic style of teaching which places heavy emphasis on grammatical rules explained in the students' own language and uses translation as the main form of exercises and testing. Consequently, it trains minds in logical thought, develops elegant expression, but meanwhile decontextualizes vocabulary owing to rote learning. It was welcomed in old style schools where learning a foreign language was regarded as a step toward cultural refinement and higher status, rather than its actual use. There is no emphasis on the development of fluent speech. As the British applied linguist

Guy Cook (2003) criticized, it aims at getting things right slowly rather than saying them fast and effectively, but incorrectly. Even today some teachers would rather limit their students' oral and writing performance than allow them to perform "in a wrong way". Eventually, such a method will make learners become a storehouse of accurate rules as well as deaf-mutes.

Stage two: the direct method: In contrast, this method encourages fast and effective learning with more tolerance for errors in performance. Its emergence about one hundred years ago was a response to the challenge of new types of students — soldiers from two world wars, immigrants, business people, and tourists, whose sole purpose was to use the language immediately after they had learned it. During the learning program the students' own languages were banished and everything should be done through the language under instruction. With more and more audio-visual equipment available, this method has evolved into an audio-lingual style that is concerned with the real-life activities the students are going to face.

Stage three: the natural approach: Influenced by Krashen's input hypothesis, this style was popular in the 1970s and 1980s. As a typical example of theory-guided practice, teachers then believed that an adult L2 learner could repeat the children's route to L1 proficiency, i.e. learning would take place without explanation or grading, and without correction of errors, but simply by exposure to "meaningful input". This means that attention to meaning would somehow trigger the natural cognitive development of the L2 system — students would work out grammar rules from listening and reading without explicit instruction. After Swain put forward her output hypothesis in 1985, this theoretically seductive method has been fatally challenged and has gradually lost its sacred aura and momentum.

Stage four: the communicative approach: As old as the natural approach, it has greater vitality. Its proposition has shifted the goal of foreign language teaching from the mastery of grammar rules to the ability to do things with the language appropriately, fluently, and effectively. Students are encouraged to apply the language first, and then learn the forms which would fulfill their needs in communication.

As a matter of fact, learning, after all, is the learner's business. Learners should have more control over what and how they learn and take more responsibility for their own learning. The teacher should play the role of a helper, an adviser, and more essentially, a task-organizer. He should be good at designing open-ended learning tasks and encouraging learners to participate in these potential-tapping activities. If students are fully mobilized, they will voluntarily use what they have learned to achieve specific goals and learn more during their participation. For example, if a college teacher encourages his students to make a survey of one problem they have noticed on campus and then write a report in their L2, similar in style to a magazine feature introduced earlier, and then present their works orally in a "conference" held by their class, the assignment will quicken the internalization of the students' L2 knowledge and contextualize all the vocabulary and structures used during the process. The guiding principles of the task are the recent developments of the communicative approach, namely the learner-centered method and task-based instruction.

15. 4 Globalized uncertainties

On the other hand, will globalization bring English everlasting dominance? Dr Robert Burchfield, former Chief Editor of *Oxford English Dictionaries*, once said, "English, as the second language of many speakers in countries throughout the world, is no more likely to survive the inevitable political changes of the future than did Latin, once the second language of the government classes or regions within the Roman Empire."

Why should that be so? Some researchers have arrived at their answers. These scholars call themselves critical applied linguists, whose viewpoints fall into at least three aspects.

1) Every individual language is deeply rooted in a specific culture. The globalization of any language will inevitably incur cultural conflicts. Germany, France, and almost all other western non-English-speaking countries are striving to safeguard the purity of their own languages, especially against the invasion of the English vocabulary into their media and popular culture. Developing countries, on the other

hand, see English popularization as a necessary step toward the world market, naively accepting the following as the key tenets of their L2 education.

— English is best taught monolingually.

— The ideal teacher of English is a native speaker.

— The earlier English is taught, the better the results.

— The more English is taught, the better the results.

— If other languages are used much, standards of English will drop.

The Danish linguist Robert Phillipson raises a cry of warning by redesignating these five tenets as five fallacies, namely, the monolingual fallacy, the native speaker fallacy, the early start fallacy, the maximum exposure fallacy, and the subtractive fallacy. They are fallacies because they artificially obstruct the natural growth of children's mother tongue, especially when the cultural universe expressed through English differs radically from that of the learners' first language. Consequently, this mismatch between the language of experience and the foreign medium of schooling imposes "cultural perception blindspots". Such fallacies, pointed out by Philipson, root back to colonial tradition.

2) Global English is none other than global business seeking world fortune and world monopoly. The exciting experience of struggling against a racist government through popularizing English as a weapon in South Africa does not always exist. Teaching English as a foreign language is normally a commercial operation. For John Hanson, former director-general of the British Council, the spread of English is the result of "countless millions of acts of choice, by students, teachers, employers and the employed who have no interest in the health, future, spread, or whatever of the English language. What 'drives' them is a view of their job prospects, their relationship with the rest of the world, their excitement in youth culture, a wish to be insiders, to be in touch." With such "ideal teachers", policy makers hope English serves people around the world as a "medium of communication about what will matter to most of us in what we hope will be the One World of Tomorrow", as well as leaving other languages as static markers of the speaker's identity. In other words, a universal second language is used by people of different places of the world "for informative communication across their own frontiers about issues of common interest

to themselves and others", while one's first language will be "a home tongue for love-making, religion, verse-craft, back chat and inexact topics in general" (Hogben, 1963). It seems a global language will not be effectively established with such an inconsiderate policy for the non-English speaking world.

3) Globalization will lead to global variation. According to Schumann, an American linguist, L2 acquisition resembles the process of pidginization. Pidgin is an auxiliary language that has been formed to provide a means of communication between people who have no common language. It has no native speakers. Such a spontaneously developed language variety is rule-governed anyway, though it usually gets rid of the difficult or unusual parts of a language; for example, the omission of verbs and the dropping of present-tense inflections.

(15.1) *You out the game.*

(15.2) *He fast in everything he do.*

On the other hand, pidgin also has useful refinements that a standard language lacks, for instance, the use of *be* to signify a stable condition in a sentence like in (15.3) and (15.5).

(15.3) *Some of them be big.*

(15.4) *He working.* (He is busy right now)

(15.5) *He be working.* (He has a steady job)

In the ex-colonies of Britain, English develops respectively. Today we can find a vast variety of Englishes beyond the British Isles — American English, Canadian English, Australian English, New Zealand English, Jamaican English, Indian English, Singaporean English, and so forth. Syntactically, some varieties move closer to Pidgin rules. Take, for example, the earliest colonial English — Irish English, in which the following sentence patterns are often used.

(15.6) *I do be living in Dublin* (= "I'm currently living in Dublin")

(15.7) *I'm after doing that* (= "I've just done that")

(15.8) *He is after writing* (= "He has just written it")

This phenomenon is pidginization. One of the most pidginized varieties — Caribbean English, turns out to be totally impossible to comprehend, with its English phonological and morphological systems drastically changed.

When English as a universal second language merges with the local cultural setting, who can guarantee that new varieties will not spring up and gradually detract from each other? Who can guarantee that a new standard international English will not be emerging somewhere, with its own rules and regularities, different from those of any of the "native Englishes"? Who can guarantee that English as a standardized global language will not be drowned in the sea of pidginization?

What kind of global language do we really need? What should we do for the co-existence of this universal L2 and our own L1? How will a global language be properly established? All these questions call for careful consideration.

Epilogue

Your conducted tour around the main gardens of the "Disneyland" — LINGUISTICS now approaches the destination. As your sincere friend and guide, we hope this book has satisfied your curiosity to see how language is studied and aroused your passion in delving into this wonderful field.

Thank you for your time and appreciation. You are welcome to come back and have a more in-depth visit next time, or, if you wish, to join the gardening team here someday, so as to add more splendors to our fields and harvest success through your own career.

EXERCISES

I. Translate the following statements into Chinese.

Applied linguistics is the study of foreign language learning and teaching in its narrow sense as well as the application of the methods and results of linguistic research to all kinds of practical areas in its broad sense.

Critical applied linguistics (CALx) is an emerging interdisciplinary approach to English applied linguistics. One of the central concerns in this approach is exposing the power dynamics of mainstream applied linguistics.

II. Fill in the blanks with the linguistic terms you have learned.

1) Applied linguistics should not merely be to transmit findings from linguistics to those involved with language related problems. It should rather be to _____ between linguistic theory and professional practice, making each relevant to the other.

2) The study of foreign language learning and teaching can be understood as the _____ view of applied linguistics.

3) _____ is a speech-system that has been formed to provide a means of communication between people who have no common language. It has no native speakers.

4) Grammar-translation method was the traditional way Latin and Greek were taught in Europe. A typical lesson consists of the presentation of a grammatical rule, a study of lists of vocabulary, and a translation exercise. It emphasizes reading rather than the ability to _____ in the target language.

5) Communicative approach emphasizes the process of communication, such as using language appropriately in different types of situations; using language to perform different kinds of tasks, e. g. to solve puzzles, to get information, etc. ; using language for social interaction with other people. It aims at developing learners' communicative _____ .

III. Give your own analysis to the background facts below.

Background one: The statistics of English are astonishing. Of all the world's languages, it is arguably the richest in vocabulary. The Oxford English Dictionary lists about 5,000,000 words; and a further half-million remain uncatalogued, which are mainly technical and scientific terms, as well as variants and obsolete words. According to traditional estimates, neighboring German has a vocabulary of about 185,000 words and French fewer than 100,000.

1) Please try to explain this amazing phenomenon with the knowledge you have hunted from this book or other readings.

2) Is the largest vocabulary a prerequisite for a language to be a global one?

3) Analyze the advantages and disadvantages of the huge English vocabulary.

Background two: Among the half a million to one million English words, only 3,000 are most frequently used (frequency rate: 95%+).

4) Please explain the striking contrast between words available and words actually used.

5) Clip an article from any English newspaper and try to identify the words which do not seem to belong to the most frequently used ones. Discuss why these words are used in the article. Can they be replaced by words or phrases that are used more often?

6) If you are learning another foreign language, try to recall how many words you have encountered that are similar to English words in spelling. Are they frequently used in that language? Discuss your discovery.

IV. Give a summary of less than 150 words to Section 15.3.

V. Challenging work.

You are among the numerous English learners in China. Have you ever thought about the following topics?

1) Why are you learning English?

2) Do you view English as a course or as an essential prerequisite for a successful career?

3) Do you sometimes worry the English you speak will become a mark of non-native-ness?

4) If you only know about grammar and words, you are deaf-mutes. If you are only good at listening and speaking, you are illiterates. If you speak and write with a hybrid register, or rather, without knowing how to use your second language appropriately in different types of situations, you will run the risk of unknowingly becoming somebody's laughingstock, let alone becoming a flexible diglossia. Isn't that the case?

5) These perceptions are why some people arrive at the conclusion that language is power. A powerful second language learner should acquire a powerful second language. Do you think so?

6) Then, you hope your child will fulfill your dream. You plan to send your son or daughter to the "immersion program" of a private school where every course is taught in Queen's English. But, remember Phillipson's warning: it will artificially obstruct the natural growth of children's mother tongue. Then what will you do?

7) Perhaps a competent second language learner should at first be an excellent first language user. Do you agree?

8) Perhaps a lasting global second language will turn out to be a blessing for speakers of all languages rather than a curse for some of them. Then how can that be attained?

Write an essay on your own contemplation.

■■

H. Widdowson

Henry. G. Widdowson is renowned in the fields of applied linguistics and language teaching, esp. one of the pioneers of the Communicative Approach to language teaching, and is the author of numerous books and articles, many of which are on other (though related) subjects such as discourse analysis and critical discourse analysis, the global spread of English, English for Special Purposes and stylistics. The Routledge Encyclopedia of Language Teaching and Learning calls him "probably the most influential philosopher of the late twentieth century for international ESOL".

Widdowson obtained his first degree at King's College of Cambridge University, and spent eight years working with the British Council in Indonesia, Sri Lanka and Bangladesh. In 1968, he became a lecturer at the University of Edinburgh and got his PhD there in 1972. In 1977 he was appointed to the chair of English for Speakers of Other Languages at the Institute of Education, University of London, and from 1993—1998 was also concurrently Professor of Applied Linguistics at the

University of Essex. In 1998 he was appointed Professor of English Linguistics at the University of Vienna. He retired from teaching in 2001 and is now Professor Emeritus, University of London, and Honorary Professor, University of Vienna. He is a prolific author of works on stylistics, language and language teaching spanning almost four decades. He is the editor of two series of works for Oxford University Press: *Oxford Introductions to Language Study* and, in conjunction with Chris Candlin: *Language Teaching: A Scheme for Teacher Education*. His books include: *Teaching Language as Communication* (1978); two volumes of *Explorations in Applied Linguistics* (1979, 1984); *Aspects of Language Teaching* (1990); *Practical Stylistics: An Approach to Poetry* (1992); *Linguistics* (1996) and *Defining Issues in English Language Teaching* (2003).

His most recent book is entitled *Text, Context, Pretex: Critical Issues in Discourse Analysis* (2004), published by Blackwell's.

==

Reading recommendation

Beginner-friendly:

D. Crystal. English as a Global Language. Cambridge University Press, 1997; 外语教学与研究出版社, 2001 (王逢鑫 导读)

P. Trudgill & J. Hannah. International English. 3rd edition. Edward Arnold (Publishers) Limited, 1994; 外语教学与研究出版社, 2000 (秦秀白 导读)

G. Cook. Applied Linguistics. Oxford University Press, 2003

More challenging:

Robert Phillipson. Linguistic Imperialism. Oxford University Press, 1992; 上海外语教育出版社, 2000

V. Cook. Second Language Learning and Language Teaching. 2nd edition. Edward Arnold (Publishers) Limited, 1996; 外语教学与研究出版社, 2000 (高远 导读)

Glossary

A

accusative：（宾格）The case showing that a word is the direct object of a verb.

affix：（词缀）A bound morpheme that changes the meaning or syntactic function of the words to which it attaches. Prefixes, infixes and suffixes are the three types of affixes.

agglutinating language：（粘着语）A language in which various affixes may be added to the stem of a word to add to its meaning or to show its grammatical function (e. g. , in Swahili the word *tulimpenda* (meaning "we love him") consists of *tu-* = "we", *li-* = "past", *m-* = "him", *-pend* = "love", *-a* = verbal suffix).

allophone：（音位变体）One of a set of nondistinctive realizations of the same phoneme. For example, Spanish /b/ appears as /b/ when adjacent to a consonant or word-initially, but as [β] when between vowels. So [b] and [β] are allophones of the phoneme /b/. Allophones are designated with ordinary phonetic brackets ([ ]), rather than slant brackets (/ /).

alveolar ridge：（齿龈脊）The ridge just behind the upper front teeth.

analytic language：（分析语）Another term for **isolating language**.

anthropological linguistics：（人类语言学）*See Ex I, Chapter 14 for definition.*

aphasia：（失语症）Inability to perceive, process, or produce language because of physical damage to the brain.

applied linguistics：（应用语言学）*See Ex I, Chapter 15 for definition.*

argument：（论元,主目语）A term used by linguists to describe the role played by particular entities in the semantic structure of sentences. Verbs require 0 to several arguments. It is the number and nature of the arguments they require that distinguish them grammatically. For example, the verb *give* requires three arguments. In the sentence, *He gave me a ticket yesterday*, *He*, *me*, and *a ticket* are the three arguments, but *yesterday* is an optional element which is not part of the sentence's argument structure. Information about the arguments required by verbs is contained in our mental lexicon and plays a vital part in the construction of well-formed sentences.

aspiration：（送气音）A puff of air that follows the release of a consonant when there is a delay in the onset of voicing. It is symbolized by a superscript h (e. g., $[p^h]$).

B

babbling：（咿呀学语）Speech-like sounds produced by very young children.

bootstrapping：（自启）To promote and develop by use of one's own initiative and work without reliance on outside help. In language acquisition, it denotes a baby's spontaneous acquisition of the meaning and structure of adults' simple utterances.

bound morpheme：（粘着词素）Morpheme that always attaches to other morphemes, never existing as a word itself.

Broca's area：（布罗卡区）The region of the brain located at the base of the motor cortex in the left hemisphere that controls the production of spoken language.

C

case：（格）Grammatical category that shows the function of the noun or noun phrase in a sentence. Common cases in different languages include nominative, genitive, dative, and accusative.

collocation：（搭配）The way in which words are used together regularly.

comment：（述题）Part of a sentence that says something further about the topic of the sentence.

communicative approach：（交际法）An approach to foreign or second language teaching which views the ability to communicate successfully as both the means and the end of language learning.

complement：（补语）In X-bar theory, a syntactic unit that is defined as the sister to the head of a phrase.

complementary distribution：（互补分布）The occurrence of sounds in language such that they are never found in the same phonetic environment. Sounds that are in complementary distribution are allophones of the same phoneme.

compound：（复合词）A word that is formed by combining two or more words.

connectionism：（连通主义）A theory of cognition which draws inspiration from the way the billions of neurons in the brain are interconnected in complex ways to produce a network of associations. It holds that the complexity of language emerges from associative learning processes being exposed to a massive and complex environment.

connotation：（内涵意义）The additional meanings that a word or phrase has beyond its central meaning. These meanings show people's emotions and attitudes towards what the word or phrase refers to. Some connotations may be shared by a group of people of the same cultural or social background, sex, or age; others may be restricted to one or several individuals and depend on their personal experience.

content word：（实词）Words which refer to a thing, quality, state, or action and which have meaning when the words are used alone. Content words are mainly nouns, verbs, adjectives, and adverbs.

contrastive analysis（CA）：（对比分析）The identification of structural differences between languages, seen as points of potential learning difficulty. Developed and practiced in the 1950s and 1960s, as an application of structural linguistics to language teaching.

conversational implicature：（会话含义）The act of implicating something via the conversational maxims.

conversational maxims：（会话准则）Grice's principles of Quantity, Quality, Relevance, and Manner that govern cooperative talk-exchanges.

cooperative principle：（合作原则）A fundamental principle governing conversational exchanges formulated by the philosopher H. P. Grice that says: Underlying a conversation is the understanding that what one says is intended to contribute to the purposes of the conversation.

coordinate structure：（并列结构）A grammatical structure consisting of two or more units of equal rank joined by a connecting word.

complementizer：（标句词）A particular category of clause—introducing word such as *that/if/for*, as used in sentences such as *I think **that** you should apologize, I doubt **if** she realizes, They're keen **for** you to show up*. In X-bar theory, the position for a complementizer is labeled by COMP or C.

CP（complementizer phrase）：（标句词短语）A phrase/clause headed by a complementizer (or by an auxiliary or verb moved into COMP).

critical applied linguistics：（批判应用语言学）*See Ex I, Chapter 15 for definition.*

critical period hypothesis：（关键期假说）The theory that in child development there is a period during which language can be acquired more easily than at any other time. According to the American neurologist Lenneberg, the critical period lasts until puberty (around age 12 or 13 years).

D

denotation：（指示意义）The core meaning of a lexical item that relates it to phenomena in the real world or in a fictional or possible world. For example, the denotation of the English word "*bird*" is a two-legged, winged, egg-laying, warm-blooded creature with a beak.

derivational morpheme：（派生词素）Morphemes that change the meaning or lexical category of the words to which they attach.

descriptivism：（描写主义）The policy of describing languages as they are bound to exist.

descriptive grammar：（描写语法）A grammar which describes how a language is actually spoken and/or written, and does not state or prescribe how it ought to be spoken or written.

diglossia：（双语体）Situation in which two varieties of a language are used for clearly defined functions. One variety is used for more prestigious functions, as for example in education, politics, and literature；the other is used for less prestigious functions and predominantly for everyday conversation.

direct method：（直接教学法）A language-teaching method with the following features：1) only the target language should be used in class；2) meanings should be communicated "directly" by associating speech forms with actions, objects, mime, gestures and situations; 3) reading and writing should be taught only after speaking; 4) grammar should only be taught inductively.

Discontinuity Hypothesis：(非连续假说) A theory proposed by the linguist Roman Jakobson. The theory claims that in babbling, infants produce a variety of speech sounds. However, as soon as the child produces meaningful speech and starts pairing sounds with meanings, the infant abruptly stops producing all kinds of different sounds.

discourse：(语篇) A continuous stretch of (esp. spoken) language larger than a sentence.

displacement：(时空置换) Ability to communicate about things that are not physically or temporally present.

distinctive feature：(区别性特征) A particular characteristic which distinguishes one distinctive sound unit of a language from another or one group of sounds from another group. For example, in the English sound system, one distinctive feature which distinguishes the /p/ in *pin* from the /b/ in *bin* is VOICE. The /b/ is a voiced stop whereas the /p/ is a voiceless stop.

dualism：(二元论) A philosophical system that recognizes two ultimate and independent principles in the scheme of things, such as mind and matter.

E

empiricism：(经验论) Philisophical and psychological position which holds that the psychological development of humans arise primarily from experience and learning.

endowments：(天赋) The natural quality that a person is made rich of from the birth.

E-language：(外化语言) Also **externalized language**. Language viewed as a set of possible sentences. This concept is still an abstraction, distinct from actual utterances.

epistemology：(认识论) Epistemology is one of the core areas of philosophy. It is concerned with the nature, sources and limits of knowledge.

error analysis (**EA**)：（错误分析）The systematic interpretation of the unacceptable forms used by someone learning a language. It was developed in 1960s based on the assumption that many learner errors were not due to the learner's mother tongue but reflected universal learning strategies.

F

face：（面子）Sociolinguists often discuss politeness phenomena in terms of face. Face is what you lose when you are embarrassed or humiliated in public. We may distinguish your **positive face** (your need to maintain and demonstrate your membership in a social group) from your **negative face** (your need to be individual and independent, to get what you want without offending anyone).

fossilization：（僵化）Incomplete L2 acquisition featured by the fact that progress in a certain aspect of the target language stops and the learner's language becomes fixed at an intermediate state. It can take a number of forms, such as fossilized accent or syntax. Fossilization can be a permanent feature of the learner's language.

free morphemes：（自由词素）Morphemes that can stand alone as a word.

free variation：（自由变异）Term used to refer to two sounds that occur in overlapping environments but cause no distinction in the meaning of their respective words (e.g. the sounds [p] and [pʰ] are in free variation in the two pronunciations [lip] and [lipʰ] of the word *leap*).

function word：（功能词）A word which has no descriptive content and which shows the grammatical relationship in a sentence or between sentences. Conjunctions, propositions, and articles are common function words.

functional categories：（功能范畴）In X-bar theory, a projection of a functional head (e.g. I-bar, IP, C-bar, CP, D-bar, DP, etc.).

functional grammar：（功能语法）*See Ex I, Chapter 8 for definition.*

G

generativist approach：（生成学派）The approach based on the belief that the structural universals of language are intrinsic and that the exploration of the universals should go beyond the study of individual languages and into the human mind.

glottis：（声门）The aperture between the vocal folds.

grammar-translation method：（语法翻译法）A language-teaching method which makes use of translation and grammar study as the main teaching and learning activities, and emphasizes reading rather than the ability to communicate in a language. A typical lesson consists of the presentation of a grammatical rule, a study of lists of vocabulary, and a translation exercise. It was the traditional way Latin and Greek were taught in Europe. In the 19th century it began to be used to teach "modern" languages such as French, German and English, and it is still used in many countries today.

H

head：（中心语）The constituent in a phrase which is chiefly responsible for the nature of that phrase and from which a phrase is named (e. g. in a verb phrase, the head is the verb; in a noun phrase, the head is the noun).

homonyms：（同音同形异义词）Two or more distinct words with the same pronunciation and spelling but different meanings (e. g. *pool table* and *swimming pool*).

homophones：（同音异形异义词）Two or more distinct words with the same pronunciation but different meanings and spellings (e. g. , *two*, *too*, *to*).

I

icon：（图像符号）A sign whose form mirrors its meaning in some respects; e. g. a diagram of an engine is the icon of the real engine.

idiolect：（个人语言）The linguistic system of an individual speaker.

idioms：（习语）An expression which functions as a single unit and whose meaning cannot be worked out from its separate parts.

I-language：（内化语言）Also **internalized language**. Language viewed as a set of rules and principles in the minds of the speakers, i. e. a computational system internalized with the brain.

illocutionary act：（以言行事）What a person is trying to do by speaking.

illocutionary force：（言外之力）The intended effects the utterance or written context has on the listener or reader, such as requests, commands, orders, etc.

I-meaning：（内化意义）The semantic properties of words used to think and talk about the world in terms of the perspectives made available by the resources of the mind.

implicational universals：（蕴涵式语言共性）A type of language universal with the form "if a language has property P, then it must also have property Q". For example, if a language has front rounded vowels, then it also has back rounded vowels.

index：（标示符号）A sign which is closely associated with its signified, often in a causal relationship; e. g. smoke is an index of fire.

infix：（中缀）A type of bound morpheme that is inserted into the root.

inflecting language：（屈折语）Also **fusional language**. A language in which the form of a word changes to show a change in meaning or grammatical function.

inflection：（屈折变化）Modification of a word to express grammatical relationships to other words in the sentence.

inflectional morphemes：（屈折词素）Morphemes that serve a purely grammatical function, never creating a new word but only a different form of the same word.

instrumental motivation：（工具型动机）Wanting to learn a language because it will be useful for certain "instrumental" goals, such as getting a job, reading a foreign newspaper, passing an examination.

integrative motivation：（结合型动机）Wanting to learn a language in order to communicate with people of another culture who speak it.

interlanguage（**IL**）：（语际语、过渡语）The language system produced at an intermediate stage of second-and foreign-language learning, different from both the mother tongue and the target language.

International Phonetic Alphabet（**IPA**）：（国际音标）A system of symbols for representing the pronunciation of words in any language according to the principles of the International Phonetic Association.

IP（**Inflection phrase**）：（屈折词短语）A phrase/clause which is a projection of I. Thus, a sentence such as *It might rain* is an IP—more specifically, a projection of the I constituent *might*.

isolating language：（孤立语）Also **analytic language**. A type of language in which words consist mainly of one morpheme and sentences are composed of sequences of these free morphemes. Grammatical relationships are often indicated by word order. Examples are Chinese and Vietnamese.

I-sound：（内化语音）The phonological properties of words which are naturally perceived by the resources of the mind; e. g. rhyme.

L

L1：（第一语言）A person's first language.

L2：（第二语言）A person's second language. To be more specific, one could refer to a person's L3, L4, and so on. However, the general term L2 is frequently used to refer to any language learning or use after the first language has been learned.

language competence：（语言能力）Knowledge of language; the linguistic capacity of a fluent speaker of a language.

language performance：（语言行为）What a speaker actually does in uttering or comprehending an expression.

language transfer：（语言迁移）The use of the first language（or other languages known）in a second language context.

larynx：（喉头）The part of the trachea containing the vocal folds.

lexeme：（词位）Also **lexical item**. The smallest contrastive unit in a semantic system. As an abstract unit, it is regarded as the same lexeme when inflected. In a dictionary, each lexeme merits a separate entry or sub-entry.

lexicon：（心理词库）Mental listing of the words in a language, including information about their meaning, grammatical function, pronunciation, etc.

lingua franca：（通用语）A language which is widely used in some region for communication among different groups of people speaking a variety of languages. It could be an internationally used language of communication（e. g. , English）, or the native language of one of the groups, or a pidgin.

linguistic relativism：（语言相对论）A hypothesis that states that the structure of our language to some extent determines the way we perceive the world. Also called

linguistic relativity hypothesis, **Sapir-Worf Hypothesis** or **Whorfian hypothesis**.

locutionary act：（以言指事）The saying of something which is meaningful and can be understood.

M

markedness：（标记性）The property which distinguishes between what is neutral, natural or expected (=unmarked) and what departs from the neutral (=marked) along some specified parameter.

mentalism：（心智说）Psychological and philosophical concept picked up and developed by Chomsky (1965), which attempts to describe the internal (innate) language mechanism that provides the basis for the creative aspect of language development and use.

minimal pair：（最小语对）Two words in a language that differ only by a single distinctive sound (one phoneme) in the same position and have different meanings, e. g. , *pin* and *bin*.

modality：（情态）The grammatical category associated with the expression of obligation, permission, prohibition, necessity, possibility and ability. Many languages contain a specific set of modal auxiliaries (e. g. , English *can*, *may*, etc.) for expressing these concepts.

modularity of language：（语言模块论）Many linguists, e. g. Chomsky, believe that language is a modular system, by which they mean that first, language is a self-contained system largely independent of other cognitive programs of the human brain, such as seeing and computing; second, language systems operate various subroutines which are separately wired in the brain and which interact with each other to produce language.

modularity：（模块组合性）The property of being composed of separate components, or "modules". A modular system is one which consists of several largely independent components which interact in such a way that the whole system performs some task or tasks successfully. Since the early 1980s, the concept of modularity has become prominent in linguistics and cognitive science.

monism：（一元论）A general name for those philosophical theories which deny the duality of matter and mind.

morpheme：（词素）Smallest linguistic unit that can have a meaning or grammatical function.

morphology：（形态学）*See Ex I, Chapter 4 for definition.*

motivation：（动机）The factors that determine a person's desire to do something. In second language acquisition, learning may be affected differently by different types of motivation.

N

nativism：（天生论）Philosophical and psychological position which holds that cognitive development of humans arises from "innate ideas". The nativist position has been used to explain how children are able to learn language and contrasts with the belief that all human knowledge comes from experience (empiricism).

natural approach：（自然法）Language "teaching" without explanation, grading, or correction of errors, but only presentation of "meaningful input".

neurolinguistics：（神经语言学）*See Ex I, Chapter 10 for definition.*

nominative：（主格）The case showing that a word is the subject of a verb.

P

palate：（硬腭）Also known as the "hard palate" or the "roof of the mouth"; the upper surface of the mouth where there is bone beneath the skin.

parameter：（参数）A dimension of grammatical variation between different languages or different varieties of the same language.

perlocutionary act：（以言成事）The results or effects that are produced by means of saying something.

phoneme：（音素，音位）The smallest unit of sound in a language which can distinguish two words.

phonetics：（语音学）The study of speech sounds; how they are produced in the vocal tract (articulatory phonetics 发音语音学), their physical properties (acoustic phonetics 声学语音学), and how they are perceived (auditory phonetics 听觉语

音学）.

phonology：（音系学）The study of the sound system of a language; how the particular sounds contrast in each language to form an integrated system for encoding information and how such systems differ from one language to another.

pidgin：（皮钦语）A language developed by speakers in contact on a regular basis who otherwise share no common language, usually with a limited vocabulary and a reduced range of grammatical structure.

pidginization：（皮钦语化）The development of a grammatically reduced form of a target language in second language acquisition. This is usually a temporary stage in language learning characterized by, for example, a limited system of auxiliary verbs, simplified question and negative forms, and reduced rules for tense, number and other grammatical categories.

pitch：（音高）The auditory sensation of the height of a sound.

pragmatics：（语用学）*See Ex 1, Chapter 9 for definition.*

prefix：（前缀）An affix that attaches to the beginning of a stem.

prescriptivism：（规定主义）The imposition of arbitrary norms upon a language, often in defiance of normal usage.

presupposition：（预设）A particular type of inference. The information that a speaker/writer assumes to be already known to the receiver of the message.

projection：（投射）A constituent which is an expansion of a head word. For example, a noun phrase such as *students of linguistics* is a projection of its head noun *students*.

proposition：（命题）The basic meaning which a sentence expresses. A proposition consists of (a) something which is named or talked about (known as the argument, or entity) (b) an assertion or predication which is made about the argument. A proposition comprises a predicate V and a set of arguments. Besides, a sentence may express or imply more than one proposition.

psycholinguistics：（心理语言学）*See Ex 1, Chapter 10 for definition.*

R

reconstitution：（经验重组）Ability to obtain a complete description of an event far displaced by combining a lot of small pieces of information.

reference：（指称关系）the relationship between words and the things, actions, events, and qualities they stand for.

referent：（指称对象）The entity (idea, object, etc.) to which a word or linguistic expressions relates. The referent of the word *table* is the actual table existing in the physical world.

register：（语域）The words, style, and grammar used by speakers and writers in particular conditions, namely, a socially defined variety of language.

Rheme：（述位）A term of systemic functional grammar, referring to the part of the clause in which the Theme is developed.

root：（词根）Also **base form**. A morpheme which is the basic part of a word and which may, in many languages, occur on its own (e.g. *man*, *hold*, *cold*, *rhythm*, *lock* in English) or be joined to other roots (e.g. *house + hold* → household; *bio + rhythm*→biorhythm) and/or take affixes (e.g. manly, unlock).

S

semantic feature：（语义特征）Also semantic component. An element of a word's meaning, e. g. *girl*→young, female, human.

semantics：（语义学）*See Ex I, Chapter 7 for definition.*

semiotics：（符号学）The study of the social production of meaning from sign systems.

sentence：（句子）The largest linguistic unit which is held together by rigid grammatical rules.

sociolect：（社会方言）Also **Social Dialect**. Variety of a language defined by social factors such as age, religion, ethnicity, or socioeconomic status. Sociolects may be classed as high or low (in status).

socialinguistics：（社会语言学）*See Ex I, Chapter 11 for definition.*

soft palate：（软腭）Also **velum**. The flap of soft tissue which forms the continuation of the palate at the back of the mouth, and may be lowered to permit nasalization.

specifier：（指示语）The grammatical function fulfilled by certain types of constituent which (in English) precede the head of their containing phrase.

speech act：（言语行为）An utterance defined in terms of the intentions of the speaker and the effect it has on the listener.

stem：（词干）The part of a word that serves as a base for forming new words by the addition of affixes. For example, *work* is the stem of *worker*; *worker* is the stem of *workers*.

stress：（重音）The increased duration and loudness of a syllable compared to other syllables in the same word.

stylistics：（文体学）*See Ex I, Chapter 11 for definition.*

subject-prominent language：（主语突出性语言）A language in which the grammatical units of subject and predicate are basic to the structure of sentences and in which sentences usually have subject-predicate structure. For example, English is a subject-prominent language.

suffix：（后缀）An affix that attaches to the end of a stem.

suprasegmental：（超切分音位）A vocal effect extending over more than one segment, e. g. , tone, length, and stress.

syntax：（句法学）*See Ex I, Chapter 5 for definition.*

synthetic languages：（综合语）Languages in which affixes are attached to other morphemes, so that a word may be made up of several meaningful elements including inflecting languages and agglutinating languages.

T

thematic role（θ-role）：（题元角色）The semantic role played by an argument in relation to its predicate.

Theme：（主位）A term of systemic functional grammar, referring to the element at the beginning of a sentence that serves as the point of departure of the message; it is that with which the clause is concerned.

tone：（声调）The distinctive pitch level of a syllable.

tone language：（声调语言）A language in which word meanings or grammatical contrasts are conveyed by variations in tone.

topic：（话题）In describing the information structure of sentences, the topic of a sentence is part of it which names the person, thing, or idea about which something is said.

topicalization：（话题化）A device which marks something as a topic by simply moving the topic to the front of the sentence, as in *This book I can't recommend.*

topic-prominent language：（话题突出性语言）A language in which the grammatical units of topic and comment are basic to the structure of sentences. For example, Chinese is a topic-prominent language.

trachea：（气管）The "windpipe" passes up from the lungs to the vocal tract beginning with the larynx.

triggering：（触发）Input as a stimulus that will reliably provoke parameter setting in language acquisition.

typologist approach：（类型学派）The approach to investigate the structural universals of language through the classification of languages according to their structural features. Languages can be classified into different types, such as their genetic relationships, the kinds of structures they exhibit, and whether or not they are tone languages.

typology：（语言类型学）*See Ex I, Chapter 14 for definition.*

U

Universal Grammar（**UG**）：（普遍语法）The genetically endowed information consisting of principles and parameters that enable the child to deduce a grammar from the primary linguistic data.

universal：（共性）A property found in the analysis of all languages.

unlearning：（习失）An unconscious process that some L1-transfer errors gradually disappear.

utterance：（话语）A particular piece of speech produced by a particular individual on a particular occasion. When we speak, we do not strictly produce sentences; instead, we produce utterances.

uvula：（小舌）The small lobe hanging from the bottom of the soft palate.

V

vocal folds：（声带）Also **vocal cords/lips/bands**. Two muscular folds in the larynx that vibrate as a source of sounds.

vocal tract：（声道）The connected passages inside the head which form the system used to produce speech. It starts at the larynx and includes the pharynx, the mouth, and the nasal cavity.

W

Wernicke's area：（韦尼克区）A region of the brain found in the left hemisphere at or around the posterior end of the Sylvain fissure that controls language comprehension.

X

X-bar theory：（X-阶标理论）An approach to syntax which attempts to show the general principles of language rather than deal with the structures of one particular language. "X" is a variable denoting any word category concerned.